The Best of
Captain Capitalism

"Top Shelf"

Aaron Clarey

ISBN:
ISBN-13: 978-1480058873
ISBN-10: 1480058874

DEDICATION

To all the Junior, Deputy, Aspiring, Official or Otherwise Economists,
and to all our Lieutenants, Agents in the Field, and Men in the Field

Thank you for your continued support and readership...
Did you buy something on Amazon today yet???

Preface
(Do not skip!)

If you were like me when I was a kid, chances are you would skip the "preface" or the "foreward" when given a reading assignment.

Why?

Because we all know the only reason the author put in a "foreward" or a "preface" or other such nonsense in his book was SOLELY to make your homework take longer and ensure you spent a higher percentage of your life studying instead of having fun.

However, because of the scope of this writing project some items about "The Best of Captain Capitalism – Top Shelf" do need to be addressed, necessitating this preface.

First, understand the primary purpose of "The Best of Captain Capitalism" was to have all my blogging literary works backed up incase open-minded liberals at Google deemed my free speech inappropriate. It was also to have a physical copy of these works in case the economy collapsed so badly or the government became so oppressive access to the original online/digital version of these works would either be deleted, inaccessible, banned or destroyed. It is my hope that people buy this book not so much for my own personal profit or gain, but to have thousands of copies of the wisdom, observations, and empirical data that has been accumulated on "Captain Capitalism" out there for the public to consume no matter what the political or economic environment.

Second, this book is merely the first of a series. With over 3,500 posts it's nearly impossible to consolidate it all into one, digestible tome. Therefore it has been categorized into logical pieces. "Top Shelf" is simply the first of this series containing my absolute best posts that not only need to be backed up, but are good enough to warrant an enjoyable book unto itself. "Top Shelf" will be followed by "Super Awesome Economic Genius" and a yet-to-be-titled book on courting and The Manosphere. Additionally, some posts fall into *multiple* categories and will be included in *multiple* books in the future resulting in some repeat posts. This is not out of laziness, but thoroughness I've included them in more than one book.

Third, because blogs are capable of multi-media and books are not, there are some features that will obviously be missing in this book. Notably, links, embedded videos, and any images I may have pilfered from the internet. All of my charts or government-made charts are included, however, there are many instances where the text will be referencing a link or a chart that is simply not there because the chart was proprietary and I deleted it. Additionally, all charts and graphs are in black and white and will obviously cause confusion as to which line is referring what data series in which chart. I apologize in advance but you should be able to look up the post on the internet and see the chart online and in color. The only other option was to charge $55 for this book in that's how much it would cost to have colored charts in this book. I may in the future do a colored version as more of a collector's item, but that is on the back burner.

And finally, I knew it would upset people and loyal readers if I changed and tweaked any of my original writing. I know how important it is to readers and literary scholars that an author complete a work, and then not constantly re-tweak it and re-polish it. So out of respect for these people and the literary profession ALL TYPOS AND GRAMMATICAL ERRORS HAVE BEEN KEPT IN THE BOOK to remain true to the original Cappy Cap works.

Take that you grammar Nazis!

Top Shelf

Vast Prosperity Begat "They Mystery"

One of the more popular local radio shows in the Twin Cities area is called Garage Logic. And one of the running gigs they have is "the Mystery." "The Mystery" is where you would have people lobbying their city council to ban leaf blowers because of the pollution and noise. Or middle-aged, gray ponytailed Baby Boomers protesting the war on the bridges spanning over the Mississippi. Or overzealous do-gooders passing smoking bans.. At first it seemed to confuse the host so much that I wrote this theory as to explain "The Mystery." Then it dawned on me that if "The Mystery" were solved, the whole "Mystery" gig wouldn't fly anymore. Kind of like preventing Niles and Daphney from ever getting together. However, I think the insights provided in my explanation does explain these people's behavior and to a larger extent what ultimately drives liberals. Hope you enjoy.

The epitome of the mystery is that there are people out there who act, say, and believe things that are completely illogical. They then give you an incredibly weak or obscure rationale as to why they do, say or believe such things. This can range from a government worker demanding higher pay when they're already paid 30% more than their private sector counterparts, to a mob of students destroying the downtown Seattle area in protest against globalization, to an environmentalist claiming that cutting your lawn with a weed whacker emits 2 million pounds of greenhouse gases into the environment.

At first glance they are seemingly unrelated. However, there is a common thread they share and this is the solution, the reason why there is the mystery;

They refuse to adhere to reality because they are lazy.

It is quite a link to claim that an environmentalist who insists a sole weed whacker emits 2 million pounds of greenhouse gases does so because he doesn't want to adhere to reality because his is lazy, but let me make several daring and dangerous links.

First off, there is a reality. There is a real world. It is the world we all live in, and whether we accept it or not, we have no choice but to abide by it.

Governing this real world are many laws, but two undeniable laws in particular are related to The Mystery;

One, in order for a society to survive they must produce the goods and services necessary for survival and produce them more efficiently should society wish to improve standards of living.

Two, it is human nature to be lazy – i.e. to get more for less.

It is these two undeniable (and diametrically opposed) laws that necessitate an economic system that is based in reality. This economic system must be based in human nature and what they are prone to do, not in human kindness or what we would hope for them to do. It is because of this that capitalism is the most efficient and successful economic system and any attempts otherwise, as evidenced by the former Soviet Union, current day North Korea, former Marxist Ethiopia, Cuba, etc., are bound to fail.

Therefore, capitalism is not debatable, it is reality.

However, capitalism is not infallible and has one great weakness;

It has a tendency to spoil its participants.

Be it a Baby Boomer who had the luxury of growing up during the post WWII economic boom turned 60's radical, leftist, anti-war hippie, or their modern day suburbanite anti-globalization protestor equivalent, both share a common trait;

They largely owe their unrivalled standards of living, employment, and wealth to capitalism, ie-vast prosperity.

Yet at the same time capitalism is so successful that it effectively shields them from the harsh realities of life. And without having to work, strive or suffer for that wealth, these people, especially when growing up, not only take such high standards of living, employment and wealth for granted, but consider them rights and entitlements.

It is this dichotomy that creates the environment in which The Mystery can form. On one hand, capitalism is providing for the livelihood of an individual. But at the same time spoils the individual so much that he/she can afford to revert back to their lazy human nature and purport the most outlandish theories and ideologies that are not based in reality but rather in their own selfish, human nature desires. This disconnect from reality and intentional ignorance of how capitalism/the real world works effectively allows a person to "have their cake and eat it too." The result is a person can then live off the system, using whatever excuse or rationale to forego responsibility and hold beliefs or live a lifestyle that runs contradictory to what we Garage Logicians know to be fact, truth, reality and logical.

Having said that, it would seem only spoiled children can be Mysterians presuming that once they entered the real world, and were forced to get jobs to support themselves they would become adults and grow up. However, two things effectively prevent this. One, capitalism is so successful that a good portion of the population can (and in some cases are) being taken care of by their parents' money well into their 40's, and some trust fund babies, indefinitely. Two, over the course of the past 30 years, a system has been installed in our society that allows people (wealthy or not) the option of never having to get a real job, with real work, effectively shielding them from the real world for the entirety of their adult lives, namely what I call the "non-private sector;"

Academia, NGO's, the public sector, non-profit industries, etc.

Thus, instead of real jobs in the private sector where competition inevitably forces production, efficiency, and the reality that one must work hard to succeed, one can now major in philosophy, women's studies, Hyphenated-American studies, sociology, communications and the uber-Mysterian "peace studies." And no longer do they have to get jobs as a machinist, an accountant, a doctor, a janitor, a chef, a customer service rep or somebody else that produces and contributes to society. But rather they can become sociology professors, psychology professors, philosophy professors, diversity counselors, grant writers, professional protestors, activists, lobbyists, journalists, career politicians, trial lawyers and a plethora of other equally worthless careers which compose the vast majority of Euphorians' and Mysterians' employment.

While this explains the incentives or at least the rationale of the Eurphorians and Mysterians it does not explain why they make such outlandish statements or are so adamant in their protests. Why they are so vocal, and zealous in establishing their cause. Why we see some many examples of The Mystery so frequently. However, this is very simple to explain;

Job security.

Realize the vast majority of these Mysterian careers are NOT demanded by the free market and must be imposed on the taxpayer by force via the government or people must be guilt-tripped into donating money to their cause. Therefore lobbying, protesting, and legislating are part of the game to protect their "industry." Furthermore, in order to GROW their "industry" they use a technique that provides us with the majority of instances of The Mystery today;

Criminalizing other entities, industries, groups of people, etc.

Tobacco companies, fast food companies, oil companies, white men, rich white men, rich white oil men in Texas, the WTO, the IMF, the military, the CIA, John Ashcroft, big business, capitalism, pharmaceuticals, NAFTA, America, cars, Haliburton, SUV's, even mold, are all targets of the Mysterians because they represent future or at least potential cash flows in the future, but at minimum, a continuation of their "causes."

The problem with attacking or criminalizing these groups is that these groups aren't evil, malicious, or criminal. All things being said they are products of reality and the free market. At worst they are a government policy attempting to respond to reality. The SUV is in response to the demands of a free people in a free market. Unhealthy fat food is in response to the demands of a free people in a free market. The military is in response to the fact people don't like us and the government attempts to protect us. And rich white men are more often than not the result of hard work, studying, and creativity. And thus, in order to criminalize them Mysterians must fabricate a rationale or reason that is not based in reality, or at best has some really shoddy evidence to support their claim. This is where you see cardiac-arrest-inducing examples of The Mystery at play in the real world:

Global warming exists and is brought on by the automobile.

You are fat because McDonald's made you that way.

You are poor and your life sucks because of racist, sexist white men.

People who drive bigger cars are endangering those of us who drives SPECS.

This, if for any other reason, is why we have been unable to solve The Mystery. Because we focus on the cause or crusade and its inanity and not what drives the people behind it. Realize, it doesn't matter what the cause or crusade is because the cause or crusade is fabricated for an ulterior motive. It could just as well be global warming as it is sex discrimination, because the ulterior motive is nothing as noble as protecting the environment or advancing the well-being of women. It's not about eliminating racism. It's not about the ethical treatment of animals. The only thing it's about is the Mysterian. Providing and securing the Mysterian a career for some fabricated cause. Giving them some self-concocted sense of pseudo self-worth. Furnishing them with an utterly hollow rationale that somehow "they're contributing to society." In short providing them a lifestyle void of responsibility and reality.

It is nothing as noble as helping 3rd World children and absolutely nothing resembling the real world or the truth.

This is why you have The Mystery. This is why you will never see the NAACP or Jesse Jackson even admit to an improvement in race relations. This is why schools will always be underfunded and will cry bloody murder and child abuse if you just hold their budgets steady. This is why the environment will forever be on the apocalyptic verge of destruction even if we ban the automobile. This is why you can have a women's studies professor claim she is 100% independent while in reality she is the trophy wife of the public sector. This is why you have Arriana Huffington and Mark Dayton inheriting their money going on political crusades to make themselves feel better. This is even arguably why you have the son of a rich Saudi millionaire flying planes in our buildings to make up for his inability to survive without his Daddy's money. Simply because people are lazy and do not want to put forth the required effort to face up to and succeed in the real world nor do they want to succumb to a career that they view as "beneath them." And it is just so much easier to ignore reality, claim you're a victim, claim you're a crusader for some "noble cause," villanize targeted groups, and just outright lie especially when a system is in place to foster and encourage such behavior.

I hope this helps explain The Mystery or at least maybe proposes some new theories about it.

Good luck!

Revised Empirical Proof

Many years ago I had taken the 5, 10 and 15 year averages of government spending and receipts as a percent of GDP for all the OECD countries and correlated against their corresponding 5, 10 and 15 year average RGDP growth rates.

It confirmed something that everybody knew;

Countries with lower taxes grow faster than countries with higher taxes.

Correlations came in around -.3.

What got me about this data is that very few Republicans, Libertarians and other varied sorts of capitalists knew of this data and would largely rely on anecdotal evidence to support capitalism as the optimal economic system. Sure, they'd use logic. Or cite the utter and dismal record of communism in the glory days of Stalin, Chairman Mao, or modern day Kim Small Jong II. But never really went out to see, "well, what tends to happen when countries are taxed at a higher rate."

Anyway, so I updated the figures with the most recent OECD data and, well, yeah, communism still sucks. Sorry dems and libs. When you argue against the truth, well, it's uhh...kind of hard to win.

Correlation Coefficients			
	5 yr	10 yr	15 yr
Expenditure	-0.38	-0.31	-0.36
Receipts	-0.32	-0.21	-0.26

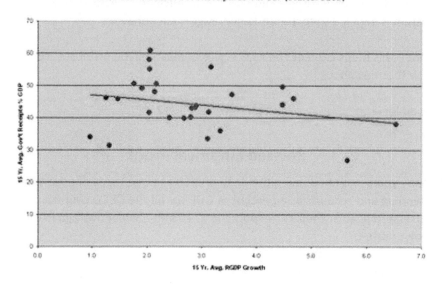

15 Yr. GDP Growth v. Gov't Receipts as % of GDP (Source: OECD)

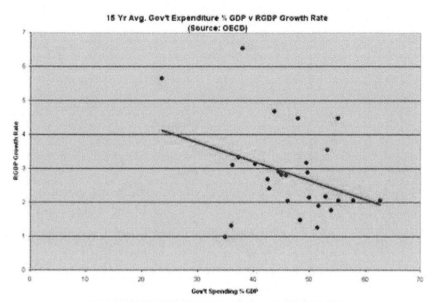

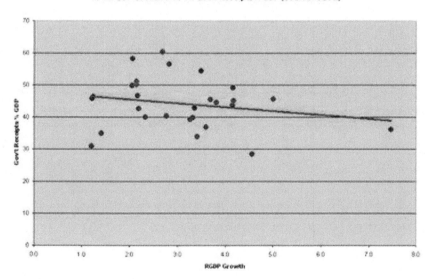

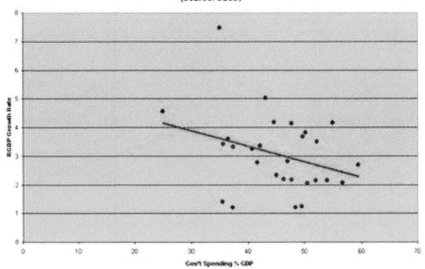

10 Yr Avg. Gov't Expenditure % GDP v RGDP Growth
(Source: OECD)

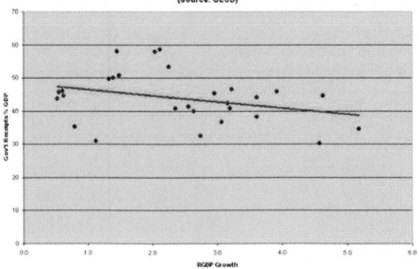

5 Yr Avg. GDP Growth v. 5 Yr Avg. Gov't Receipts % GDP
(Source: OECD)

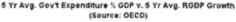

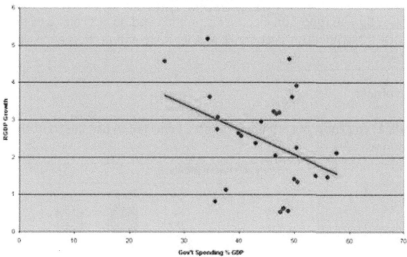

Economics for Idiots - 101

Now I know that all you aspiring and junior deputy economists out there are smarter than your average bear.

And I know that economics, when it really boils down to it, is REALLY not that difficult.

So for your average person, economics should be a pretty easy concept to grasp and usually, it is.
Unfortunately, not everybody is gifted as us. We have people that are not necessarily as smart as us. Some people are poorer and never learned to read. Additionally, the public schools do their darnedest to turn out idiots, and thusly something as simple as economics is like trying to understand quantum physics for a lot of people.

So, because I am a kind, charitable soul, I thought I'd offer a lesson for the stupid people in the world. Kind of an "Economics for Idiots" lesson, so that not only can geniuses like you and me understand economics. Not only can average everyday people understand economics. But complete freaking retards and mollusk can understand economics.

This need for "Economics Lessons for Idiots" was brought to my attention when I got an e-mail from American Progress.org highlighting the recent Census Bureau report on income distriubtion and poverty and wealth as PROOF POSITIVE Bush's economic policies are creating Nazis and killing babies.

The proof?

Well, as you know my affinity for charts, I decided to use the chart they sent me;

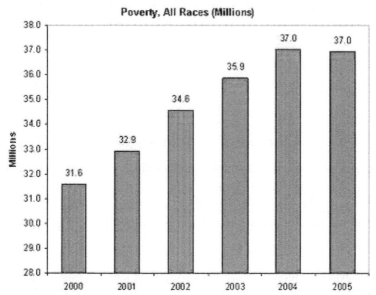

A pity. Shame shame shame. Obviously the work of a retard...or a mollusk.

OK, so, let's begin the lesson in Economics for Idiots - 101 because it is glaringly obvious we need one.

First, if you're going to make a chart, don't manipulate it by changing the scale on the Y-axis so that it shows this dramatic increase when in reality, it is quite small. If you are an idiot, you would look at this chart and think poverty has tripled under the Bush presidency. When in reality it's only gone up by 20%.

Now the idiots over at the Center for American Progress will still probably get all in a tizzy over that fact right there, a 20% increase in poverty. They'll salavate over it, *HEE HEEE HEEEE HEEE! 20% increase, WE HAVE BUSH NOW!!!!*

Well, that's because they're idiots.

Any person of average intelligence would say, *"hey, hasn't the population of the country been growing? And wouldn't a more accurate measure be some kind of, you know, "**poverty rate**," you know, like the percent of the population that's under the poverty threshold?"* And by golly, those good men and women at the Census Bureau have calculated just such a thing. They call it;

THE POVERTY RATE!

Those crafty devils!

Well here's a chart FROM THAT SAME DAMNING REPORT that shows the poverty rate.

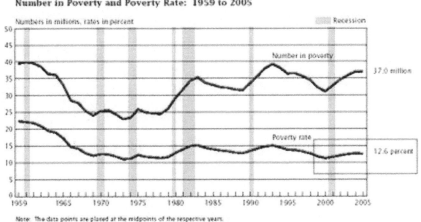

Figure 4.
Number in Poverty and Poverty Rate: 1959 to 2005

Note: The data points are placed at the midpoints of the respective years.

Source: U.S. Census Bureau, Current Population Survey, 1960 to 2006 Annual Social and Economic Supplements.

Not quite so damning is it? The poverty rate doesn't show this dramatic increase in poverty as the Center for American Progress would have you believe. Who would have guessed a communist institution like the Center for American Progress would misrepresent data?

Second, also notice another thing, aspiring and junior deputy economists. Notice how the chart from the Center for American Progress goes back a whopping 5 years. While the good men and women of the Census Bureau go back to 1959. See, this is what we call "context."

With context we see that the poverty rate, though ever so slightly up, is still technically at a historic low. Thus, official economists would come to the professional conclusion that;

"People should shut the hell up and stop their whining. Poverty is not a problem in America."

Third, no doubt you've heard this Census Bureau report being paraded by the left for the fact that incomes have remained stagnant or slightly dropped in the past 4-5 years. Again, PROOF POSITIVE that Bush is out hurling rocks at the elderly and kicking dogs. But do you see a trend here? The left keeps going back only 4-5 years. Might it be time, once again ladies and gentlemen, to use that "context" we learned about earlier?

Well, here's the chart;

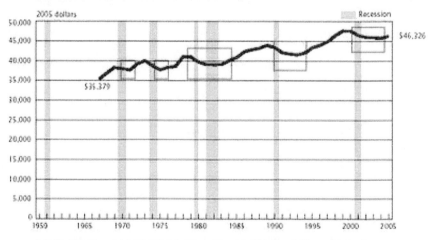

Figure 1.
Real Median Household Income: 1967 to 2005

Note: The data points are placed at the midpoints of the respective years. Median household income data are not available before 1967.
Source: U.S. Census Bureau, Current Population Survey, 1968 to 2006 Annual Social and Economic Supplements.

When you look at it you'll notice them nice slim shady lines. Those are recessions. Notice after each recession how real incomes historically have dropped and then recovered, as you WOULD NORMALLY EXPECT THEM TO DO???? So perhaps this is just a function of a normally functioning economy and not Bush hurling rocks at the elderly?

You see folks, this what happens when you have publicly educated children who never grow up and major in El Crapo studies in college while working for some non-profit or the government because they have no skills of use that the private sector would actually want to fork over good money for. People who find nothing wrong with misrepresenting data and reality to the detriment of society because it makes them feel good and feel like their lives actually have a purpose. Because they feel like they're crusaders. Because they feel like they're heroes fighting some imagined evil (If you need an amazingly interesting reference to this cowardly psychology, please feel free to read this post).

Fourth and finally. This will be your assignment in Economics for Idiots - 101. What might the effect be on poverty levels AND WAGES OF THE LOWER INCOME QUINTILES if 10.5 million illegal aliens have entered the country AND if the Census Bureau does NOT exclude non-citizens from the data?

The Best of Captain Capitalism - Dear Penthouse Forum

This was arguably the most popular post and taught me a great lesson in the economics of blogs;

Smut and sex sells and ain't none of you honyakers interest in economics as much as you are dirt on people's dating lives.

Alas, what am I to do, a true capitalism responds to the market.

It was several weeks ago I was sitting at one of my favorite jazz clubs. And as always I was reading the most recent issue of The Economist. I had set it down on the table and turned my attention to do some tax work when an rather attractive Asian woman walked by. But while I was looking at her, I noticed that she was looking at the cover of The Economist.

At first I was hopefully impressed, thinking that somehow this may be the legendary "video-game-playing, Economist-reading, sexy-lingerie-wearing, totally hot babe capitalist economist that likes to serve Irish economist men martinis while they listen to Frank Sinatra." The one that the **Holy and Sacred Elder Economists of Yore** spoke so much of. But when I saw what was on the cover of The Economist, "China and the Key to Asian Peace" I realized she must be Chinese and was naturally just looking at the cover.

She proceeded to sit down at a table about 10 yards from me and ordered a glass of wine. She was dressed provocatively enough that I figured she had a date or was meeting some friends, so I just left it at that and returned to doing some tax work. However, 20 minutes had passed and I noticed that she was still sitting by herself.

Did her date fail to show up?

Were her friends the tardy types?

Or...could she be like me! *A Napoleon Solo type character who is actually secure and cool enough with themselves to go to clubs and read The Economist?!?!*

Realizing that my finite resource of time was being used up, I decided to gather up the courage and ask her if she was alone. Upon asking her, she said she was waiting for friends, but they were very late. And in my politest, least forward and non-threatening way, I asked her if she would like to join me so that I may keep her company until her friends arrived.

She agreed.

Happily we sat down at the couch I had previously ornamented with my papers and files and started talking. A very nice and attractive woman, but what impressed me the most was that she was not bashful about asking me about myself, alleviating me of the typical male duty of keeping the conversation going. And within one minute of asking me questions, it seemed the prophecy of the **Holy and Sacred Elder Economists of Yore** were to come true. For in that brief minute of conversation it was established that;

1. She reads The Economist
2. She was a financial manager at a money management firm
3. She had her undergraduate in finance
4. She was getting her masters in economics

The next hour of conversation was tantilizing and insanely intelligent. We talked about econometric modeling. We talked about efficient frontier theory. We talked about Miller-Modigliani. And then she talked about her specialty, behavioral economics.

I love it when chicks talk dirty to me.

And thinking that the night could not get better, it did. Her friends showed up. All of them finance majors and all of them just as capable of holding intelligent conversation which lasted the next hour.

But I knew inevitably I would have to make my play. And at a table full of economists and finance majors you're not really going to impress anybody by quoting correlation coefficients between GDP growth rates and unemployment figures because that's just par for the course for them. So I decided to play my trump card. My master stroke of genius. My coup d'etat.

I can dance.

Fortunately for me there was a jazz band. And fortunately there was a dance floor. So sitting there patiently, engaging in conversation, I waited for the perfectly timed song to play and then asked, "do you know how to dance?"

The expression on her face could not be repeated.

"No, but I would love to learn how!"

So I said, "I can teach you."

"Well, not now, but I'd certainly love to go dancing sometime later."

And boom! There was my in.

The scenario could not have been more perfect;

* I established we had insane amounts in common.
* We established we could have that insanely rare thing called "intelligent conversation"
* I mingled well with her friends
* I established that I was unique and could offer her something fun that would make for one hell of a date.
* She wanted me to take her out dancing.

And like George Castanza, knowing that he should exit at the top of his game, I proceeded to give the woman my card, said I would love to take her out dancing, and bid her and her friends farewell.

Leaving the jazz club I had a smile on my face. I was supremely confident she would call.

Which reminded me of a theory I had developed back in my college days;

"If you are supremely confident a girl will call, she won't."

Sure enough, time had passed, and no call.

Alas, I concluded she must not have been too smart, for how stupid do you have to be not to call a *dancing, video-game-playing economist*? Especially one with *his very own subscription* to The Economist! I mean come on, ladies, how can you resist?

But don't cry for me Argentina, for there is good news to this story. For immediately after I had left the jazz club, and while I was still riding high on the prospects of meeting a potential intellectual equal, I felt it necessary to share my experiences with those who I thought at the time were at least in part responsible for making this meeting happen; the kind ladies and gentlemen at The Economist. In a drunken stupor, I had sent off a letter to London detailing my exploits that night, not expecting what would happen two weeks later.

For two weeks later, at the insanely early hour of 10AM, I was awoken by a call from none other than the ***chief editor of The Economist*** asking if I had taken her out yet! It seems the good blokes and dames at The Economist had a running wager on me and whether I'd be successful in getting her out on a date. The chief editor, recognizing the obvious fact that anybody who subscribes to The Economist and who is in fact an economist himself, is so studly that they would practically be guaranteed of getting a date, wisely bet on me. Sadly, perhaps he is too wise, for he is 72 years of age and perhaps still subscribes to the romantic notions of the 1940's; chivalry, tradition, romance, and other such BS. Whereas his younger, less senior counterparts are fully aware of the insanity of modern day women and their incapability to appreciate the concept of carpe diem, and thus bet against me.

But regardless of the outcome, as an economist, one must think. For while girls that shoot me down are a dime a dozen, how often is it that you get a call from the chief editor of The Economist?

As far as my econometric models tell me, that's worth getting shot down at least 348 times with a 2.5% margin of error.

Best of Captain Capitalism - Payment in Kisses

Back when I was young and foolish I fell for a girl.

And it's an interesting thing how a person, a song, or just about anything will trigger the release of endorphins or whatever neurochemical that effectively gives your brain an immeasurable boost and soon your brain it churning out pure genius.

You don't know how.

You don't know why.

You almost feel as if somebody else is in control and you are a helpless by-stander watching your brain work at the speed of light producing pure, unrivalled genius. It's like watching a movie in 3D.

But there your hands go, hammering away at the keyboard, almost as if somebody else were commanding them to write a masterpiece.

Well such a masterpiece I wrote in my foolish folly fancying of a female.

And frankly it did not get the attention it truly and rightly deserved, because it really is that good.

For what, I ask you, is better than the mixing of;

1. Romance
2. Cappy Cap wit
and
3. Economics

IN

POETIC FORM NO LESS!???!!!?

Nothing is the answer.

Thus, I present to you all aspiring, junior, and official economists, the best economic poem ever written. (all aspiring, junior and official male deputy economists have permission to plagiarize this masterpiece as long as it is used to score with a dame).

"Payment in Kisses"

Oh the girl so quickly dismisses
My offer for payment in kisses
However, she'd be much smarter
Realizing the merits of barter.

Oh my dear it's so simplistic
For my kisses are so intrinsic.
Oh baby we would have it made
If you'd accept my payment in trade

Chorus;

Oh, I'd gladly overpay
And then you'd owe me some "change"
Come on baby don't you know?
It's the universally accepted medium of exchange.

Oh I'll show you where they're minted
And I'll show you how they're printed
They come fresh hot off the presses
The only currency that caresses.

The IRS has no rules
My kisses weren't taught in the schools.
Accept my kisses as money
You'd be the world's richest girl, honey

Chorus;

Oh, I'd gladly overpay
And then you'd owe me some "change"
Come on baby don't you know?
It's the universally accepted medium of exchange.

The Dinar, Dollar and Shilling
I know how you like your billing
No Euro, no Kiwi nor Sterling
It's my kisses that you are yearning

So don't delay,

There will come the day;

that you accept my kisses as legal and tender.

The Best of Captain Capitalism - Support Your Local Cynic

This was sent to me by a reader and reminded me not of the playboy post, but this one, support your local cynic. I caught a lot of flak for this post from women, but (as is many of the times) they don't realize my main aim in this post was to save future women (and men as well) from wasting their precious time and money on such worthless degrees. Oh well, tough fatherly love is out of fashion in today's DesperatehousewivesDawsonsCreekTeenIdol America.

Often I have been accused of being a cynic. And not necessarily in a positive light either. No, usually it is followed by some commentary that I should "let go" or "loosen up" otherwise I shall "blow a gasket" and my "blood pressure will skyrocket" and "do I really want to live life this way?"

So to disprove the doubting Thomases and to help us once again advance our understanding about economics I shall demonstrate why cynicism and those that participate in it, cynics, are necessary and right in their insistence on being cynical.

First off, the majority of people you view to be "cynics" are not really cynics at all. No, those of us who seem to have a negative outlook on life and pummel those that come up to us with their brainwashed ignorant smiles saying, "Hey, don't worry be happy" are in reality REALISTS.

The reason for this is instead of being placated by Desperate Housewives or Teen Idol and satiated by marrying and having the 2.2 kids in the suburbs as our cookie-cutter American counterparts have done, we think ahead. We survey the land. We ask ourselves questions, "what do we want in life and what will happen in the future and what action should be taken to best navigate that future." This leads any independent-thinking individual to study and take note of various sociological and economic factors, some of which will certainly be; the pathetic savings rates we have, the impending social security crisis that is looming, not to mention the Medicare/Medicaid crisis, all under the shadow of a property market bubble, and an increasing parasite class nudging the US ever closer towards socialism.

And no, don't tell me to loosen up.

However, the deteriorating economic fundamentals of the future US is not the reason for my bringing up cynicism. The reason is a talking point that I have heard now one too many times in the talk radio world and that is somehow that men, or rather, boys, are being neglected in schools and this results in (ready for the sound byte???) women earning the majority of college degrees.

Usually this is set in the context of reverse discrimination where boys are forced out of their traditional male role models at school and then usually an accusation of some leftist policy that heralds girls over boys, and then the ensuing "woe are we poor men/boys being discriminated against by the leftist educational machine."

I have two major points of contention with this;

One, we on the right are not whiners. It's one of the key things that separates us from the left. You want to call us names? Fine. You want to make the playing field unfair? Fine. But we are not going to bitch and whine and feel sorry for ourselves. That's the job of the left, liberals, and their bevy of political allies. We on the right get up off the ground and go back into the fight, regardless of the odds. So cut as many men jokes as you want. Post as many oafish, tail-behing-the-legs Ray Romanos on TV as you want. We don't care, because frankly men know better and we are actually secure with ourselves and needn't any pity or affirmative action hand out and can let whatever unfair practices in the schools roll off our backs for that is what makes us men. And radio talk show hosts should know better.

My second point of contention was started when a little voice in the back of my head said, "something ain't right about that" when I heard Michael Medved complaining about how men were trailing women in earning college degrees. Certainly he was right, women do earn the majority of college degrees, but something was amiss. Something didn't add up. Something I couldn't put my finger on.

Fortunately, I have that trait that all people seemingly are hell-bent on hating and beating out of me, cynicism. And whilst many of you want to just "let go" and be blissfully happy, ignorant to the realities around you whilst you hold hands around the camp fire singing Kumbya and participate in candle-light vigils, some of us were being vigilant.

For as a cynic I remember college and I remember the majority of the women I dated were frankly, morons. Now one could make the argument, this was a sample bias since only morons would go out with me, but I contend another theory. That the majority of girls I dated in college were morons not because only morons would go out with me, but rather because the majority of women majored in what I call "crap studies." Fields such as "sociology," "communications" and my all-time favorite, because you've only been speaking it for 18 years, "english."

In other words, the reason why more women are earning more degrees than men is because they major in subjects that are easier.

"WHY, HOW DARE YOU!!!! YOU CYNICAL ASS YOU!!!!"

Yeah, well, like I said, the majority of cynics aren't pessimistic, but realists. For you see, to test my theory I called up the University of Minnesota with its some 50,000 students and asked them if they could send me a breakdown between the types of degrees awarded and gender. And after a little number crunching it seems my theory was not a theory at all, but reality.

When broken down the majority graduate degrees that are awarded to women are in "fluff" or since I'm subsidizing their education, I call them "crap" fields such as psychology, women's studies, urban studies, etc., while the majority of real degrees in fields such as engineering, medicine, accounting, etc., with practical applications to the real world are awarded to men.

(charts on next page)

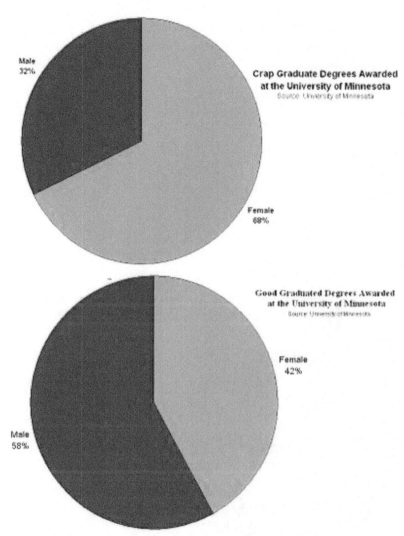

Male
32%

**Crap Graduate Degrees Awarded
at the University of Minnesota**
Source: University of Minnesota

Female
68%

**Good Graduated Degrees Awarded
at the University of Minnesota**
Source: University of Minnesota

Female
42%

Male
58%

Similar statistics are shown in undergraduate degrees, where again the majority of "crap" degrees are earned by women and the majority of real degrees are earned by men.

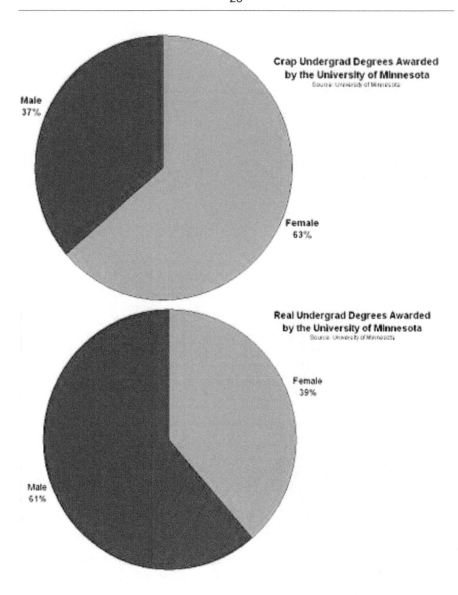

As an economist I have a particular respect for engineers since they compose not only the majority of my friends, but I deem it the field most productive to society (and the labor market agrees with me based on their starting salaries). Alas, men outdo women 5 to 1 in these fields.

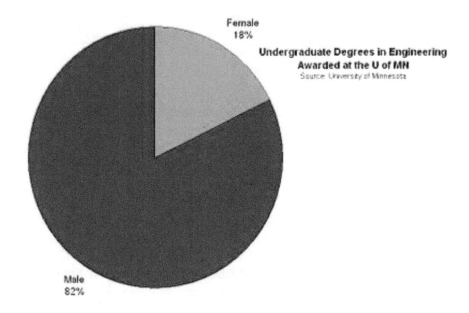

Now you can go ahead can contest that I've tainted the data. That somehow the University of Minnesota is not a representative sample of an American college, and who am I to say degrees in Chicano Studies are not as warranted as chemical engineering (you racist cynic you!). All I can say is that if you are offended, well you should be, because it's not the falsities of life that are truly insulting, but rather the truth. The question is whether you want to deal with it, or go watch some more Desperate Housewives.

"Your are a cynical person, Rick, if you forgive me for saying so."
"Oh, I forgive you."

Sinking the Men of the Yamato

Through my own personal conversations, the conversations retold to me of other men, and even those conversations I've heard on the Tom Leykis Show, all of us men have at one point in time or another been asked by women,

"Who screwed you over in the past?"

or a variant

"What girl did this to you?"

Usually this happens when women ask you about your opinions of dating, courtship, romance, etc., and when you speak the truth they are shocked and horrified that you have such a cynical or pessimistic attitude towards dating or women in general. The logic they employ leads them to only one possible solution or explanation:

That ONE girl completely screwed you over and thus, unjustifiably and unfairly, soured your opinion of ALL women.

They believe there was this ONE, SINGLE, SOLE perpetrator that did not represent or resemble the majority of women and that is why you have this "irrational" or "inappropriate" response or view of women. That the majority of women are too numerous and prevalent that it was only sheer dumb luck you ran into a single, sole, renegade operator who warped your perception of women so unjustifiably so.

So let me introduce a little reality into the situation.

For the most part, I believe most women subscribe to the theory that "ONE" person did this to you, and therefore scarred you for the rest of your life, because it's simple. The human brain (male or female) is more prone to select the simpler theory because it takes too much effort to accept and rationalize complex ones. This is not a criticism of women, because men are just as susceptible to believe in a "simple" theory than a complex one. But it's just easier to believe there was this ONE, SINGLE, MEAN, BADDIE of a girl that did something really mean to you and thus you swore off women forever.

The REALITY is however, quite the opposite.

Yes, there are men who unfortunately suffered one, single death-knelling blow and they never got up again. But for the majority of men, it is more akin to the sinking of the Yamato than anything else.

The Yamato was the premier Japanese battleship of WWII. It was more or less unsinkable from sea and thus they had to resort to aerial bombing to sink her. She took an AMAZING amount of punishment. Three separate waves of attacks, from air and sea and she still kept on going.

Inevitably she DID capitulate and sink, but understand it was no one single bomb or torpedo that did her in. It was a relentless, constant, repetitive, barrage and assault that essentially bludgeoned her into submission and defeat. And thus is the way of most men you will face today above an age of 25.

The sheer hell and punishment, NOT in terms of single punishing blows, but in terms of constantly repetitive, NEVER ENDING attacks is what molds or galvanizes men into what they are today. The accomplished Hugh Grant-like bachelor that eschews meeting your friend that is "perfect for him" was not sunk by a single woman, but a barrage of flake outs, stand ups, drama queens and suicide threats. The confirmed bachelor who prefers to hang out with his buds instead of go to a club and meet a girl has had his deck strafed repeatedly. The 40 something executive, committed to his job and his career and maybe calls you when he's in town, remembers starkly those days of getting the hell bombed out of him by ditzy girlfriend after cheating girlfriend after money-sucking girlfriend.

Did some girls cause more damage than others?

Yes.

Did any one of them sink the individual man?

No.

And so in the end if you look at the autopsy of this former "good guy" or "reliable man," you'll find that the cause of death was no single girl that hurt his feelings "really bad" back in college, but a never ending litany of flakes, frauds, drama queens, liars and just plain evil women/girls that were never strong enough or significant enough on their own to cause major damage to such a vessel, but a never ending barrage of them that just plain wore him down to the point of defeat.

Ergo, stop trying to blame the sinking of "good men" on mythical single, sole villains and start casting a wider net. It is a problem that is more pervasive and wide-spread than most women will admit. And much like Christianity did, and Islam must in the future -have a reformation- so too must modern day women purge and shame through their ranks the women who find it fashionable, funny, entertaining and enjoyable to bomb, strafe, torpedo and attack men.

Because understand, those of us men of the Yamato class are simply forced to make a decision based on statistics and probability. Enough girls attack, drop their bombs, and shoot torpedoes into our sides, we have no choice but to treat you all as enemies and give no one the benefit of the doubt, even the genuine and true "good girls." And so there you sit at the age of 32 wondering "where have all the good men gone." Whether you're a good girl or a bad girl, it doesn't matter. By this point in the game it's revenge by proxy time. If you're upset about that, then take it up with the feminists and evil women in your ranks that found it so necessary to villainize, mock, stand up, play mind, etc. with young men/boys, not the sinking Yamato's themselves.

Regardless, I sure hope it was fun (not to mention, worth it) playing with young boys' feelings and emotions in middle school through college. Hope it was fun with the drama and suicide threats, and ultimatums and mind games and sh!t tests and whatever else Cosmo told you to do. I hope "playing hard to get" and stringing along men/boys provided invaluable entertainment. Because there couldn't possibly be a consequence to all that now could there?

You lovely western ladies enjoy that decline!

My Goldman Sachs Story

I was at my bar last night. Technically I don't own it, but I like using the possessive pronoun in the phrase "my bar." It also happens to be in "my town" which too, unbeknownst to all the townspeople is owned by me. It's all mine, the bar, the town, the roads. Everything, I freaking own it all!

Anyway, I was at my bar last night talking to some buddies of mine. And we were exchanging stories about" interviews from hell." Most of them themed or centraled around stories of some idiot 24 year old HR generalist idiot that knew nothing of your field or specialty asking you;

"If you were in this situation, what would you do and why?"

"Have you ever been in a situation and you disagreed with your boss?"

"What is your favorite color and why?"

Meanwhile you'd sit there and be amazed the entirety of the US labor market hasn't come to a screeching halt due to the inefficiencies and incompetence of its gatekeepers; HR.

So I told my worst interview story, which begat requests that I put it up on the blog (as some in the crew were investment bankers) and so I've decided to oblige them.

I was all of 21 I think, maybe just recently turned 22. By this time I was coming upon the end of a hellish experience known as college. And it WAS hellish and I mean it in the most sincerest and literal sense. Most people say, "It was hell" when in reality it was just an annoyance. College WAS hell (hell, I even wrote song about to sing whilst on patrol)

Regardless, the primary (although not only) reason college was hell was because I worked full time while going to school full time. I had dropped down to 118 pounds my sophomore year because I couldn't afford much in the way of food and my job required me to bike about 50 miles a day. This was on top of a credit load that most preppy suburbanites would get crushed under, so after three and a half years of this (and sleep deprevation) the light at the end of the tunnel was coming. Add to this I had a 3.96 GPA and 3 interships under my belt, I thought the last thing I would have to worry about was a job. So as luck would have it, I got an interview with the chalice of all finance majors; Goldman Sachs.

Now the bulge bracket doesn't bother with the U of MN because frankly, nobody in the world has heard about the "Carlson School of Management." And as far as the East Coast is concerned the only schools are Wharton, Chicago, Darden, Harvard and Nepotism U. And if I recall correctly I had a buddy either hack or somehow provide me the password and username from the U of Chicago's job posting board which ended up in me getting the interview for a "GLOBAL EQUITIES ANALYST" at none other than Goldman Sachs.

Now this was right up my alley. I had a passion for finance and international economics (heck, I interned under the international economics department at Wells Fargo and had subscribed to The Economist since I was 19), and so I was naturally excited about being the one non-ivy leaguer to break into the Bulge Bracket. To be the one guy from Carlson to say, "Oh no, I don't work at Piper Jaffray or Dain Rauscher or one of those wannabe investment banks. I work at a "real" one." But there was one slight problem.

You see, at the time, Goldman Sachs was still a privately held company. So there was no way to know how much they made. And they fed me this line, "well, if you'd like to interview with us, then you'll have to fly out here for the interview on your own expense."

Of course, 5 years later they go public and I find out they made $47 trillion in earnings and could have damned well afforded my flight with my own personal team of redheaded Irish cheerleaders to cheer me on for the interview, but being a naive 22 year old, what did I know? So I fell for it.

Now the thing is, I didn't make $47 trillion in earnings in 1997 either. And I couldn't afford a flight out there, so my only option was to load up my rusty but trusty 1985 Oldsmobile Cutlass Supreme with some Moutain Dew, some deodorant (no tapes or CD's cause there was no deck), my best suit and head on out.

I scheduled myself two days to get there and two days to get back.

Of course there are logistical problems with planning a cumulative 5 day road trip and making only $16,000 per year without parental support. Namely, you can't afford lodging, which means you sleep in the back of your 1985 Cutlass Supreme. (which is actually quite comfy).

The first rest stop was a small town in Pennsylvannia, Clarion.

I stopped there because there was a state college campus and I figured it was just as safe as any place to stop and sleep. I woke up the next morn around 830AM to the sounds of other students my age making noise and making their way to the gym of the parking lot I had decided to park in. So I decided to wake up, head into the gym and see if there were some lockers where I could maybe take a shower, freshen up, change clothes and hit the road again.

The problem is I'm a particularly young looking 22 year old at the time, wearing what amounted to cut off sweats and a t-shirt and didn't materially differ from anybody else walking into the gym at that time. Little did I know I was about to be assumed into the Badminton 101 class with the rest of the college students.

Little did they know that I was the badminton champion at my high school.

"Hey you, grab a racket!"

"Uh, OK."

So, after 1 hour of summarily defeating the best U of Penn Clarion had to offer (and getting some odd looks that nobody could recognize me or remember me), I hit the showers (which was my original purpose in the first place) cleaned up, hopped back into the Gutless Cutlass and headed out.

I made it to Union City and due to my then-infant economic spidey senses I was able to find a place to park for 50 cents a day. The problem was it was already getting dark and hotel rates I observed along the highway were around $180/night. But I did recall a way side near a town called Dover a couple miles back. So I decided to head back to the way side, sleep, wake up the next morning park my car in Union City and take the train into New York for my interview.

The next morning I did wake up. By this time I was wearing the same clothes for the third straight day and would have to clean up somewhere between Dover and NYC. Started making my way in and right before I got to Union City I stopped at a McDonalds. Went in with my suit and shaving kit. Washed up my body best one can in a washroom in McDonalds. Shaved, put on my suit and headed across the Hudson into Battery Park. Found Goldman Sach's HQ, went in, said I was in for an interview with some high ranked schmutz or another and was escorted upstairs to his office.

Now, I had never been to New York, but I knew this guy was probably pretty highly ranked. His office had a perfect view of the Statue of Liberty. It was right on the coast of Battery Park. And he actually DID have his own redheaded Irish girl cheerleading squad! I'm not kidding, they were right there! I did however remember him having a two floor red carpeted office.

So there I am, sitting in this guy's office. Looking around and he comes in. We introduce ourselves and he says, "So, what was on the front page of the Wall Street Journal this morning?"

"What?"

"What was on the front page of the Wall Street Journal this morning?"

I didn't know. I was driving in from Dover. I was in a McDonalds washing my arm pits with cold sink water and shaving. And making sure I had enough time to make it into Manhattan so I wouldn't be late. And this guy wants to know what's on the front page of the WSJ?

I said, "I don't know."

"Do you read the Wall Street Journal?"

Which I didn't because the Wall Street Journal, frankly, sucks. It's a paper. Even in 1997 it was outdated. I got most of my news from the Internet and if I read anything it was The Economist.

So I lied and said, "uh, yeah."

"What was on it yesterday?"

By this time I wanted to reach across his table, grab him by the lapels and say, "Listen you blue blood schmuck, I just drove 2 days across half the freakin' country because you're too damn cheap to fly me out here. I had to sleep in two way sides, act like I was in a badminton class, essentially shower in a McDonalds' sink and drop who knows how much in gas and Mountain Dew to have your Ivy League pampered ass look at me and ask me what was on the front page of the Wall Street Journal? I don't know what was on the front page of the Wall Street Journal, but I can tell you what Dover, New Jersey looks like at 3AM!"

But by that time I knew it was pretty much over. There was a whole different set of unspoken professional rules out there in the Bulge Bracket that they must have taught you in the Ivy League. And it wouldn't have mattered much if I did know what was on the front page of the Wall Street Journal, because I presume there would have been another eccentric trip wire of the east coast I-Banking world I would have tripped. I got through the rest of the interview with no questions about what I knew about sovereign risk analysis, model programming, valuation techniques or any of my other fortes. And now that I think about it, the suit I interviewed in was from JC Penny. I'm sure I ruined any chances of future U of MN students ever getting an interview at Goldmand Sachs.

And so defeated I left the Big Apple, confident I would get a rejection letter in the mail, which I did one week later.

Now one would think that a kid with the gumption and determination to drive 2 days for an interview, who would sleep in way sides and shower at a McDonalds would in that action itself warrant employment with most employers. But it seems employers nowadays are more concerned with protocol, about procedure, about HR standard questions of "*what would you do if you were in this situation*" or "if *you saw an employee do something unethical, what would you do and why*?" or in the case of Goldman Sachs "*what was on the front page of the Wall Street Journal*?"

Who knew the bulge bracket was no more efficient than the HR department.

You Suck at Suicide Bombing

Sorry, short on time and time for a repost. The best of. Preparing for a big time trip out west. Glacier National. Yellowstone. Grand Tetons...what they hell is a teton?" Anyway, hope you new readers enjoys, you old readers reminisce, and all you junior deputy economists forward it to somebody! (Seriously, I'd be curious to see the statistical ramifications to see if people just insisted on forwarding it to somebody else. Forget whether you have a genuine interest in the post, but if people DID forward it to other people just out of curiosity to see just how many people it would reach.)

It was during the closing few moments of what I call "The Dark Days" in Captain Capitalism's life that I substitute taught at the public schools in the Twin Cities metro, thinking that perhaps I would want to become an economics teacher. Only to find out that what goes on in the school system is not so much education or teaching as much as it is baby sitting children's children and making sure you don't upset anybody or do anything that anybody would disagree with or perhaps even be slightly uneasy about. It also gave me a grudging respect, or perhaps pity, for the impossible situation public school teachers are in;

Try to teach children who never have been disciplined in their lives without meting out discipline yourself.

Impossible.

However, while I quickly found out I would NOT like teaching, I found something I did like.

Something I didn't know I would have liked before.

Grandchildren.

I was substitute teaching kindergarten one week, not really thinking much about it before my first day. Just go in, deal with the little runts, collect my check and go home. But outside banging up my shins something fierce on the "kindergarten furniture" which is all 1/3 scale adult size, I actually found the little snots pleasant, borderline fun.

The reason I came to realize why is that they're still innocent, they're still curious and, frankly, they're so trusting you can manipulate the heck out of them.

Such trust came to my advantage when we were making snowflakes for the teacher (who was sick). Soon I realized that it was winter and that it's a 45 minute procedure just to get them into their winter garb because none of them know how to dress themselves;

One needs help putting on the boots
The other is trying to put snowmobile pants on with their boots already on.
You ever see a kid put a jacket on backwards and sit there for a full 30 seconds looking at their front wondering where the zipper went?
"And no Jimmy, those are gloves, they go on your hands, not your feet"

Regardless, that was a 45 minute process and the buses were coming to pick them up in 55 minutes AND the room was a mess with little paper schnerbles a strew on the floor.

What is a substitute teacher to do?

So I came up with a brilliant idea and said to the kids,

"OK guys, you want to play a game?"

Their eyes shot wide open, all of them, "oh yea yea!!!! We want to play a game WE WANT TO PLAY A GAME!!!!"

Using cunning reverse psychology I said,

"Oh, wait, I don't know. On second thought it really is more of a FIRST GRADER game. Never mind, we can't play the FIRST GRADER game."

That alone had them eating out of my hand. Practically jumping out of their seats, borderline some of them going into cardiac arrest,

"oh oh oh!!!!! Oohhh!!! We want to play the first grader game!!!!! PLEEEEASSEEE!!!! Let us play the first grader game."

"Wellll, I don't know. I could get in trouble...you have to promise not to tell the teacher when she comes back."

"OH OH!!! WE PROMISE WE PROMISE!!!!!!! WE PROMISE!!!!"

"OK, well raise you're right hand."

Which I didn't foresee would be a problem with half the students.

"No, no your RIGHT hand. OK, repeat after me;

"I"

"I"

"Promise"

"Promise"

"Not to tell anybody"

"Not to tell anybody"

"We played the first grader game"

"We played the first grader game."

Once I had their oath, I was pretty sure I'd be able to clean the room and have them in full gear and on the bus in time.

"OK, you 5 are blue team."

"we don't want to be blue team"

"Uh, ok, how about red."

"I don't like red."

"ALRIGHT, FINE, GREEN? IS GREEN OK?"

Yes, they were satisfied with green.

"You guys are yellow team, you guys are red team, and you guys are blue team"

Which ever team picks up the most pieces of junk off the floor wins a prize!

"OH OH !!!! What's the PRIZE WHAT"S THE PRIZE????"

Waiting, looking around to make sure nobody was looking or listening in I said,

"It's a SUR-prize"

"OOOH!!!!! OOH!!!!! "

Before they blew their little gaskets I figured it best to let them clean up the place. And with no forewarning I said,

"123GO!!!"

Boom! Place was clean in under 4 minutes.

Once the room was picked up to my satisfaction I called an end to the game and inspected each team's pile.

"OK, ok, very good there red team. Honorable mention. Yellow team that's a fine pile. Blue team, very good, but I think the winner is GREEN team."

All of green team went more rabid than a bunch of drunken Germans at a British soccer match.

"What'd we win, what'd we win!!!????"

And looking straight into their trusting, excited and hopeful eyes I said,

"You win my dignity and respect."

Dead silence.

And one of them sheepishly peeped up,

"That's not a prize."

Of which there was no time to debate because the bells rang and it was time to get geared up for the buses.

It was this experience, the concept that I could have that much fun with a bunch of little disease spreading snots AND send them on their way to have somebody deal with them and actually pay for them made me think that having children would suck, but having grandchildren could almost be tolerable.

The next day it convinced me grandchildren would be a blast.

For the next day was the FIRST SNOW FALL OF THE YEAR. And here you have these little 5 year old kids, who for them is a big experience. For it was one thing when the snow first fell when you were 3 or 4. But when you're in school and it's the first snow fall, then it is the eleventh commandment that you must go out and have a snowball fight.

Leave it to the nanny-Nazi's to spoil our fun. I was already scheming a massing snow ball fight with red team, blue team and yellow team, but the iron maiden principal came over the intercom.

"I'm aware that it is snowing, but as you know it is school policy there will be no snowball fights and no recess outside. Recess will be held in the gym."

You might as well have taken each of these kids and shot their pet from home right in front of them.

This first big time experience, the first snowfall of their first year in school. And this fascist bitch who kowtowed to her hyperactive, over sensitive, leftist, commie bastard overlords "all risk must be eliminated at all cost" thought nothing of denying these kids their God-given right to a snowball fight on the first snow fall of their first year in school.

The hell they weren't getting a snowball fight. And I had the perfect alibi, "I'm just a dumb substitute teacher."

Now, you think it's a big ordeal getting 30 snots geared up in winter gear in preparation for the buses. Try doing it clandestinely so the principal doesn't find out.

Cripes.

Bring all the gear into the classroom, put the gear on in the classroom. Keep them quiet while you're walking through the halls. "No, Jimmy, that's a glove damnit again!" Hope to God no one sees us making our escape out the back door. But once we were out, the fruits of our labor paid off.

The little snots running around in the snow, making snowballs faster than they could throw them. Using the substitute teacher as a shield. Ganging up on the substitute teacher. The substitute teacher, perhaps, maybe grabbing the occasional kid to use as a shield for incoming snowballs. Their little unformed arms throwing snowballs with the accuracy of Republican Guard tank gunners. The runt of the little, some little girl that couldn't have been more than 2'9" with a huge grin on her face, even though I don't think she managed one direct hit. All the meanwhile little faces you could see smooshed up against the windows from inside the school. Pointing at my students that got to have a snowball fight. Begging their teacher to let them join the free world. Only to have the teacher deny their request and conform to Nazism.

But not my students, they were going to have their day...of course I was going to have my day too.

27 years old and I'm still getting called down to the principal's office.

Despite the lecture I got about "rules" and "legal liability" and everything else that has taken whatever vestiges remain of childhood and thrown them in the toilet, I still stood by my decision. I frankly, by this time, didn't care, because I had also substitute taught babysat for middle school which quickly made up my mind that I was not going to pursue a teaching career anyway.

But it did clinch my decision that grandchildren would be the best thing in the world.

Of course the paradox is that the pleasure and fun grandchildren would bring, is not worth the pain and agony regular children would give. And so, as a way to circumvent this cruel law of nature, I have lobbied my sister to start having nieces and nephews. Heck, I may even start donating time at an orphanage, but I must maintain my image of an evil, fascist capitalist, so I would have to do it clandestinely.

Regardless, the whole point is that, accidentally, I happened upon this little joy of life. Who would have known little snots could be so fun. As long as they go home to their parents, and I can veto authority and do away with the rules you can have a blast with the little wealth-consumers (as long as it isn't your wealth they're consuming). Grandchildren are hands down one of the best things on this planet to enjoy.

Then will somebody please explain this to me?

A woman, 57, who is a grandmother of 41, decided to blow herself up to attack Israeli soldiers.

Now I know that this is the Gaza strip, and I know that this is a different culture, but it is insane to me that if you have 41 grandchildren, with such a potential for such fun and happiness in life, not to mention at the relatively young age of 57, why on God's green earth would you kill yourself and not just deny yourself such a grand time of snowball fights, vetoing parents, and tricking them into cleaning up their rooms, but deny them a grandmother?

And of all things to "lightly wound 3 Israeli soldiers????"

You end your life, pass up a great life and deny 41 grandchildren their grandmother to "LIGHTLY WOUND 3 Israeli soldiers?"

First you suck at suicide bombing. All the training, all the psychological preparation, all the gear, and you just "lightly wound" 3 Israeli soldiers? I mean you REALLY pissed your life away.

I can see them immediately after you blew yourself up;

"Hey Bob"

"Yeah?"

"Looks like you got a little shrapnel in the leg there."

"Oh, didn't notice. I think it's just a piece of grit. You sure I'm wounded?"

"Yeah, I think I see a little blood. Better go and get it checked."

"You think?"

"Yeah, better be safe."

Bob goes to get it checked, doc looks at him;

"What they hell did you come in here for this scratch for??? Here's a band aid, get your ass back on patrol."

Secondly, look what she gave up for "lightly wounding" 3 Israeli soldiers.

41 grand children.

Cripes, I had 30 little snots under my command. It was a blast. How could you pass up all the fun games and times you could have had with 41 of them???? The holidays, the games, the reverse psychology. You name it, the possibilities for fun are endless with 41 of those little tykes running around!!! But no, you opt to blow yourself up.

So I tendered this question to my audience on my radio show. Why would this woman do this? Why would she pass up 41 grandchildren to LIGHTY FREAKING WOUND all of THREE, count them, 1, 2, 3 Israeli soldiers?

And I got two answers.

Jamall called in saying she did it to protect her grandchildren. That the Israeli's were going to hunt these kids down and kill them anyway and this was the only thing she could do to protect them.

Ignoring the brainwashed conspiracy theory aspect of this, I just poked at his logic a bit and asked him, "well, wait, wouldn't she have done more damage if she was a sniper or just stay at home with a shotgun?"

"Well the Israeli's have all the guns and weapons. That's why they throw rocks."

Sure, fine, but why do I see Hamas and Islamic Jihad with AK-47s ripping off rounds into the air? And if the people in the Gaza strip are "stripped" (har har har) of their weapons and Isreal's goal is to destroy them, what's stopping Israel from coming in there and wiping them out?

Of course the answer is that Jamall wants to believe in what he wants to believe, which points to the fact he has an agenda and really isn't concerned with logic or the truth. Just, I presume, coming up with a reason to blame Israel and the US.

Regardless, it still didn't answer my question to my satisfaction. Why did this woman give up her life that would have involved 41 grandchildren?

I was toying around with the idea of brainwashing. That maybe with her 9 children and 41 grandchildren she was destitute and poor. There was nothing to live for, so why not take the express train to Allah?

Then the wife of a former Israeli soldier called in;

"They're paid $25,000 by Hamas to go on suicide runs."

Now, call me cynical. Call me an Israeli sympathizer. Call me an infidel. But take your political and religious leanings out of it and ask yourself which explanation is more palatable?

"This woman killed herself because she was trying to protect her grandchildren?"

Or

"Hamas paid her $25,000 to do this and it would go to help her family?"

Of course the second makes the most sense, and is probably true. But despite the bounty of $25,000 and a "guaranteed audience with Allah" I'll still take happiness provided by the now orphaned 41 snots.

ROI of a Vasectomy

It was determined a while ago that Captain Capitalism would not sow his seed for despite high demand by the ladies, a little Jr. Captain Capitalism would wreak havoc upon my life and no doubt be turned to the Dark Side by the public schools requiring a kind of Obi Wan Kenobi versus Anakin Skywalker ultimate showdown in the end, where no doubt I would surely win for I am on the Good Side of the Force and he would be a product of the public schools.

Having said that, it was determined a while ago that Captain Capitalism would have a vasectomy and his friends in St. Paul got the brilliant idea of having a *"Vasectomy Fund Raiser Party"* where the theme was akin to "He doesn't want to breed, and the World doesn't want him breeding either! Save the World! Donate to Captain Capitalism's Vasectomy Fund!" Alas as the time nears, it got me thinking, "how much am I going to save by having this vasectomy?"

Or more specifically, "what kind of rate of return am I going to realize on a little snip-snip?"

So with a little number crunching and research I figured that by plopping down $1,200 for the vasectomy, and assuming I would have had the 2.08 children that is the US average, I would save about $577,000 (or $945,000 if I was stupid enough to pay for my 2.08 childrens' way through college). This translates into a whopping total Return on Investment (ROI) of 48,177% (or 78,762%, respectively).

Of course, not everybody has 2.08 kids. Some are microscopically wiser only spitting out one. Others are complete morons producing 5 children and no doubt requiring me to subsidize them. Thus I calculated the total

ROI's for varying levels of children as a handy dandy reference guide for those of you pondering having children;

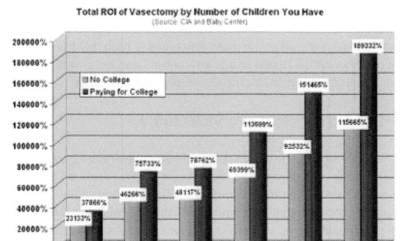

I also annualized these rates of return so that you may compare them against the performance of your 401k/403b funds, and even that of the seemingly "unbeatable" S&P 500 (and no, it's not a mathematical error that paying for college results in a lower annualized rate of return).

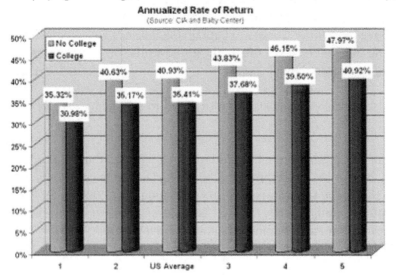

Look out Warren Buffett. There's a new sheriff in town.

How SWPL's Can Predict Bubbles

SWPL (or "Stuff White People Like") when I first read their site I found to be viscerally HILARIOUS. I would just guffaw and heartily so because I found the stuff just so damn funny and so damn accurate. On a deeper level though I didn't really know why it resonated with me so well, but after sitting here at the hospital waiting for a buddy of mine to come out of the urgent care, my super awesome economic genius mind has come up with it.

SWPL exposes the fake, shallow tastes of either faux intellectually elitists or the brain-dead, automotonic herds and delivers to them the mockery and insult they so richly deserve.

For example - "Grad School." HOW GREAT IS THAT? You have some idiot that chose an undergrad degree that was so worthless, they go back for MORE of the same. In reality they are an idiot, BUT, because they have a masters in "fillintheblankhere" they think they're smart.

Or for the "brain-dead herd of lemmings" crowd - Professional sports. Again, how great is that? You have some idiot whose entire LIFE'S WORTH is based on whether or not one group of big guys throws the ball better than another group of big guys, discernible only through the color of the jerseys they wear. But, ohhhhhh wrath upon thee that dare insult the team that these morons have vested so much emotion, psychology and (foolishly) cash into simply because they wear the blue jersey!

But the ultimate kicker for SWPL is that these people are COMPLETELY oblivious to their idiocy. They don't realize they're being made fun of and most of them even think they're smarter than the average person (ever go to a "wine and cheese party?") They just plain don't get the fact that they are the butt of the joke.

Of course there's a problem. SWPL's are not some small group of people. They're the majority of people! And because this is a democracy and a relatively free market we genuinely intelligent people must suffer their idiocy.

For example television.

Um, please somebody explain to me why there are **GLEE PARTIES**?????

You want TV shows to throw parties over? Try Firefly. Try Cowboy Bebop. Try Venture Brothers. Try classical Bugs Bunny. Try Hogan's Heroes. Try Family Guy.

But GLEE????

Another example - the movie industry.

Why am I relegated to marginally good movies starring Jason Statham and cartoons like Despicable Me? Why is it for every "Saving Private Ryan" there's a score of "Eat PRay Love" or "Sex in the City 14" movies?

Going green anyone? Great, I get to pay higher gas prices, higher heating bills, higher electric costs all because it's fashionable to hate fossil fuels.

Even voting patterns.

Why do I have to face a 9+% unemployment rate and a doubling of the national debt?

Because Obama and socialism is just the latest SWPL craze.

Now I could go on, but hopefully I've managed to do two things;

1. Entertain the regular and genuinely intelligent readers that visit the ole Capposphere and
2. Anger and insult SWPL types to the point you might actually be listening now BECAUSE

I am going to lay down some super economic genius that is going to benefit EVERYBODY.

401k's are SWPL.

Yes, sorry to say, 401k's, 403b's, IRA's and whatever other retirement plan you've put together for yourself is SWPL.

Now, this is not to say saving for retirement is foolish, it's not. BUt what we have here is the "brain-dead herd SWPL" members flooding a market to the point purchasing stocks in the US just plain ain't worth it. Specifically, since the government gives tax breaks to invest in (primarily) stocks, what has happened is by default the government has ordained stocks as the defacto retirement vehicle.

Now I've pointed this **out before and to great lengths**. I also pointed it out probably **5 years ago** and the article, though pure genius, went nowhere (because it wasn't SWPL). But now MAYBE, JUST MAYBE, people will listen to me.

This recent run up in the stock market from a DJIA of 7,000 to 12,000 has people very happy and excited. The problem is that the reason you buy stocks is NOT because you will sell them for more in the future. You buy them because of the profits they will (hopefully generate)

To measure this ratio of the price you pay to the profits you'll make, there is a thing called the P/E ratio. It takes the price of a stock and divides it by the earnings per share, showing you essentially how much you are paying in stock price for $1 in earnings. The higher, the worst the deal, the lower, the better.

Now the average has been since 1880 a ratio of roughly 15. Meaning you paid $15 in stock price for $1 in earnings. However during the peak of the Dotcom Bubble the P/E peaked at 45. That bubble burst, bringing the ratio down to 22, STILL NOT A GOOD DEAL.

But, ANOTHER SWPL fad came in - home ownership and condos and mcmansions!

THis drove the P/E ratio up again to 28, only until we found out the SWPL fad of buying a house you can't afford was not a sustainable economic behavior.

The Dow Jones dropped to 7,000 and with it the P/E ratio reached 14!

HURRAY!!!! LOOK AT THAT!!! THE STOCK MARKET IS *ACCURATELY* VALUED!!!!

NOT **UNDERVALUED**

ACCURATELY VALUED.

And so what do people do with stocks that are neither a steal nor overpriced, but just sanely valued?

A buying frenzy.

They drive the Dow Jones back up to 12,000 because SWPL's like to pay high stock prices for low earnings resulting in a P/E that is now around 24, implying a 30-40% overvaluation (denoted by the latest quick jump at the end of the chart).

S&P 500 P/E Ratio (Source: Shiller)

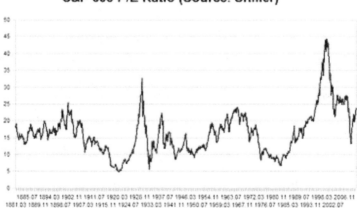

Now Professor Robert Shiller, who is a real intellectual, not only provided this information, but logically concluded stocks are now overvalued again.

But ohhhhhh, my goodness! The SWPL's don't like that! They want stock bubbles! They want happy fuzzies for everyone! They want unicorn 401k's where you never have to work and solely rely on forever increasing asset prices to pay for your retirement. And they **go out of their way to find a rationale or reason to continue living in SWPL Land**.

Well, there's just one more problem with that guys.

See, while arguments can be made about whether you use earnings, EBIT, EBITDA and other things that aren't the bottom line, ultimate what drives stock prices are DIVIDENDS.

Because (and here's the economic lesson of the day), it is the only real cash flow a stock generates.

Oh, sure, you may sell the stock to another person generating a capital gain. But that didn't come from the stock. It came from another person. And the only reason that person paid you money for that stock is why?

Because the only thing a stock really generates is dividends.

And it is here, the only one TRUE cash flow that makes it to the stock holder and the only one TRUE cash flow that provides a stock with value that the situation is dire.

Below is the "dividend yield" for the S&P 500. This mathematically is the dividend per share divided by the price per share. In other words the rate of return you can expect from dividends.

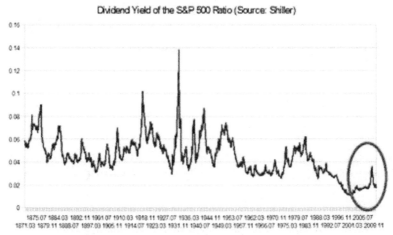

Dividend Yield of the S&P 500 Ratio (Source: Shiller)

And while the history of the dividend yield shows a rough average of about 5%, notice the general trend downward?

It reached a low back in the Dotcom bubble of 1.8%. Wow, that's a GREAT return! Let me get my checkbook out!

Of course there was a dose of sanity when the stock market collapsed this last time around, driving the dividend yield up to a whopping 3%.

But oh no. We can't have that! That's not SWPL! SWPL's like over valued stocks! We don't want any of those icky yuck gross dividends! And so with the reinflation of the stock market bubble the Dow Jones magically doubled in 2 1/2 years with no real economic growth, no real improvement in our economic future, sending the dividend yield back to 2%.

Now economists can go ahead and pull out their hair (like I did) about why the American public just plain doesn't get it and keeps on investing in overvalued markets. They can rack their brains asking, "did these people NOT just go through two massive bubbles??? Did they not learn their lesson? How did they DOUBLE the value of the stock market when the economy is in such dire shape and there's really no economic hope for the future?" But they will simply increase their blood pressure.

For there is no "logical" or "sane" reason these bubbles persistently and constantly form. It's much simpler. It's the same thing that causes people to make "going green" a hobby. It's the same thing that sends millions of people to fork over $10 a ticket to see mediocre movies. It's the same thing that makes people listen to something as boring as public radio.

It's SWPL!

Enjoy the decline!

A Friendly Reminder - If Corporations Really Cared About Global Warming...

Given the price of gas going up and we're facing $4 gallon of gas, I thought this little post I made a while ago might convince those corporate social responsibility types up in the executive offices about just how much they're contributing to global warming by forcing millions of Americans to pointlessly commute. Think of how much publicity your corporation would get if you made telecommuting an official corporate policy!

What I don't get is power.

Money I can understand, but power, that is something very human, maybe the key to evil.

The reason I say that is I look at all the people running for office and you wonder, why would some of these people even bother? They're so loaded, you'd think the last thing they'd want is a full time job and instead should be off on a cruise somewhere soaking up the rays, eating sushi till their death.

John Edwards is the perfect example. Multi millionaire, set for life and yet he chooses to work.

His senior running partner from a presidential election ago, John Kerry, had the sweet set up. Married to a ketchup heiress. Why run for senate, let alone the 80 hour work week president?

And a local here in Minnesota, though he is no more on the political scene, Mark "Daddy's Boy" Dayton, heir to the Dayton empire, decided to buy himself a senator's seat two terms ago.

Alas they still run, by the droves. Pretty much everybody in congress and the presidency don't need the job, but they fight, lie, cheat and take donations from illegal sources to maintain their position of power like there's no tomorrow. Alas, I cannot figure out why.

But "power" isn't an addictive drug that just affects politicians. You look at pretty much any institution and "power" is a reward unto itself. Government, non-profits, political organizations, corporations, militant groups, you name it. But the place I see the irrational addiction to power most flagrantly violating common sense is in corporate America, particularly when it comes to telecommuting.

I don't think I've had a job in the past 10 years where I HAD to be at the office to do it. With "today's" technology (which has been available for about a decade) the vast majority of office and corporate jobs could be done from home.

E-mail, attaching documents, conducting research, calling people, presentations, etc., all the duties, functions and responsibilities of your typical office job can be done from home. And not to mention pretty much every American household has the computer, fax and other machinery to accommodate this. But try to get your boss, let alone anybody with the power who could make it a corporate wide policy to endorse telecommuting is like getting congress to get a flat tax; it would all make our lives incredibly easier, but the politics of power block it every time.

However, this time there is a little political twist. Far from the comfort, job satisfaction and happiness of millions of workers everywhere being the impetus to implementing telecommuting, global warming is providing the political incentive to cut back on greenhouse gases and gasoline consumption. And with this political twist, corporations are bending over backwards to present themselves as "green" companies. NBC with their ridiculous "black out" during a football game comes to mind. However, wouldn't it make sense, such an unbelievably, incomprehensible simple, simple sense to endorse and aggressively pursue implementing a "maximum telecommuting policy?"

I mean, come on. It's a win win win win win situation.

The corporation not only gets to feign being green, IT ACTUALLY IS BEING GREEN!

Employee job satisfaction would rise like you wouldn't believe, not to mention the resulting increase in labor productivity.

Greenhouse gases would drop more than any worthless Kyoto Protocol or "Carbon Trading Indulgences...errr I mean "permits" would cause.

TRAFFIC! Good Lord! Could you imagine the elimination of rush hour from every major metropolis? Nobody would be going to work!

The TIME saved from wasting your time commuting. Instead you could spend it sleeping, improve your health, and spend more time with your family instead. Maybe even divorce rates would go down?

And let's not forget about the costs we'd save on the transportation budgets at the state, federal and local levels! We wouldn't need any new roads, it would just be maintenance. Tax cuts all around, or if you're a lefter leaning sort, "more spending for more worthless social program X."

And if corporations really, REALLY wanted to help the nation become independent from oil, how about not requiring us to drive to your lousy, stinking office in the first place? Could you imagine what would happen to the price of gas if we didn't have to commute?

All these benefits are certainly achievable, but there's just one thing blocking the way;

Power.

Specifically corporate power.

For whatever sick twisted reason, I have to drive to the office. I certainly don't need to. I have a computer at home, a fax at home and even a web cam. But no, my boss insists I drive to the office. Why?

So I can do what I would have normally done at home.

Of course when confronted with the option or request of telecommuting, there is no good reason they can give you, other than they want you to be under their control. They want you to be there, where they can see you, because lord knows that if you were working from home, you'd be drunk, high and bringing hookers over on a coke while you play Halo 3 all day and sell corporate secrets on E-Bay.

And if you think my claim that corporations do this for purely power and political reasons, consider the most obvious and egregious use and abuse of power by corporations;

The meeting.

Cripes. Does a bigger destroyer and depleter of productivity, GDP and work exist? The meeting must have been a creation of communists in a desperate attempt to slow down capitalist economies.

The meeting works like this;

Big time, gray haired bosses like to see how much of other people's time they can send into a black hole. ALL people, no matter how irrelevant their job is to the presumed purpose of the meeting are required to attend. Nobody is listening to the current speaker because it's irrelevant to their job. Meanwhile, the brown nosers, who like you have no purpose of being at the meeting either, ask a litany of questions or blather on about their project to make themselves sound busy and productive, which only lengthens the pain and suffering of those who actually have REAL work to do. Meanwhile the boss sits there, laughing inside, knowing he or she is exercising their power forcing you to waste your time and made you spend the money on gas to attend the meeting.

It is proof positive the only reason you commute is because irrational corporate power wants you to jump through hoops like meetings, commuting, participating in "corporate charity events."

So my fellow junior, deputy, aspiring, official or otherwise economists, just like the US' tax system, just like the raj system in India and just like Kim Jong Il in North Korea, the masses are expected to suffer some more for irrational power. For while a life of never commuting again, spending more time with your family, sleeping in for a full 9 hours a day, eliminating the country's dependence on oil, not to mention finally ending this stupid debate about global warming, as well as the limitless economic benefits telecommuting would provide we're going to continue to pointlessly drive billions of miles for the sole reason of petty, corporate power.

When I am King

I went to a wedding tonight and if there is something that must be extinguished from society it must be this;

In lieu of table favors, Lee and Amy made a donation to the Crohn's and Colitis Foundation of America. This foundation desires to support and fund Research in order to find a cure for Crohn's and Colitis.
For more information visit www.ccfa.org

CROHN'S & COLITIS
FOUNDATION OF AMERICA

"I donated money to a charity and give this donation to you as a gift."

OK, seriously, when I'm king, you are one of the first people I'm going to send to the gallows.

This is not to belittle the Crohn's and Colitis foundation, but rather those that engage in such fake "altruistic" behavior. Seriously, WTF??? There are many reason why this is so dishonest.

1. What if I wanted my freaking gift? Huh, did that occur to you? Who are you to determine whether I want a genuine bona fide table gift or a donation (no matter how honorable it may be) to some charity? Truth is I don't care about the table gift. I wouldn't have even known there was a table gift to begin with. But then you say there WAS a table gift, but that was taken away from me and given to something else? Hello, how, precisely is that a "gift" for me?

2. Don't give me this gloating "how selfless and altruistic are we" BS that you were so "kind" and "charitable" to donate money in my name to a freaking charity. It's a cop out. Plain and simple. Additionally the condescending tone of it, "how dare you expect a gift when there are

people suffering." No, I'm sorry, I'm a selfish, evil, capitalist, hate-filled, racist, dog-tripping, old-people punching, nose picking, booger-eating, goose stepping bastard. Where's my freaking gift?!

3. Not to accuse this particular party, but, I'm sorry, this is too rife to be abused. All I have to do is donate 30 cents to the "Captain Capitalism's Whiskey Fund" and write on some piece of paper that says "Your gift is a $5,000 donation we made to the 'Jones Cancer Fund'" I won't have kids, but I fully expect to have nieces and nephews. And when I do, Uncle Cappy is buying them X-box and ice cream and video games and fishing trips and Swiss army knives and splat ball guns and pocket bikes and water cannons and home made rockets and all the other cool stuff kids want but parents forbid. I'm not making a freaking-a charity donation in their name.

4. The concept of a gift is that you at least TRY to guess what the person genuinely wants. This is why I always advocate giving the gift of cash. Nobody is a better determiner of what one needs, than oneself. And think about what that person wants all you want, you'll never, in the quite literal economic sense give anybody a better gift than cash. In donating money to a charity of fund, you take away the semi-purchasing power of a true and genuine gift and force that person to donate their would be gift to something that is in reality nothing more than something designated to make you feel better about yourself. ie-quit giving a gift to you for yourself you cheat skate hypocrite. Either get them what they want, or cash, or nothing at all.

When I am king, "donating to a charity" as a gift will be punishable by death.

Sex Causes Economic Growth

I was always curious what would happen to the economy if all of the sudden women decided to dolls themselves up in french maid or naughty librarian outfits and upon their husbands or boyfriends walking through the door started, ahem, "making with the bam bam."

My theory was this would make men much happier and trigger a productivity boost which would translate into economic growth. I then pondered being the president of the Federal Reserve and creating indices measuring the sales of french maid outfits as an economic indicator.

Regardless, I did inevitably get around to finding a "frequency of sex rate" and compared it to the average economic growth of about a score of OECD nations. And as I surmised, the correlation between the frequency of sex and economic growth is positive.

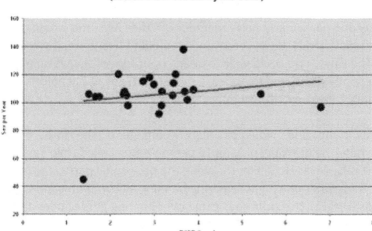

Frequency of Sex per Year vs. 15 Year Avg GDP Growth
(Source: Durex Sex Survey and OECD)

A correlation coefficient of .2 no less.

Now don't ask me to adjust for outliers. And don't ask me about the confidence interval. Just shut up and appreciate what we got here; Empirical, conclusive indisputable proof that sex causes more economic growth.

Alas, when I am president, there will not be any of this impotent "stimulus" package nonsense. I shall just merely decree a "Naughty Nurse" holiday.

Daddy's Little Girl Gone and Got Herself a Degree in Sociology...EXCELLENT!

I will confess!

Many years ago when men were giants and women were angels "The Guys" all lived in this house in St. Paul.

The house was a holy and sacred temple to bachelortude.

Owned by one particularly savvy member of "The Guys," he would rent it out to 4 other friends. However, even if you didn't live there, if you were one of "The Guys" you could walk in at any hour (doors always unlocked), crash there any night, and to appease the **Great Gods of Bachelortude**, occasionally bring a sacrifical 12 pack of beer.

Thusly, my friends and I would pay nightly homage to "**The House of Bachelortude**" by drinking, playing 16 person X-Box linked Halo Fests till 3 AM, WarCraft, Texas Hold 'Em, throwing the occasional party, and I explicitly remember one night requiring banning all communications with girlfriends (UNLESS the girlfriends came over bearing gifts of beer and food which would earn them a 5 minute audience with their boyfriend, whose dumbasses should have been covering my approach to the blue team's base with the sniper rifle while playing Sidewinder in Halo, but oh no, somebody has got to go talk to his girlfriend, meanwhile I'm run over with a tank and the Blue Team has the bazooka and shotgun and is heading over to our base...I'LL NEVER FORGIVE YOU KILGS!!!!!!)

And life was good.

But as this was **The House of Bachelortude** the magazine subscriptions were not exactly The Economist or the Journal of American Political Economy...actually it was FHM and Playboy.
Not that we had a choice in the matter you understand. **The Great Gods of Bachelortude** DEMANDED IT! So what were we to do? You don't want to incur the wrath of **The Great Gods of Bachelortude**!

Anyway, as I said before I will confess, that while waiting for the pizza to show up, or being recently defeated in a game of Texas Hold 'Em I would peruse the most recent issue of Playboy that would be strewn on the table (to appease **The House of Bacherlortude** of course).

While not as attractive as some of the charts I've seen in The Economist, I will admit some of the girls were OK looking. Of course as any good economist would do, I read the footnotes to make sure the source is reputable, the methodology sound, etc. But instead of reading "SOURCE: RETROACTIVELY APPLYING STANDARDIZED UNEMPLOYMENT RATES IN SWEDEN, OECD SEPT 12, 2006" the footnotes to these Playboy models was;

"BAMBI JONES, AGE 23, HEIGHT 5'2" WEIGHT 105 POUNDS. DEGREE - BACHELORS OF ARTS IN SOCIOLOGY FROM THE UNIVERSITY OF ARIZONA."

And then my economic spidey senses started tingling. For fresh in my memory was when I was stood up, not once, not twice, but thrice by a drop dead, Playboy-esque girl who had went to school for cosmotology. This observation, combined with my utter disdain for fluffy majors got me thinking;

Was there a correlation???

Do Playboy Playmates pursue easy degrees?

And if so, do they pursue these degrees because they're dumb?

Or are they just bidding their time in college majoring in philosophy whilst scoping out for a husband effectively earning themselves an MRS. degree?

Furthermore, should they not find a husband are these degrees so worthless that they resort to baring it all to make ends meet?

And finally, can what daddy's little girl major in be a predictor of whether millions of young horn-dog guys will see daddy's little girl spread eagle on a centerfold?

So I set forth to conduct this serious study. Selflessly dedicating my time for the sake of advancing our understanding of economics. And took it upon myself to study all the Playboy Playmate's profiles and see what they majored in.

No no, you don't have to thank me. It's my patriotic and American duty to foist this heavy burden upon myself. And it is the least I can do to repay the great freedoms our forefathers fought so valiantly for.

The results?

Here is a breakdown of what Playboy Playmates studied in college;

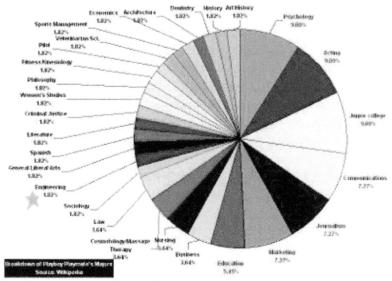

*Note, the vast majority of Playmates either didn't attend or list whether they attended college. This includes all the data found on Wikipedia for all playmates going back to 1980. An interesting side note, the further back you go, less and less playmates went to college reflecting the increasing trend in labor force participation by women. Total number of playmates that listed a major was 54, understand this does not mean they finished college or earned a degree. It just mentioned college.

What is amazing is how there is not one, **NOT ONE** COMPUTER PROGRAMMER OR PRE-MED OR PHYSICS OR OR ACCOUNTING OR ENGINEERING MAJOR (bar Cindy Crawford who spent 1 quarter in chemical engineering, but never graduated). The majority of playmates pursue degrees in utter fluff, the biggest pulls being "psychology," "acting/theater," "journalism," "communications," "education," "junior college," and that weak pathetic worthless degree that tries to score some credibility as passing itself off as a "business major;" marketing.

I further simplified this chart between what I like to call **"Fluffy El Crapo Degrees"** and **"REAL DEGREES THAT WILL GET YOU A FREAKING JOB."**

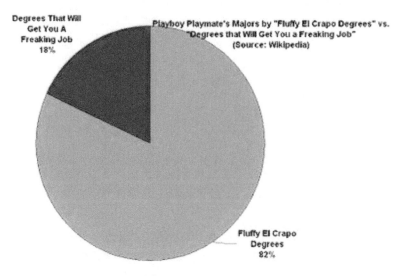

A full 82% of the playmates that went to college, effectively wasted their time and pursued worthless degrees, whilst a paltry 18% actually went and did something useful with their time (sadly even this can't be said as most of them didn't graduate with those degrees, when you adjust for this it literally is only about 3%).

So what lesson can we take away from this fellow aspiring and junior deputy economists?

How can we end this post so that in a Stan and Kyle like way we say,

"you know, I think we learned something here today."

Well, for one, maybe Larry Summers shouldn't have been punished for his truthful statement that women just aren't cutting it in the real sciences. Maybe good ol' Larry was just trying to prevent some of these young girls from having to resort to posing nude to make ends meet or make a living. Maybe Larry was trying to actually do something **tangible** that would help close the wage gap between men and women by getting more women into the sciences and engineering.

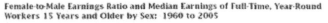

Female-to-Male Earnings Ratio and Median Earnings of Full-Time, Year-Round
Workers 15 Years and Older by Sex: 1960 to 2005

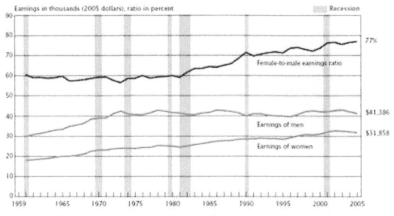

Note: The data points are placed at the midpoints of the respective years. Data on earnings of full-time, year-round workers are not readily available before 1960.
Source: U.S. Census Bureau, Current Population Survey, 1961 to 2006 Annual Social and Economic Supplements.

Secondly, maybe we ought to cut back on fluffy subjects in not just the high schools but the colleges as well. Enough of the "pscyhology" or "sociology" or "communications" crap. And certainly do away with "peace studies" programs. Maybe instead of enticing women with the false illusion that they're going to make it big or even make it period with touchy feely degrees that we show them just what caliber go and pursue such worthless degrees and encourage them to pursue careers that would actually increase their incomes and make them TRULY independent women.

Third, upper middle income fathers who think "daddy's little girl can do no wrong," think daddy's little girl is superior to all other humans, and think nothing of preparing his little girl for the real world beyond giving her his credit card for a trip to the mall better pull his head out of his ass and start fathering instead of thinking his arrogance and bank account is going to carry through his little suburbanite princesses. That you might want to instill a little work ethic in her and teach her the merits of work and self-reliance before you go and buy her a little Honda Del Sol or Pontiac Sunfire.

And finally, if daddy's little girl goes into the fluff-stuff for college, be aware that the day might just come when you go to the office and all the other guys will see just how much your little princess has grown up.

However, there is a way to prevent this embarrassing situation. Note that the sciences;

engineering, computers, medicine, physics, chemistry, etc.

are like a vaccine practically innoculating your little girl from ever showing her assets to the entire world and all the horn-dogs at **The House of Bachelortude**. Again, Cindy Crawford is the only one to major in engineering, and she gave that up because she had the rare opportunity to become a bona fide supermodel. And although I didn't add it up, the majority of "post playboy careers" a lot of these playmates had were either "dancers" or "strippers."

Only problem is we keep on telling women that math is too "tough" for them and channel them to the majors and careers that are less paying than subjects that have traditionally been pursued by men.

Of course, when we say this, everybody gets in a hissy fits and demands blood. Larry Summers lost his job over it. Feminists and leftists don't like it because women entering the sciences would result in more capitalists and Republicans and take away from the liberal arts.

Besides which...it just occurred to me...if we encouraged girls to major in the sciences, where would we get our Playboy Playmates?

Uhhh..sooo...ummm, yeah, on second thought ENCOURAGE YOUR YOUNG DAUGHTERS TO MAJOR IN FLUFF! We wouldn't want them getting real jobs with real careers. We men need them desperate enough to disrobe for our viewing pleasure.

Besides which, **THE GODS OF BACHELORTUDE** DEMAND IT!!!!!

How Wine Proves Women are Communists!

I ordered some wine.

And the reason I ordered some wine is because I wanted some wine.

Now let us review that simple statement.

"And the reason *I* ordered some wine is because *I* wanted some wine."

Not

"I ordered some wine because I wanted *somebody else* to have my wine."

Not

"I ordered some wine because I wanted to *SHARE* my wine."

Not

"I ordered some wine so I could go and share it with the masses and we all sing kumbya while talking about how dreamy Obama is."

I wanted some wine for me, because *I wanted some freaking wine.*

But sure as bears and popes, the girl slowly reaches across the table, going for *my* glass of wine.

Not even asking.

Not even requesting permission.

Just sloooooowly moving her hand across the table, making a bee line towards MY wine.

I waited patiently for her hand to make contact with it, but once it did I said,

"Whoa, whoa whoa whoa whoa! Just what do you think you're doing?"

Almost with a shocked look on her face she said, "I was just going to have a sip of your wine."

Now let me explain something to ladies out there. You see, I ordered MY wine because I wanted some wine for ME. When men buy themselves something, they intended it for them. Not for you. Not to be shared. Not to make us have warm fuzzies in our stomachs as we all capitulate to Marxism and spread the wealth. It's for us! Not you.

So I explained the concept of how I forfeited some of my finite life in exchange for the money to buy this wine for ME. That I gave up a part of my life in the form of labor to earn the money that bought me this wine and ergo, I was 100% entitled to all of it. Every single drop. I went so far as even to offer to buy her, her own glass of wine if she wanted one. But then she dropped the Ultra-Marxist bomb on me;

"But I want to taste yours."

You see, this is why women deep down inside are communists. They don't want to pay to taste some wine. They don't want to even have their entire whole glass of wine. No, they want a "little sip" of *YOUR* wine.

So I asked said girl,

"Said Girl, why is it you want a sip of MY wine when I am more than willing to buy you your own glass of wine?"

And the Leninist across the table from me responded,

"Because I just want a sip. Besides it tastes better when it's somebody else's."

This confirmed something I knew all along. Communists derive an additional utility from the same volume of consumption if what they're consuming is somebody else's. It's a sick and twisted masochistic aspect of the weaker political ideology.

I was always intuitively aware of this as the same thing happened with fries. Lord knows you couldn't just sit there on a date in high school, about to engorged yourself with those heavenly McDonald's fries, and then, sure as bears and popes some your 16 year old steady is burrowing into YOUR fries like a badger in a hole. But now I had proof, a confession, self-admitted guilt she was gunning for my wine because it was MY wine.

And don't think for a second this is just relegated to fries or wine. Oh no no no no! Ice cream. My god, has any man in the history of America been able to enjoy 100% of his own, labor-bought-and-paid-for ice cream? Can't get one bite before "she" wants to "try" some of "your" ice cream.

Any pie left in the fridge? Go ahead and try to have a full piece of pie. Oh no, you can't. Not in a million years. Even though there is a whole 3/4ths of a pie in the fridge and she could very well have her own entire piece of pie to herself, no, she wants "just a little bite" of yours.

And don't think it's just relegated to food. Ha! If you had a favorite shirt she likes, yeah, well pal, you HAD a favorite shirt. Now it's a communal shirt. That nice little sporty convertible you have out there. If it's 85 and sunny, she's going to want a little taste of that. Nothing is safe from their Marxist reach.

Of course, try to then share something that was intended to be shared and she wants none of it. Video games are the perfect example. Designed to bring the masses together, designed to make us all players, designed to increase camaraderie and bonding and bring us all closer together, arguably the key to world peace, but oh no, she wants none of that. No, it has to be something that she covets. Your ice cream. Your wine. Your martini. Your convertible. Your favorite old ratty sweatshirt from college.

Oh, and you may be laughing now, but they're out there men. And it all starts with just a "little sip" of your much-coveted wine.

Time to Start Cheering for the Good Guys

Whilst tirading against the bailout and mourning the slow and inevitable slouch towards socialism the US seems hell-bent on, a reader made an excellent point that deserves further attention. I'm paraphrasing, but it basically went like this;

"You're like Hank Rearden when he realizes that it's not society that is behaving irrationally, but given the bail outs, corporate and social welfare, taxation rates, etc., it is your economic behavior that is irrational."

Now I confess I have not read Atlas Shrugged, but the point was still very well made. I, as well as all of you out there are suckers. We're rubes. We're the dumbsh!ts for working hard, paying our taxes, living only in houses we can afford, spending within our means, and otherwise supporting ourselves. That with all the benies government pays to the losers and parasites of society, why on God's green earth would we be working in the first place?

It's an outstanding point. I look back at my life and see just how much work and sweat I put into college, my career, my side jobs, only to have what is essentially the parasites of society lob off 33% of it, and now $700 billion more, and I have a hard time seeing how it was worth it. I'm trying to find out why I slaved and toiled working full time and going to school full time, when I could have just taken the easy way out and said "screw it, I'm collecting welfare and going on MinnCare (Minnesota's state health care) and refusing to work a day in my life." I'm trying to find out why I paid WaMu religiously and timely for every mortgage payment in the past 7 years, only to have their deadbeat leaders come to the government with a cup in their hand and ask for more of my money. I should have just defaulted like everyone else and stayed at home and played video games all day. But the key point is that whereas we berate and loathe such behavior, given the progressively socialist environment foisted on us by the government, how could a rationale person NOT avail themselves of all those benefits? Yes, we detest the parasite, welfare, sub-slime deadbeats who lived in better houses than we did, drove nicer cars than we have, and did it all with no ability to pay, and ultimately on the dime of us responsible members of society, but can you blame them?

And thus, why the entirety of this whole financial/banking/housing situation is so enraging. We did the right thing. We worked hard, we paid our bills, we budgeted, lived within our means and adhered to other simple concepts that 3rd graders can understand. The losers of society, whether knowingly or ignorantly (though I'm going more with knowingly), spent themselves into oblivion. And while they enjoyed luxury cars, sushi diners, trips to Europe and SUV's, we scrimped and saved and conserved, only to ultimately subsidize and bail out these degenerates. But to add insult to injury, as we look back at it, we were the ones who were idiots. We were the ones who were taken. To do the right thing, to work hard, to pay taxes, to pay your mortgage to live within one's means for the past 5 years was laughable and idiotic. We were voluntary hosts to parasites. It is arguably the most angering and depressing feeling a lot of us are feeling right now.

Alas, we are faced with a choice. Do we become "rational" human beings and capitulate to this wave of socialism sweeping the nation? Do we tell our mortgage company to ef off and refuse to pay our mortgage? Do we go out and sign up for welfare and state-paid health care? Or do we continue in our idiotic, archaic, obsolete 1940's old-school-American ways and continue to work hard and live within our means? Let me argue for that "stupid" "old school" Americanism.

First off you must realize the honor that comes with being one of those dwindling few that support themselves. If it weren't for us, the entire human race would cease to exist. I'm not saying this as hyperbole or rhetoric, I mean that dead-seriously. If it weren't for the producers, the human race would cease to exist. There'd be no New York, there'd be no X-Box, there'd be no ice cream there'd be no wiener dogs. The reason is very simple; if you don't produce, if you don't support yourself, then by definition you will die. And the same thing applies on a society wide level. I've always asked myself "what would happen to the country if all the Libertarians, republicans, conservatives and other varied sorts of capitalists, just ceased to exist?" And the answer is very simple; there'd be no country. We are the people who work and make this country go. We are the people who made America great. It is the workers and producers and entrepreneurs of the world that are the sole reason for advances in technology, creations in medicine, democracy, flight, cars, scotch and everything else. Everybody else is in the most literal sense, irrelevant to humankind and human history.

Second, is the nobility of independence. I don't know how many times back in college I heard some little 20 something girl, fresh out of a women's studies class bravado about how she was "independent."

Oh sure, dad bought her a brand new car.

And paid her rent.

And paid her credit card bills.

And her tuition for her worthless sociology degree.

Oh, but she was "independent."

And the womens studies professors. Certainly even more adamant about their independence than their student.

Oh sure, nobody in the private sector would hire them.

And the only thing they do is teach a study whose only function is to be retaught to the next generation of kids with no practical application outside academia.

And in most cases, these professors are in the public schools thereby necessitating the only way they'd get paid is if the government forces tax payers to cough up the money for something they wouldn't have spent money on otherwise.

But they're independent.

And those preppy frat boys soon to become Wall Street's finest as they kiss ass and suck...errr...I mean "work real hard" pulling off C's and D's in college because they know daddy has a job lined up for them in the end, so why work anyway?

Oh yeah, they're "independent."

Especially when they go to the government and need a bail out for Bear Sterns, Lehman Brothers, AIG. Oh yeah, real independent.

Let me tell you who is really independent.

The burger flipper at McDonald's who is slaving away to make ends meet and doesn't have the luxury of being a suburbanite prince or princess. He's independent.

The security guard who works the third shift so s/he can go to school during the day so they might be able to better themselves. They are independent.

The blue collar family that lives within their means and BUDGETS (any of you parasites ever hear of that word), to ensure they don't spend more than they make. They are independent.

And the capitalist or entrepreneur that saves their money, starts a company, fails but then doesn't go to the government for a subsidy or a check. He is independent.

Independence is arguably the most noble trait to have. It means you are truly and genuinely supporting yourself and do not rely upon others. Furthermore, it means you are a contributing member to society. Even if you think it a menial task or job you have, the burger flipper at McDonald's has done more to advance society than the highly paid Wall Street investment banker who's asking the government for a bail out because he's truly and genuinely INDEPENDENT. And it is because we are truly independent (not just "told" we're independent by some academian putz) that makes us (and I mean this seriously) better people than those who are dependent no matter what our financial background.

Finally, to give those of you who are independent, self-supporting contributing members of society one final thing to think about; who would you rather be?

I've often opined what would it be like to be a welfare bum or suburbanite prince/princess or "professional activist" on their death bed. To have all those years of lying about, not producing, not making anything of this one, precious finite life you have, and then when the end of that life is upon you, don't you have just a little bit of remorse or lament you've pissed it away?

When I die, I will be proud. I have taught thousands of people how to dance. I've taught thousands of people about personal financial management. I've gotten hundreds of little kids interested in paleontology and fossils. I hope I **educate millions about the housing crisis.** And for my day job (though it sounds nerdy) I've allocated capital efficiently. I can point to something so when I'm on deathbed I can say, "hey, good or bad, sub-prime deadbeats parasiting off of me or not, I achieved some amazing sh!t."

The dependent, the deadbeats, the losers who we are currently bailing out, can't say that. All they will be able to say is "I sat around and watched TV while collecting a government check."

"I helped bring the world's largest economy to recession as well as the global economy while I pocketed $100 million in a severance package."

"I filed for bankruptcy 3 times and had the consumer eat the extra costs."

When you die, you will leave a legacy. Maybe you aren't Tony Stark. Maybe you're not Bill Gates. But in the end, you will be able to point to your life and say, "I didn't waste it." You will go down in history as one of the producers. One of the independents. Alas, rational or not, there's nothing wrong with wanting to be Hank Rearden.

Kill the Bankers

I was angry before, which prompted me to **write my book**. But now I am livid. With a potential $1 trillion bill facing the taxpayers, I am at a loss for words to describe my sincere hatred for bankers. And thus, without words, that leaves only actions;

I want to kill the bankers.

I don't mean that in a funny, ha ha, way. I don't mean that in a sarcastic way. I mean that in an old school American, wild wild west, you killed my father-prepare-to-die, deadly serious way. I literally want to grab my gun, get a lot of bullets, find some bankers, hunt them down and kill them. I even know the bankers I would hunt down. I know their names and where I can find them. I would do with a smile on my face. I would enjoy the action of it, I would savor it. I would go home and pour myself a well-earned drink and sleep just as soundly as I ever have, if not, probably better. I would not have one pang of guilt.

Now I know that violence and hate and revenge are officially outlawed in this country. When we get attacked we're supposed to ask what we did wrong. When we get bombed we're supposed to apologize. And when bankers screw us out of $1 trillion, we're supposed to forgive them and get over it and maybe bend over again and to make easier for them the next time around, perhaps spread our butt cheeks.

Not me.

No.

I'm steaming.

And the particular reason why is that bankers are unique because of their hubris and arrogance.

Say you have a deadbeat on welfare. Fine, I have no respect for that individual, I may not really like that individual, but for the most part while they're living off the taxpayer, they're not really living a jet set life style. Bankers on the other hand, insist, almost demand that they live the jet set lifestyle, regardless of whether they produce a profit or not. They drive Beamers, they drive Mercedes, they wear fancy clothes, all to put up the image, all to tell themselves in their minds that they are hot sh!t, whether or not they're actually a good banker. Yet the fact so many of them were so poor at their job that it is potentially going to cost the real working American's $1 trillion shows you their entitlement mentality.

"What? Turn down a loan on account we're ultimately guaranteed by the FDIC and thus the taxpayer and we owe it to the country not to destroy the economy? Why that would get in the way of my commission! And me

having the latest in Armani and Trophy Wife apparel is more important than you dumb working schleps! Why, I'm a BANKER, I'm an important guy! I work on Wall Street! I'm not some peon like you!"

Additionally, it is the attitude of the holier than thou crowd of the now-crumbling elite "Bulge Bracket" of Wall Street. I remember many years ago applying to the likes of Bear Sterns and Lehman Brothers only to be turned down solely because I went to a state school and not "the Ivy League." I wasn't a Rockefeller or a Winthrop the III or a Kennedy. I, and presumably the rest of blue collar America, was not "good enough" to work for these firms. Now these firms and their incompetent, moronic blue blood ilk are coming up to us with a cup in their hand for a $1 trillion bail out? These "elites," the "smartest people from the best schools" have effectively caused a recession? They are the bottom of the barrel. They're incompetent. They're losers. They're not good at anything but living off of mommy and daddy, and when they can't produce anything of value, parasiting off the real men and women who work.

Regardless, this mentality these bankers have is the exact same as an entitled socialist, but with the unfathomable arrogance that they're entitled to riches as well at the expense of society and the taxpayer. They are entitled to a fancy I-banking job whether they have the skill for it or not. They are entitled to limitless wealth because of their profession. They are entitled to drive a luxury car, even though pretty much every bankers' beamer out there is paid for with 100% of somebody else's money. It is arguably the epitome of evil and why I seriously would not have any problem killing some bankers.

Of course, the problem is "killing" is "illegal." Much as I (and no doubt some of you) would like to go out with our rifles during "Banker Season," we'd all end up in jail. Thus, I have a solution, that although would not be quite as effective as "The Great Banker Purge of 2008" in fighting moral hazard, I think the effects will be the same as it is worse than death itself;

Tax them.

Tax the living snot out of them.

We know who the bad bankers are. It's not that hard. The Feds are investigating scores of banks and while the criminal bankers have left or been fired, you can still track them down, garnish their wages and make them pay for their mistakes. It is only fair that for once, instead of repeating another S&L bail out where we give bankers another cup of moral hazard, we make them pay, and make the price so dear they never forget. That instead of them parasiting off society, they sleep in their own bed and deal with their own mess. That instead of driving their Escillade around for selling the taxpayers another $40 million worth of worthless CDO's, they drive an old used Chevy Caprice and have to budget, and conserve and feel the constant threat of poverty the rest of us have known, but they never have. I want them to pay the $1 trillion tab, not when they're making $10 million a year in bonus, but when they have to work as a security guard during the 3rd shift for $8.50 and hour.

Of course though, we don't really have a choice because our beloved elected leaders are going to once again bail out the financial system on account of it being "too vital a component to the economy." But bankers beware, if a revolution ever comes and society crumbles, something tells me it won't be rabbit season, or duck season, or Elmer Fudd season.

It'll be **banker season**.

But I Thought Italian Guys Were Hot?

Karen is a nice sweet buddy of mine. Bit brash, bit loud mouthed, but those are the flaws that make her all the more endearing to me. From an upper middle income family, she has visited Europe several times whereas I've never been. Also from an upper middle income family, she was afforded the opportunity to go party in her 20's and even to this day goes to the Boom-Chicka-Boom bars that I usually eschew.

However, though very different, we get along swimmingly because she works hard, she is self-supporting and she hates communism. Also in talking with with her I get a glimpse into a world I have never been in, and she gets a glimpse into a world she's never been in. But one of the more interesting observations, if not, addictions she has is "Spanish Men" or "Italian Men."

Not too long ago she went to Spain and hung out for a week. She absolutely loved it, particularly the laid back attitude and culture of the Spaniards. She said,

"Oh, Captain, you would just not fit in there. Everything is relaxed and laid back. You're supposed to take siestas during the day and have some wine. And they're always critical of American's attitudes. *"Oh, you Americans. You are so tight and anxious. You work too hard. You need to relax and learn to enjoy life."* They go out dancing every night and party and then wake up at 10AM and go to work. They know how to live."

Interestingly enough, it is the same with the Italians (or so I'm told by the ladies who have been there). The Italians are laid back, they know how to enjoy life. They drink their vino and drive their Vespas, they love life, blah blah blah.

Of course Karen and the varied female friends of mine are also fans of the Spanish and Italian men. Accents, olive skin, charming, they know how to have a good time. Oh yes, the Ladies of America love the Men of the Mediterranean. But there was a another funny observation she had. When I asked her,

"Well, how do they afford all this vino and dancing? How can they afford a lifestyle of just lying around and getting to work at 10AM if rents are so high in Madrid?"

She said,

"Well, all these Spanish guys all live at home with their parents. A lot of them work for their moms or fathers as well. They absolutely love their families, it's wonderful."

And that's when the epiphany hit me, as it should be hitting you right now.

It is well known and documented that the charming Men of the Mediterranean live at home in higher numbers. So much so it affects the birth rates of come countries because you can't be **making babies when mom is sleeping upstair**s. However, this is NOT a criticism of those men, as I do not believe it is because these men lack ambition, drive or work ethic. It is the direct consequence of having a government so large and invasive that it crowds out the private sector. This not only makes finding a job difficult, but also provides great financial incentive to not work as hard or leave home. Free health care, free education, free food, free this, free that. Why go to school, become a doctor, and buy a house when you can live at home and enjoy 4 siestas a day during a 4 hour work week?

But what is truly great, what is truly juicy is the utter hypocrisy the young women of America display. Not consciously of course, because I don't think they connect the dots. Additionally, I don't think they're contemplating the socio-economic reasons why tall, dark, handsome and charming Rafael lives at home with mom as they salsa dance with him in Barcelona tipsy on vino. But there is a hypocrisy. Anybody see it yet?

Well, let me connect the dots.

"Fernando" 30 year old accented hot Italian/Spanish guy with olive colored skin, is a great cook, rides a Vespa, drinks vino, knows how to dance and "live life" and loves his mother. **Oh Fernando, take me away**!

"Jon Jones" 27 year old stupid lazy American who doesn't have a job, can't find one, doesn't have a degree, plays video games all day, drinks beer, watches sports AND **STILL LIVES WITH HIS MOTHER!** *Jon Jones, you **need to man up** you slacker!!!*

What the ladies fail to see is that Fernando and Jon are the exact same guys, just an ocean apart. Oh sure Fernando has an accent, olive skin and speaks Italian, but they both "live life" (Jon plays video games, Fernando seduces naive female tourists), they both drink (Jon prefers Budweiser, Fernando red wine), they both live at home (though we interpret this as and applaud Fernando for "loving his mother"), and I guaran-freaking-tee you they BOTH play video games. Probably MW3 online, they're probably doing a co-op mission right now.

Laugh as we might, there are several economic lessons or observations to be gleaned.

One, is how Italy and Spain are down the road further than the US when it comes to the state replacing men. Men are no longer the primary bread winner of the family. That is the state. Men are no longer the kernel of the household. That is the state. So with the state replacing the primary roles men used to play in Italy and Spain, AND with the financial largess they provide to people, is it any wonder these guys "live life" and bang on their drums all day?

Two, is it any surprise Italy and Spain are part of the PIIGS suffering from imminent financial collapse? Yes, what a wonderful life it must be to drink vino all day, work 20 hours a week, have free health care and **be able to retire at 57** AND have everything paid for. You don't need to be a PhD in economics to understand why they have such HUGE debts - because the countries come nowhere NEAR producing what is necessary to pay for all the crap they've promised themselves under the Tuscan sun.

Three, how women (in a very admitted and general brush) generally are unable to see how voting for socialism drives men to the couch, video games, beer and their parents' basement. If you keep voting for socialism you do two things to make men perpetual Peter Pan's who will never grow up. One, you will essentially pay them with a bevy of government benefits so they don't HAVE TO WORK. Two, even if they wanted to work, THERE ARE NO JOBS BECAUSE YOU'VE DRIVEN AWAY THE PRIVATE SECTOR AND INVESTORS WHO WOULD NORMALLY LIKE TO INVEST, BUT NOT IF 50% OF THEIR PROFITS ARE GOING TO BE CONFISCATED!

Four, boys, this is an important one. If you want to impress girls here but live at home, all you have to do is keep doing what you're doing now, but fake an accent, take some tanning pills and instead of saying, "I live at home with mother because I can't afford rent," say, "I live at home with mother because I love her and want to take care of her." Then POOF! You've magically gone from a "Grade A American Loser" to an "Exotic Foreigner Who Loves His Mother."

My Bondage-A-Go-Go-Girl Story

Occasionally, kind of akin to Michael Savage when he talks about his days as a youth, my friends suggest instead of a lecture on economics, that I regale my audience occasionally with more personable stories. And after telling a group of new friends my bondage-a-go-go girl story, they all demanded I put it up here, so pour yourself a martini, light up a cigar if you have it, settle in and enjoy.

It was 1998 and I was all of 22 years old. I frequented a club called "The Front" in Minneapolis for it was the very first place to have swing dancing. It was a great place (still is) with a Tiki-Martini Lounge theme and they had live bands like **Tony DeMarco**, **Vic Volare** and a whole host of other bands. But it was also called "The Front" because it was the front part of a larger club called "Ground Zero." Ground Zero was an industrial, techno-rave discoteque that had this kind of "dance-girls-in-cages-men-wearing-leashes-bondage" theme. The upstairs of which you could pay a scantily-leather-clad dominatrix or dominator (depending on your preference) to torture you in front of the masses. Things like electrocuting clamps, pouring hot wax on you and so forth. It was quite surreal.

In any case, in my youthful age of 22, I ended up dating Jackie who was the bartender at The Front and was also 30. Giddy as a school boy, we only dated about a month or so, until she broke my poor youthful heart on the grounds I was too young for her and she felt guilty dating me. Regardless, she was a nice gal, almost church going, and all we did was date and smooch a little bit, but alas, that's all it was meant to be.

So fast forward 7 years and me and my buddy Tony (the singer of the club who I befriended) were reminiscing about the good ole days at The Front.

I said, "Do you remember The Front."

Tony responded, "Yeah, I remember The Front. Those were good days back then."

I said, "Nothing exciting, but I used to date Jackie. You know, that cute blond that was the bartender at The Front."

Tony, kind of surprised, turned and looked at me and said, "You dated Jackie the dominatrix?"

I said, "No, no, I dated Jackie, the bartender at The Front."

He replied, "You dated the dominatrix!"

I said, "No, Jackie, the bartender at The Front! She was the girl serving drinks at The Front. That's who I dated."

Smugly he then replied, "Jackie, the bartender at The Front, WAS the dominatrix!"

In disbelief, I said, "Wha?"

"You mean to tell me, you were dating the dominatrix and you DIDN'T KNOW!?"

Tony who was, and still is, one of the most somber, darker individuals I know, never laughed so hard in his life.

I said, "Well how the hell was I supposed to know! She didn't have whips or anything in her house! It's almost as if she was going to church or something!"

Never before had I felt so cheated. I almost felt more cheated out of that, than the social security I'll never get. She seemed like a normal, almost quiet-like girl. And then, seven years after the fact, I found out I was dating Minneapolis' premiere dominatrix.

And thus concludes my bondage-a-go-go girl story.

A "PhD in Manosphere Studies"

So I am hiking and in the back of my mind a thought or observation is trying to get out. It's centralled around the purpose or reason why one would get a degree in "Women's Studies." And I don't know if it was a neuron that was jolted into place or perhaps the Rumpleminze finally wore off of one of my neuron receptors, but the epiphany finally exploded to the frontal lobes:
BLAMO!

"How stupid would a PhD in "Manosphere Studies" be?"

The question seems obvious or maybe simple. People have been kicking around a "male studies" department recently and most of us on some level know to poo-poo the idea because it is outlandishly stupid. "What would be the point" most men would ask, and we'd dismiss the idea and its originator as stupid. But the epiphany is not so much in the question being asked, but taking the same logic, consequences and ramifications of asking that same question and applying it to "women's studies."

If it sounds ludicrous to offer a "PhD in Manosphere Studies" then how galactically stupid of an idea was it for somebody to come up with "women's studies" as some kind of viable or legitimate field? Additionally, how naive and gullible did millions of sheeple have to be in order for it to grow legs and make it this far a legitimate academic field? In short, the idea of a man (or a woman) getting ANY kind of degree in "Manosphere Studies" is so outlandish, so stupid, it provides the clear vantage point, void of blinding politically-correct bias, needed to realize the true foolishness and stupidity in treating "women's studies" as a legitimate field.

And so Lieutenants, Agents in the Field, and Junior, Deputy, Aspiring, Official or Otherwise Economists, let us go down into this rabbit hole with the intent of fully exploring it and snuffing this rabbit out.

First is the inanity of the idea. To offer a study of one's traits half the population are born with is on the level with offering a college program in studying the color of the sky. As I said in "**Worthless**" (SPECIFICALLY warning minorities and women about the pitfalls of spending $100,000 in studying hyphenated-American studies that have NO job prospects) traits are something you are born with.

You're not special because you're "female."

You are not special because you're "Hispanic."

You're are not special because you're "straight."

You are not special because you are "male."

And you are not special because you're "black."

You just simply ARE these things.

You didn't "work" at becoming them. You didn't study or engage in academic rigor to hone your skills at being "male" or "black." You just "are." So to study mere traits you had nothing to do with and then somehow champion them as "skills" or something to have "pride" in or (worse) to turn these mere traits into "achievements" deserving of reward is nothing more than a childish, lazy, selfish, self-absorbed, ego-driven, love-fest. It serves no practical purpose except to stroke your ego. It's ludicrous.

But again, don't listen to mean ole sexist me, view it from the perspective of majoring in "Manopshere Studies."

Not only would I, but every other guy out there (I'm guessing) would say,

*"Why the hell would I study myself? I already know enough about myself, live with myself 24 hours a day, and **I don't really define myself by my race or gender**. I'd rather study something new, develop a skill or consume new knowledge. What could I possibly gain by paying some washed up professor $4,500 a class to learn about "being me" or "being male?" It's stupid."*

Regardless of which approach we want to use, ANY study of a person's gender has no practical application. The concept of such studies is point blank absurd. They should/should have NEVER existed in the first place.

Second, the absurdity and the lack of any outside, practical purpose in women's studies behooves the question:

What type of people major in this crap?

But before we can ask who majors in it, I have a very thought-provoking question - who started it and how did it all get started?

I mean, who woke up late at night with a brilliant idea, rushed to their bedside table, broke out the pen and paper and wrote down:

"Let's create a college program so poor female college students can spend thousands of dollars getting a degree in themselves! And not just that, but we'll offer MASTERS and DOCTORAL programs in what it means to be female! Of course there will be no employment prospects to such a

degree. And of course the same could be achieved merely in reading books about female philosophy and psychology. And heck, it's not like we don't converse about this anyways amongst ourselves. No, let's make women PAY FOR IT!"

I want to know who came up with that idea.

And, on a related note, how do you just "poof" make a new college program without "experts" or "predecessor experts" who established the study? Who were the first professors? Without PhD's in women's studies, did some women just self-decree themselves as the "lords" or "masters" of the "field?'

Well Cappy Cappites, what do you think?

I already looked it up (and DAMN am I good), but let's see how good you are at predicting what the "founding mothers" of the first "women's studies departments" looked like (not physically, I'm talking profiles, backgrounds, psychologies, education, resumes, etc.)

I'll give you a couple seconds.

Go ahead, jot down your predictions.

Think hard. Take from lessons the ole Captain has provided you before.

Couple spaces so nobody cheats.

Are you ready?

OK, here we go. From Wikipedia (which I know some of you have a problem with, but just let me roll here):

*The first accredited Women's Studies course was held in 1969 at Cornell University. The first two Women's Studies Programs in the United States were established in 1970 at **San Diego State College** (now **San Diego State University**) and **SUNY-Buffalo**. The SDSU program was initiated after a year of intense organizing of women's **consciousness raising groups**, rallies, petition circulating, and operating unofficial or experimental classes and presentations before seven committees and assemblies.[2] **Carol Rowell Council** was the student co-founder along with Dr. Joyce Nower, a literature instructor. The SUNY-Buffalo program was also the result of intense debate and feminist organizing led by **Elizabeth Lapovsky Kennedy**, and it was eventually birthed out of the **American Studies** department. In 1972, **Sarah Lawrence College** became the first institution to grant Masters degrees in Women's History. **Throughout the later 1970s many universities and colleges created departments and programs in women's studies, and professorships became available in the field which did not require the sponsorship of other departments***

So right there, the women's studies department was just created out of whole cloth by a bunch of 60's hippie activists. There was no precedence for the "study." There was no demand for such a field. It wasn't in response to societal need for it. It wasn't an outgrowth of an already-existing field that warranted its own department or program. And there certainly was no practical application for a field outside academia. It was merely a bunch of activists who didn't want to grow up, face the real world and get real jobs.

But what I get a kick out of (and what you should have jotted down on them there notes in front of you) is the profile of some of the people in the entry:

Worthless majors - (BA's in anthropology, Masters in Art History, etc., proving they never had any intention of working real jobs in the first place)

No Real Work - (all jobs are in academia, government or non-profit, they need OTHER people's money to live, they are NOT independent)

Crusaders - (by the fact they decided to create an unneeded program, financed by taxpayer money, NOT to help women, but merely to help themselves first and foremost)

Upper middle class/rich - (my favorite is the one where her daddy was a NEUROSURGEON. Yes, "independent" I'm sure she'll claim to be)

In short, they are nothing but crusaders.

So "let us be clear." The founders of "women's studies" departments had no desire to "bring about justice and equality for women." They are crusaders, they are hypocrites. They care FIRST AND FOREMOST about themselves and have no problem abusing a GENUINE noble cause (in this case, the equal treatment of women) so they can profit from it at taxpayer expense. They are spoiled, upper income, brats who absolutely FEARED mathematical and genuine academic rigor and instead NOT ONLY chose to major in worthless, cake easy fields, but to CREATE A NEW ONE OUT OF WHOLE CLOTH. They merely used the "oppression of women" as the Trojan Horse to rationalize it and no politician would dare call them out on it in fear of being labelled a sexist. It's the same game plan socialists, leftists, feminists, liberals and communists have been playing this entire time.

So to answer the previous question - what type of people came up with/major in this nonsense?

Answer?

Not adults, these are politically motivated charlatans. These are little children who are the opposite of independent. They are scared little children who never wanted to compete toe-to-toe, on a level playing field in the real world, and they certainly don't want to produce anything of value society might want (though I'm sure they're happy some STEM majoring nerd created their government-financed Apple products). They are hypocrites claiming to be independent (while needing constant outside sources of financing for their "careers" as they hide in academia and the public sector) and are doubly so when they claim to be for "women" (when in reality they use women for their personal profiteering and really couldn't care less about women's happiness and success). Ironically, contrast that with the theoretical would-be founders of "Manosphere Studies" and you're pitting public sector economic deadweight against engineers, programmers, doctors, soldiers, accountants, entrepreneurs, economists, husbands, fathers and laborers who actually do produce something of value in society, are genuinely independent and because of this CERTAINLY have more authority and legitimacy in starting a "Manosphere Studies" program than any feminist founder ever did a "women's studies" program.

Now, third. As my posts are prone to do, they flare up emotions (the secret ingredient is "truth"). I know truth and reality have the tendency to make people who are living lies get upset because we expose the type of people they really are. But perhaps a different approach will convince you I'm truly not biased or have some kind of vendetta against women, but perhaps (GASP!) I might actually care about women (in that I would **prevent the likes of this from happening**). So allow me to introduce some humor, though I'm no less serious about what I'm about to say.

The **PhD's passed out at The University of Man** should be recognized by the National Association of Accredited Colleges and Schools as just as legitimate as the PhD's in "women's studies" passed out at "accredited" institutions.

Not joking, I'm as serious as a heart attack. The Manosphere is just as legitimate, if not, a superior "institution" to most women's studies departments.

One, just as much intellectual thought and debate goes into the Manosphere as the average women's studies department. Matter of fact, we're more intellectually honest (in that we're acknowledging a PhD in Manosphere studies would be pretty freaking stupid) and we have no ulterior motive (sayyyyyyyy extorting the taxpayer for make-work-government-financed academia jobs that produce absolutely nothing of value?) Two, unlike women's studies, the Manosphere's aim is not political, but practical. It is NOT the oppression or subjugation of women, but merely the maximization of happiness between the sexes. Unlike women's studies, it is not an "us vs. them" or a "right the wrongs of our oppressors," but an intense desire to find out and establish the truth as to what is the optimal relationship between men and women in all aspects of life (work, marriage, friends, sex, social, etc.) so that men and women may prosper and be happy. Three, we do have more legitimacy in our founding in that the majority, if not ALL of the members of the Manosphere are independent men (and women) who work for a living and are not hypocritically willing to go through the charade of creating a whole academic department just to score ourselves some government cheese. And fourth, the fact the open-source nature of the Manosphere in it's unprofessional, non-accredited, unordained form, is providing such an intellectually equal rival or "challenge" to "women's studies" is NOT an argument for a "male studies" department, but rather, quite the opposite. It's an argument to eliminate every "women's studies" program out there because it exposes just how inane, stupid, absurd, worthless and useless those programs actually are.

Besides, even if you tried to make "Manosphere Studies" a legitimate college program you could get a degree in, it wouldn't work. Real men couldn't stomach the hypocritical and parasitical reputation that would come with it.

(This post sponsored by "**Worthless**." Want to irk a liberal arts major who no doubt is going to increase your taxes? Buy "**Worthless**" 100% guaranteed to anger, enrage and peeve your Unicorn Studies-majoring friends! Buy Worthless now!)

What Percent of Lake Minnetonka Properties are Earned?

For those of you not familiar with Twin Cities geography, allow me to lay out the Twin Cities metro to you.

In the center you have two major cities; Minneapolis and St. Paul. The Mississippi flowing through both, cutting Minneapolis in half as it flows southward, and then cutting St. Paul in half as it turns and flows northward, inevitably turning south again and making its run for the Gulf of Mexico. Surrounding the two city centers is an oval of inner suburbs, which in turn is surrounded by outer suburbs, with houses getting progressively larger and the yards bigger the further out along the radius you go. But depending where you are (north, south, east or west) of the metropolitan hub, more or less generally determines what kind of neighborhood you live in.

Bar "pockets of resistance" such as Edina, St. Louis Park, and so forth, the inner suburbs are more or less blue collar, old school neighborhoods, pock-marked with crime ridden extensions of the poorer parts of Minneapolis and St. Paul.

The northern suburbs are predominantly blue collar. The running joke in the Twin Cities is if you are in Anoka you should wear your "good" snowmobile jacket if you have a wedding.

The eastern metro is filled with farms and ranches and apple orchards, with epicenters of limousine liberal smugness manifesting themselves in the forms of trinket/antique shopping towns like Stillwater.

The south is kind of a hodgepodge of varied sorts, but you're generally solid white collar.

But the west...ohhhhh, the west. Let me tell you about the west.

For directly west there is a lake called Lake Minnetonka. And Lake Minnetonka is no ordinary lake, it is a many-multi-chambered, multi-bay, multi-isthmus lake. Tons of shoreline, nestled within coves, within peninsulas, within hidden lakes, all interconnected to allow boats and yachts the best sailing bar going to Lake Superior. If you do not have a map, you can get lost, but you won't care because it is the most beautiful lake in the state. And it is because of these traits that it was only a matter of time that it would come to house the richest of Minnesota's rich.

Every bit of lakeshore has a mansion on it that can compete with any other mansion throughout the world. You can go to various bars along the lake and see nothing but Beamers, Mercedes, Ferraris, and Lotuses being valet parked for their owners. You can see boats that are just as big as what they have on the North Shore bay in Chicago. You can go there and see the most poshly dressed and done up people and think you're in Milan. But you're not, you're in fly over country.

Naturally, if you're a normal hard working Joe, this is a foreign world to you. A world of peppered hair investment banking types ordering $15 martini's. A world where trophy wives drive their Lexus SUV's to the local towns at 11AM to meet their trophy comrades because they don't have to work. A world where 17 year old high school kids have nicer cars than you've ever had. It is a world you just can't relate to. But I have a dirty little suspicion about this world, and that suspicion is it's like the "Barbie Girl" in the "Barbie World";

It's fantastic.

But it's made of plastic.

What first aroused my suspicion to this ultra-elite world is when working in banking I would get an inordinate amount of real estate developers who claimed residency in the area. **In my book I regale the story of a man I called "Zorba the Swede"** who I titled such because he was always super tan when he came into the bank, even in January. Minnesotans do not pull off that "Greek guy in a speedo with a lot of chest hair" tan in January (let alone July). But this guy did and he hailed from Wayzata (the capitol of this elite area). Regardless, it was the likes of Zorba and his ilk and their uncanny ability to reside in the Lake Minnetonka area that raised my eyebrow. And the reason my eyebrow was raised was not the tans they were sporting, but their tax returns.

Most of them showed losses.

It seemed odd to me that if you showed losses on your tax returns that you could somehow live in the Lake Minnetonka area. Matter of fact, unless your tax return showed at minimum a $1.5 million salary a year, I don't see how you could even afford to live in the "slums" of Lake Minnetonka. But somehow they did.

But the excuse I received was universally the same;

"Oh, Zorba made money, he was just trying to low his tax bill by showing losses. But rest assured he was a very successful real estate developer/surgeon/businessman, which is why he needed an emergency $4 million loan this afternoon. You understand of course, it's just business."

Funny thing was I never understood.

I understood they weren't making money. I understood they had overleveraged themselves into property that would never sell. I understood there was a housing crash coming. And I understood that even if they had $30 million in assets, if they had $35 million in debts, they were insolvent. But I never understood how somebody who was LOSING money could afford a $10 million mansion on Lake Minnetonka, and still don't to this day.

Time would go on and sure enough there was no limit to the number of "Zorba's" out there. Real estate developers. Non-descript businessmen. Investment brokers. All showing losses. None posting profits. But invariably all living in the fanciest zip codes money could buy.

But as the housing crash started its decline, it was interesting to see how many of these "super-successful" business men failed to provide their most current tax return. Or their most up to date personal financial statement. Or just give us projections or estimates of what their current financial situation was. They would hem and haw, and ultimately balk, but according to my supervisors;

"Well, they're very successful men. They are so busy making money, they don't have time to get their tax returns in on time. That's why they always file extensions."

Funny, I never understood that either.

In any case, what I suspected ultimately proved to be true. The majority of these "super successful business men" were in short nothing but financial deadbeats. Losers who couldn't even manage a lemonade stand to profitability. Inferior little middle-aged brats who didn't have the guts, nor the aptitude, nor the intelligence, nor the skill to genuinely work up the wealth they farcically paraded around. And some were so egregious in their financial masquerading they begat the attention of their friendly neighborhood federal investigators;.

Adam LaFavre once the darling of real estate circles is under investigation for a litany of things.

Michael Parish of Parish Development plead guilty to a $50 million strawbuyer and fraud scheme.

And **Bruce Nedegaard**, convicted felon, turned real estate mogul, who, tragically died of cancer before he could be sentenced for fraud, tax evasion and a whole host of other no-no's.

But just three men do not make the 50,000 or so Lake Minnetonka area residents all financial deadbeats. There are people who ethically (or at least, legally) earned (cough cough! - inherited) their multi-million dollar lakeside homes. Genuine wealth and empires have been produced providing billions in profits and thousands of jobs. But as the housing market has collapsed and with it the economy, the wheat is being separated from the chaff and I am now questioning what percent of the Lake Minnetoka residents are genuine captains of industry earning their "elite" rank, and what percent are just a bunch of financial deadbeat posers.

Three events or observations have piqued my suspicion.

First was last week when it was a rare beautiful October day, I decided to take my motorcycle (that's right ladies, the Captain is a bad boy) and cruise around the 98 miles of shoreline on Lake Minnetonka. What amazed me was just how many homes were for sale. A brand new mansion for sale here. A partially completed dream house there. And an old school estate up for auction there. Two large "luxury condo" developments on the lake were nothing but ghost towns and I remember reading about the developers and these much heralded developments as the local paper fawned over them as local celebrities. In short, it was shocking to see Minnesota's richest neighborhood having the same, if not, a higher percentage of the homes for sale as your local suffering blue collar neighborhood.

Second was a story told to me by an acquaintance who lives in the area about a young, budding socialite couple who live in the area and live in one of the nicer houses. However, they actually don't own the $5 million home. It is owned by the mother in law who lets them live there RENT FREE as if they were a 20 year old college couple trying to pay for tuition. Worse still, the "business" the husband runs is perpetually losing money and needs a constant cash infusion from the mother in law. Meanwhile they drive around in nothing but the finest luxury cars and SUV's while wining and dining at the local restaurants where drinks are $10 a shot. Fine, the house may not be up for sale, but how many live-in-my-mom's-basement-at-the-age-of-40 "successful" investment bankers are there? I want that set up.

And finally was the now disgraced Tom Petters. Multi-billion dollar business mogul who lived in Wayzata and was recently paid a visit by the local, state and federal law enforcement representatives who were quite insistent he come with them. Posing as only a poser could, he was heralded by scores of magazines and newspapers as a "super successful" businessman (who no doubt had trouble getting his tax returns in on time too), only to turn out to be crook who defrauded billions from his victims. However, it was not his arrest that crystallized by suspicion into an outright thought, but that he had a magazine called "Lake Minnetonka Magazine."

I saw the magazine once and it reminded me of the time I was invited to one of the "popular kids" parties back in high school. Shocking as this may be, I was nerd back in 1991, and for me to be invited to this party sounded more like a set up than anything else. It turned out to be a genuine invite by one of the nicer popular kids, but when I got there, instead of this wild crazy party with the cheerleaders running around topless, all it was, was the cheerleaders watching a video of themselves cheering at a recent football game and the jocks watching the same. All they were doing was watching themselves on the VCR. It was the most boring party I had ever been to and I remember leaving only after 10 minutes to go play some Dungeons and Dragons with my friends.

Regardless, the point was this magazine was the exact same thing. A "hurrah for us" fest. A magazine where a bunch of people read about themselves and the parties they went to. It was nothing but them masturbating over themselves. Articles about "Joe Schmoe and Jane Jones-Schmoe (note the hyphenated name) hanging out with real estate tycoon Bob Bobson and his Minnesota Viking's cheerleader Bambi Bames as they discuss which boat they're going to buy." Or "banking heiress Jessica Johnson and some friends party it up at the local club – *rumor is she is dating star investment banker and most eligible bachelor, Lance Winthrop!*"

It was all of the observations mentioned above, combined with the fakeness of this magazine (not to mention the owner himself was now proven to be a deadbeat) that made me think it wasn't just a few bad apples in Minnesota's most elite neighborhood, but that something closer to 25-33% of the population were indeed posers.

Now, admittedly you cannot get rid of nepotism. Undeserving people will inherit the fortune their parents worked up. But what angers me the most about this is the attitude these elites have. I'm not talking about me being jealous or envious, I'm talking about the hypocrisy these people have. It's one thing to build up an empire from scratch, buy a mansion and drive your Lotus around and live the jet set lifestyle. You earned it. You deserved it. You produced wealth and earned so much money, not to mention employed people along the way that you deserve to sit on the docks of Lake Minnetonka while you sip your $10 martini and say, "I'm one of the best. I am indeed one of the greatest." I applaud you.

But if you are what I estimate to be that 25-33% of losers who just inherited it, or borrowed it, or worse, just stole it, not only should you have shame, you should be taken to a back alley and have every undeserved penny beaten out of you. Not because you have it (however you may have gotten it), but because of your insistence that like all the other subprime deadbeats, thieving bankers and other entitlement princes and princesses out there, that you're ENTITLED to it. And what's really goading is when you flaunt it.

The dead beat, live at home, son in law who isn't man enough to make a profit to support himself and has to live off of his mother in law driving a luxury car? Back alley with a baseball bat.

Partying it up living off of embezzled funds, posing as some big time hot shot "businessman" with $40 million in assets and $50 million in debts soon to be bailed out by the taxpayer as you throw the economy into recession? Back alley with a baseball bat.

And Tom Petters with his house he owned (well, "he" never really owned it);

(picture removed)

Back alley with a baseball bat, broken glass, rubbing alcohol and a blowtorch.

Now I've said it before and I will say it again, because I think those of us who work for a living, who manage to spend within our means, only to bail out financial deadbeats like these, really need to hear it (since it's only true)

We are better people than you.

We don't pose, we're legitimate.

We don't steal, parasite, inherit then flaunt, or borrow with no intention of paying back, we earn.

We are the ones who make this country and any other country great. And while you may have your Beamers and your Lake Minnetonka homes and your fancy parties, you're not fooling any one. Your net worth is negative. The waitress with a positive checking account balance has a higher net worth than you. You are the losers and we are the winners.

Yes, Men Do Leave the Market

As many of you know I moonlight at night in a Bruce Wayne/Dark Knight sort of way as a dance instructor. And as I've aged from 23 to my present day 33 in those now approaching 10 years of dance instruction, I've seen the first wave of Gen X'ers age out of their youthful 20's as well as seen a wave of divorcees coming online and back into the "dating" marketplace.

Now for whatever reason it may be, dance tends to attract more women than men and over the years, I've of course befriended several female students. They vary in ages anywhere from 24 to 60, but the one common trait they have is they are typically (though not always) single. And while not always, most of them took dance class half incented to perhaps find a guy.

But what is becoming a more frequent phenomenon is a question these girls ask;

"Where are all the guys?"

I never paid much attention to this, as it has always been the case that men just eschew dance classes, but it wasn't until an older dance student of mine perhaps refined the question a bit and made it more pointed. It wasn't so much "Where are all the guys," as much as it was;

"I just get the feeling there aren't any men anymore. Not just in dance class, but where are all the men from all the various social activities? They make up half the population, but I can't find any single guys to date. They can't all be married, even my female friends are running into this mysterious disappearance of men. Do they like stop trying after a while and just stay home?"

And that's when I realized what she was asking.

"Do you mean, do men give up and don't bother trying to find women any more?" I clarified.

She said, "Yes. So do they?"

"Yes" I answered.

She was somewhat surprised at my response. She said, "so they just *give up*? They don't go out anymore? Don't they want to find somebody? Anybody?!"

"Yeah, more or less."

"That's crazy! How do they ever expect to find anybody?"

I replied, "Well...they don't."

Regardless, the point was her reaction surprised me in return to see this was that shocking of a revelation to her. I always thought it was kind of common knowledge, men do indeed give up after a while, but apparently it's not. So allow me to explain.

I don't know when precisely it is, nor is it the same for every guy, but inevitably guys in a sense "burn out." Consider it a staged rocket and as the last vestiges of fuel burn out of the booster, it slowly disengages and disintegrates as it plummets back to Earth. Many things can burn out the fuel;

Divorce and the loss of one's assets
Personal finances/loss of job
Demanding/successful career
Or just plain bad dating experiences (your beloved captain has had suicide threats, gotten punched for refusing a girl sex and unknowingly dated a married woman for three months...you get the idea).

But what ultimately results in the decision to exit the market is more of an economic decision. It is the realization that as you have less and less remaining life you have to make surer and surer bets as to how to spend your time. It's no different than switching from equities to bonds as you approach retirement. Ergo, whereas when you were 18 you would stay at a party all night in the hopes of getting a girl's phone number, when you're 25 you start to think about working instead of partying, and by the time you're 30, you rarely go to clubs, dance halls, bars opting instead to play video games at home or read a book or put some more hours in at the office.

The reason is the expected rate of return of your precious, finite, and perpetually dwindling time. If you go out, hot as you may be when you're 18, you have little to no control over succeeding in getting a girl's number or a date. And as experience will tell you it's a 1/20 shot you will succeed, and that's assuming you have good game. All in all, I would estimate most 20 somethings waste an equivalent to 4 full years of full time work chasing girls to relatively little avail. A significant opportunity cost.

The X-Box 360 on the other hand is a guaranteed rate of return.

Working a couple more hours at work, is a guaranteed rate of return.

Even something as simple as lighting up a cigar with your friends and having a good scotch is a guaranteed rate of return.

And dare the Captain admit he enjoys writing for you honyakers and conversing with you as it is a guaranteed rate of return?

And this is what progressively more and more men turn to as they get older. Now I can certainly see the case where a man gets divorced multiple times, losing 50% of his assets each time as it would accelerate the burning the fuel, but this phenomenon goes beyond married and divorced men. This is merely anecdotal and I'd certainly be welcoming of any other guys out there who have noticed this, but whereas all of 10 years ago nearly 100% of my male friends were looking for a wife, now I think in my group of friends less than 25% of them are, none of which have ever been married all of which are under 45. The rationale is it was too burdensome to go out on the "prowl." The idea of paying a cover to go to a club to yell at some stranger over loud music while paying $10 for parking and having to hike 10 blocks in DT Minneapolis is not appealing.

Going to the local sports bar to feign interest in "Brandi" as she talks about the latest issue of People Magazine or American Idol pales in comparison to shooting Nazi's online with your video gaming buds.

And wasting the hour setting up a Match.com profile because your friend gifted you a free month subscription and swore you'd meet chicks is nowhere near as fun as talking politics over a cigar and scotch with intellectual friends (***and I want that hour of my life back by the way Jeff!***).

Ergo (and again, this is just what I've personally observed) there is a (dare I say) mass exodus of men out of the dating market and into their own little bachelor worlds and this may go a long way in explaining why you don't really see us out there.

Now again, this is just what I've observed and has been seemingly corroborated by the experiences of many different women I've ran into, but we could be wrong. But I would be very curious of any junior, deputy, official or otherwise bachelor economists out there have seen the same thing.

Ode to Tom Petters

Given the recent arrest of Tom Petters, I thought this repost would be very befitting for the latest "high flier" who now has to have the "Trophy Wife Chat." Enjoy jail time Tom!

Like most other people, I'm livid over the housing debacle and the prospective bail out. And in times like these where the rest of us are facing a recession, a loss of a job, or poverty because of a group of greedy scum sucking parasites, I find it helpful to point out the occasional thing that might bring a bit of happiness or humor into our lives (or permit us pure, vicious schadenfreude in watching these scumbags get what they deserve). And one of those thing is the "trophy wife talk."

You see, there this "talk" being held in thousands of luxurious suburbanite McMansions across the US and it's the *"Honey, let me explain to you the difference between debt and equity spending"* talk. This talk is where the powerful and successful investment banker, commercial banker, real estate developer (fill in the blank) has to come home and explain to his little trophy wife the difference between debt and equity spending.

The reason this talk is necessary is because despite them being a "successful" real estate developer, the truth of the matter is all they did was borrow other people's money and live off of it. And now that the market is collapsing and their empire is crumbling, they now have to shuffle back home in shame and explain to their ditzy wives why when they left for work in the morning they were a high flying, SUV driving, investment banking real estate mogul, but now upon their return are bankrupt, scumbag losers.

You see, real SUCCESSFUL **MEN** don't have to have this talk. Because we, no matter how small or insignificant our career or job may be, earn this thing called "profit." We earn more than we make. We go to our jobs, be it a high flying surgeon or a burger flipper at McDonald's, we get our pay check and we spend less than what we earned. And while some of us may only make $35,000 a year, that is infinitely more than what this plethora of real estate developers, investment bankers, and mortgage brokers made, simply by the fact it's a positive number.

But the real shame these faux business "men" face is that they were never able to make a profit in the first place. They were never able to get it economically "up." And the only way they could make it was by borrowing money. They're too shallow to admit it, but they never turned a profit. They never produced a penny of wealth. They don't even approach us in terms of being real men with real jobs who do real work.

Ahhh, but the irony doesn't stop there. For you see, these egomanics not only found nothing wrong with borrowing money to survive, but found nothing wrong with borrowing millions of dollars to live a luxurious lifestyle they never had the wherewithal to EARN.

Real estate developers are a perfect example. I don't know how many stories I could tell you of the "multi-millionaire" real estate developer who was some big shot out there who thought he was king sh!t. They all drive Beamers. They all own multi-million dollar homes on the lake and they all have drop dead gorgeous wives. But when the market started to crumble, they became desperate. And the reason they because desperate is because they had borrowed so much money to afford these unsustainable lifestyles, even with the profits they had before, they could not keep up the charade.

Now many of them would try. Again, I don't know how many real estate developers I had in my bank back in 2005-2006 that were trying to borrow any amount they could get. They would lie on their personal financial statements, grossly exaggerating the value of their real estate empire (thus allowing them to borrow even more money) so they could get the funds to continue living their faux jet set lifestyle. But in the end, it would catch up with them, for ultimately, no matter how big their operations were, those operations weren't profitable. It was just like the US auto industry. It doesn't matter how "big" GM is, it's still a lousy, money losing company.

But here is why the "Trophy Wife Chat" is all the more necessary.

Trophy wives don't know the difference between debt and equity spending.

When "investment banking man" met his floozy of a wife at the bar he didn't tell her what his "adjusted gross income" was, because there was none. When the "real estate mogul" met his soon-to-be eye candy wife at the club, he didn't tell her what his "net income" was, because there was none. Both of them just bragged, "well I work on multi-million dollar deals." "I'm a multi-million dollar real estate developer." And the reason why is that the typical trophy wife doesn't know the difference between sales and profits. The typical trophy wife actually thinks you are a millionaire when you say you "own a $4 million house" but have $4.2 million in mortgages against it.

Ergo, the typical trophy wife cannot discern between the money you spend on them on whether it is borrowed money (debt) or money you actually made (equity).

And key to understand this, is they don't care. As long as you spend the money on them, whether you earned it or not, is completely irrelevant to them.

And thus all the more shock when this "chat" occurs.

For to whet your schadenfreude appetite I have seen this happen multiple times. As the housing market crashed, I have seen at least 10 "highly successful (ahem) "men" forced to sell their luxurious mansions and move into a lesser zip code. I even remember one desperate big shot insisting that on all the paper work we had, that we list the luxurious town of "Edina" instead of where he really moved to (the much less posh town of Richfield) because he didn't want people to know he moved out of Edina. The blow to their egos was so crushing, so shameful, so rude-awakening-ish that it should at least provide some of you a bit of solace.

But the ultimate payoff is to know the conversation that must have been had and is being had across the nation. To be a fly on the wall when these fat, gluttonous, embezzling, dirtbag scumball schmutzes who dared to live off of the rest of us to the tunes of millions, had to go home and explain to their moronic wives why they had to;

1. Sell the house
2. Move to a lesser neighborhood.
3. Sell the Lexus, the Beamer, the Mercedes and buy a Buick
4. Pull the kids out of private school
5. Cancel the trip to Arizona
6. Sell the house in Arizona
7. Oh, and by the way the feds might be coming knocking at the door
8. Does your mom have a place we can stay?
9. What do you mean "divorce?"

has to at least make some of you feel better.

For I've said it before, and I'll say it again, we may not be rich, but we are real men and women who are really independent. **We are better than them**.

And if you need something of a boost like the above to get you through the day and put a smile on your face again, **please consider buying my book.** Plenty of more stories and some of my finest work.

How Horses are to Blame for the Housing Crash

In my days in banking if there was one thing that went hand in hand with rich men applying for loans, it was horses.

If you had a shady real estate developer, there was a horse.

If you had some rich doctor or lawyer, there was a horse.

If you had some trust fund baby now slowing watching his parent's fortune erode, there was a horse.

And the reason there was a horse was not because they came riding into town on one, or were racing them, but their wives, without fail bought them.

This manifested itself on the personal financial documents of the people applying for loans. Typically what you'd see was a rich man making all the money (or at least borrowing all the money) and the wife, who was literally doing nothing, running some token business on some money her husband gave her to keep her out of his hair **(I affectionately referred to this as "KHOMA" money - Keep Her Off My Ass - in my book)**. So what you'd see is the husband listing an AGI (adjusted gross income) of say $560,000 and the wife showing a perpetual loss on "Frieda's Farms" or "Heather's Horses" or some such dumb name on their schedule C.

Now while for the most part, if the husband was bringing in a decent amount of cash, I could see it definitely being worth dropping a couple grand on some horses to keep the wife out of his hair so he could effectively run the real business while she lost a grand or two on her horse hobby and play "Make Believe Businessman." But what was scary was just how many times I saw the horses (combined with other consumer spending on the part of the wife) that actually crippled and threatened the man's financial solvency.

One guy was an overweight guy and without a doubt had essentially bought his wife because he was too physically unattractive to find one. Naturally the wife, along with children, would rack up credit card bills that would wipe out what he earned, almost penny for penny. And of course the single largest expenditure was her "horse business." So when he came in for a loan for his wife's "horse" business I was curious and started asking questions;

"So does she breed the horses?"

"Uh no."

"So she races them then?"

"Uh no."

"So she uses them to teach riding?"

"Uh no."

"Well, what does she do with them?"

"Well, she rides them and maintains them."

Meanwhile he wanted us to lend against this never-profitable operation.

Another hilarious instance was when one guy actually wanted to use his wife's horses as collateral. That if he defaulted on his business loan, then we could go and repossess the horses and sell them to recoup the money.

Well "yip yip yip yip yahoo."

Just what banks and bankers wanted to do.

Repossess on a "horse," feed it, store it, and then try to sell it.

What is sad though is that because horses were so prevalent when it came to dealing with the upper classes, they inevitably became collateral for more real estate deals than most people realize. Through the personal guarantee of the borrower, sometimes they would put up "All Business Assets" as collateral for the loan. And not just all business assets, but all personal assets as well. And though horses were never intended to be the primary form of collateral, invariably they did boost personal financial statements enough to make it look like the borrowers were solvent enough to guarantee the loan.

Alas, big dumb animals were tangentially backing up various real estate and other business deals.

Ultimately what I found is that horses are more or less a tell tale sign you're dealing with a "Bon Fire of the Vanities" type couple. The wife typically cares more about the horses than her husband. The husband is feverishly working to support his wife's spending habits and keep her loyal to him. And both are so vain about their appearances that every bit of asset and property is borrowed against and leveraged to the hilt.

But what gets me about the horses is "why horses?"

What is the freaking pull?

I suppose I could be asking the same question on any kind of frivolous consumer spending such as;

"Why shoes?"

"Why purses?"

"Why a boat you'll never use?"

But there is something about horses and trophy wives that I can't put my finger on, but I know is there.

Alas, perhaps the aspiring, junior, deputy, official or otherwise economists can tender some theories.

My "You Need a Better Car" Story

It was requested I post another personal story about the Captain's previous escapades through life so here is another.

I was about 30 or 31 or so and back then I still had some youthful naivety about me and was thus still on the market, "playing the game" looking to date girls. I had my radio show at the time and invariably because I was a young and dapper radio show host who happened to moonlight as a dance instructor, the topic of lining me up with some attractive young listener of the female persuasion would continually recur.

Sure enough a caller called in saying she had the most perfect girl in the world for me that I should date her. I was reluctant as because what you learn in the radio world is that the sexiness of a woman's voice is inversely related to her actual sexiness, but this girl assured me her friend was beautiful, not fat and still on top of all that had a great personality.

I was reluctant so I told her to shoot me an e-mail and we'd discuss further. I received her e-mail within 5 minutes of the show ending, behooving me to respond and consider her friend. I said I would agree, but I wanted to see a NORMAL, FULL BODY LENGTH picture, nothing that was touched up, or an insane close up of what would be a pretty face on an enormously large girl. I wanted proof she was an attractive girl.

Sure enough, the next day I received the picture.

Stunning, cute redhead. Slim, and in very good shape. Long flowing hair. Her friend was not lying, she was quite attractive.

So I agreed that I would meet her friend and go out with her and sure enough within a couple days I had a lunch date set at Benihanna's.

We met and she was just as her pictures suggested, a very attractive woman. She worked in real estate, and at the time I was in banking, and so we had a very high end intelligent conversation about the real estate market, housing and the crash that was slowly starting to materialize. She was impressed with all my various activities and I was very impressed with her entrepreneurialism. The date lasted two hours, we more or less closed the place down for lunch, before I decided that it was getting pretty late and I'd have to return to work. We left with me fully expecting a second date.

Of course I wasn't fresh off the assembly line. I knew that the date in my opinion could have gone great, while she could perhaps have had a horrendous time, so I didn't bank on anything. That is until her friend e-mailed me complimenting me on my behavior and witicisms and conversation skills. Apparently I had impressed her friend and I should certainly ask her out on a second date, except there was just this one major thing I would have to do;

I really ought to get a nicer car.

I was then lectured by her friend that, yes, while she knew I was proud of my frugality and spending within my means, I was 30 and therefore had to drive a nicer car. Too old and experienced to be insulted or shocked, I kind of laughed inside and looked up into the sky as if I was saying to the old man upstairs, "Are you freaking kidding me?"

So I asked her, "Well, what's wrong with my VW?"

Granted it wasn't a high end Jetta or a new model, but it wasn't a bad car either. It was at the time 7 years old, in good shape, it was kept clean and ran just fine. And out of all three of my cars, it was the nicer one.

"Well, it's not like you're 25 anymore. You really need to get a nicer car. My friend kind of noticed and mentioned it. It's really something that could turn into a deal breaker."

Again, too experienced and old to really be shocked or to really care, I resigned myself to defeat and said, "Well does she still want to go out with me then or what?"

"Sure! You should call her and ask her out!"

Which I promptly did.

Now a lot of you who know me are asking yourselves, "What they hell, Captain? Why were you going to go out with this girl again after she proved herself to be so shallow? She mentioned your CAR wasn't nice enough?! Are you just trying to aim for some play? What gives?"

But have faith in your beloved Captain, have faith.

For while I had no intention of ever having a future with this girl, I decided to at least have a little fun with her.

I scheduled a date, told her I would pick her up and drove to my buddy's place to trade my Chevy in for her BMW for the evening.

I showed up in this high end BMW, pulled up to the girl's house. Walked up, rang the doorbell and as she came down, escorted to towards the Beamer.

She was looking around trying to find my presumed P.O.S. VW and when she finally realized I was making a bee- line for the Beamer she said, "Wait, is THIS your car?"

I said, "Yeah."

She said, "Well, wait, when did you get this?!"

"Today," I said. "Your friend said that you didn't like my other car so I decided to buy this one."

She was a little shocked to say the least. She couldn't understand somebody just "up and buying a Beamer" because she mentioned to her friend the guy she went on a date with had an unacceptable car.

We went on our second date and I didn't bother calling her back. Last she saw of me was me driving off in my buddy's BMW. But it teaches all of us a lesson;

It's not just stories about women who put more value on fake things like cars and clothes. These women exist. And sadly, they're passing up on some of the best men in the world because of their shallowness.

Rule #1: Do NOT Turn Men Down for Dancing

In addition to my dance classes, as my goal is to get my students to dance, I host "field trips" wherein I take my students out to various bistros, ballrooms and jazz clubs, thereby allowing them the chance to practice the moves I taught them...and grant me an excuse to write off my booze for the evening. This last Saturday I went to a Latin joint for my Latin and Salsa dance students, and though lightly attended, we all had a good time.

However, while sipping away at my Rumpleminze and talking with some of my students, I witnessed out of the corner of my eye a phenomenon that is all too common and must be eradicated immediately. An immigrant invariably of Hispanic descent, was sheepishly standing by a support column, visually trying to assess his chances of getting a group of girls sitting at a table to his right to dance with him. Inevitably he got enough courage to approach the table and as far as I could tell, didn't identify any one particular girl he'd like to dance with, but more or less just threw the option out on the table to see if ANYBODY would dance with him.

Unfortunately I knew what was coming for I had been there a million times before.

The girls looked at each other, pointed at one another, giggled and then tried to foist the "chore" of dancing with this man on their friends, all the while utterly insulting him there as he waited patiently for a grown up to arise from the group and say, "yes I would like to dance."

He had more patience than I did, as he sat there a painful 30 seconds while the little girls giggled amongst themselves and pointed at one another, but inevitably he turned away and left the girls to themselves.

Now ladies, I know it is not fashionable to provide women advice on...well...anything. And I know that because of the political climate in the US anything meant as constructive criticism is construed as misogyny. But, out of the benefit of advancing society and perhaps finding you a future love, tough. This is for your own good.

First, this is the primary reason you "can't find a man." Oh sure, you'll let Chip McWinthrop buy you a drink at the local sports bar on daddy's dime, you'll sign up for utterly pointless online dating services such as Match and E-Harmony, but when Pablo comes up to you and asks you to dance, oh, no. That's just outlandish now isn't it?! Let me explain to you how you are shooting yourselves in the foot. It doesn't get any more Cary Grant than a man who not only has the gall to approach a table of girls, but has the skill to back it up on the dance floor. A man that knows how to dance is like an automatic screener. If he has taken the time to learn a skill such as dance, chances are he is a bit more refined, intelligent, not a drug dealer, not living at home or whatever else was your ex-boyfriend in the past.

Second, I don't give a damn if you do or do not know how to dance. Sit there and wish all you want, you will never look like Ginger Rogers sitting, sipping your cosmopolitans and opining about how you'd LIKE to dance watching Dancing with the Stars, unless you get off your ass and dance. That's why men "LEAD" in dancing. About your only responsibility in dancing is to not fall down, otherwise a good lead will be able to make you look like a million bucks on the floor. Of course you can continue to sit there and look like a dime-a-dozen with your eleven other friends sipping your mojitos, but that's just me.

Third, out of pure simple courtesy, you needn't dance with us, but by god, if you dare do the giggly girl sh!t, pointing at each other saying, *"no you dance with him! No YOU dance with him! Hee hee hee!! No, she really wants to dance with you!"* while a true gentleman is standing in your presence, you earn the right to be perpetually single for the rest of your days. Be true grown up women, and afford these men the simplest of etiquette. This has not only happened to me, and "Pablo," but practically every male friend I know. And you know what the consequences are? When you finally do decide you're ready to dance or perhaps go to a fancy place and meet a refined Antonio Banderas, too bad. All the good guys quit and either don't show up or don't bother expending the calories of energy to go up and ask you to dance anymore. This is of no concern when you're 25 as 25 year old men still have it in them. But if you're 35 and you're constantly wondering "where are all the good 30 something/40 something/50 something men?" Yeah, that WAS us. We're enjoying some X-Box 360 and a scotch with our buddies over a poker game...might even invite Pablo.

Fourth. Understood. You just want to enjoy some jazz. You just want to listen to some serious Latin. You just want to hang out with your girlfriends and be left alone. Fine, we get that and can appreciate that. Then don't sit near the dance floor, while dolled up in some kind of alluring dancing attire as you gyrate to the music in your seat looking like a puppy dog begging for a bit of ice cream to fall off your cone. And for the love of Pete, don't take the token dance lesson at the beginning of the evening. It's called false advertising. Not that the men are stalking, but they do pay attention to who is taking the lessons or is exuding the body language that they'd like to dance. This way (well, in theory anyway) we only ask the girls who want to dance to dance and leave the others be in peace.

Fifth, it is a dance. That is all it is. Oh sure, we might angle to ask you out later, based on how much you try to commandeer the lead away from us. We wouldn't have asked you to dance if we didn't find you at least a little bit attractive, but it's not a proposal of marriage. It's not an indecent proposal. It's not even a date or even a compliment on your hair. It's a dance. It's about 3-5 minutes of moving around on the floor. Heck, the music is so loud, it's impossible to get to know you. So don't worry, we have no "aims" on you. We (shocking as it may be) just genuinely want to dance.

Sixth, take it from me. I've been teaching dance 10 years. And when it comes to dance ladies, the men ARE GONE when you get older. The vast majority of people in my dance classes without partners are women. The men just don't dance, especially the older they get. I have had classes so lopsided that there were 6 women for every man. And beg and plead as much as I do with my male friends to show up and pinch hit, very few of them do. Ergo, if you ever want to be the girl that is the center of attention on the dance floor, or (the ultimate coup de tat) be that girl who steals all the attention at the reception away from the bride and onto you, then by all that is Metal-Gear-Solid-sacred you do not turn down a man who is asking you to dance.

Economics Will Replace Religion

I resigned myself recently that no matter how much empirical data, history, facts and information I provide about the merits of capitalism, the desire of the masses to believe what they want to believe will override it. The appeal or the draw to such a childishly simplistic ideology that if we "just tax the rich a little bit more" everything will be alright, or the blackhole-gravitational attraction of socialism where "you DON'T have to work, but you still can eat" has this scary and eerie ability to turn what would be normally intelligent thinking adults, into greedy, selfish little children. And try to rationalize with them though I might, the exercise is largely futile as charts correlating tax rates versus GDP growth figures just pales in comparison to Obama promising everything under the sun.

Ergo, since trying to reason with them doesn't work, there are only two ways I've found that works.

One is to bet them. It's one thing to advocate socialism and socialist policies, but when a savvy, educated economist challenges a socialist on their philosophy and forces them to put their own hard earned money on what they "know" to be "true," you'd be amazed how many of these zealots won't even wager $20 on something they not only feverishly support, but insist on forcing the rest of society to live under.

The second is to just let them have their way, as no matter how pretty your charts, and beautifully scripted your power point presentations, nothing convinces socialists they're wrong like a collapsing economy, a Stalinist regime, 40 million people dead from starvation and the TRUE elimination of their social freedoms. Give them a little bit of their utopia and they'll be BEGGING for full force free markets to come back.

Now, it takes a while, and as humans are prone to do, they may have to repeat their mistakes several times to finally learn a lesson or two (Tulip Bulbs, Dotcoms, Beanie Babies, and Housing), but inevitably they learn from them, and if they're smart, they start teaching and instilling these hard-learned lessons to future generations, allowing them to avoid the mistakes of the past (and make whole new ones).

But it was this line of thought that got me thinking about economics and how if we mastered it, or at least instilled some basic, simple economics principles in our society, it would not only eliminate a whole host of social problems and ailments, but basically be the guiding force to govern society. I still contest to this day, a population adequately educated in economics could inoculate itself against recessions. I still contest to this day, that I don't care how "mature" the US economy is, RGDP growth of 7% per year is possible. I still contest to this day that if we mastered economics as a society we could have income per capitas of $250,000 per person and effectively eliminate poverty, not to mention extend life expectancies to unfathomable ages. All these benefits are possible if we just master economics.

However, as these advances in economics occur (more so, instilling what we already know about economics in the masses), it will be at the expense of a much larger and older institution; religion.

If you think about it, religion was not created by a "god" or "gods" by which to govern the people. It was created by people to govern people - and not necesarily without merit.

Disagree with religion much as you would like, it provides an otherwise unorganized society a means by which to organize and progress. Religion provides laws, it provides order, it keeps peace, etc. Religion in other words was nothing more than the ancient version of government. ie- it's no coincidence that in the olden days (and even in many archaic societies today) religion WAS the government. The Ten Commandments and other remnants of Christianity are instilled in US government to this day. Not to mention, rules and laws such as how to butcher animals and swine in Jewish texts were not done so because "god" ordained it as such, but rather because it was for the health benefits of society at the time (pre-refrigeration).

However, religion has one primary flaw; in order to give it teeth, and give its clergy "authority" or "legitimacy" to rule over the masses you had to create things like "hell" and deities and wrath, largely things that could not be proven until (conveniently) somebody died and went there. The problem is technological advances in science have not only made some of these rules obsolete, but have disproven or dismissed a lot of the tenets by which religions are founded on. We no longer need to butcher various animals certain ways due to refrigeration. We no longer have to worship the sun as, well, as it turns out it's just one of a gazillion stars out there. And no, AIDS wasn't created to hurt or banish any one group of non-believers or another, it's frankly just a really bad virus.

However, this spells trouble for religion in that as humans learn more and more about the universe and solve its mysteries, it disproves and obsoletes more and more aspects of religion all together. This relegates religion to the position it's in now, second to most governments and secular law, and more a means by which to provide moral guidance and comfort to its followers.

The question is as religion goes the way of the dinosaurs (or adapts to become more acceptable and marketable to the modern day masses - a perfect example being a church in the Twin Cities that has "pet baptismals") what will provide the matter by which we create the laws to most efficiently govern society. And that is where economics steps in.

Economics is such an encompassing study that it is more or less the only thing that could replace religion. It's designed to allocate the resources of society to not only advance it, but keep it from regressing. It's purpose is to enrich the most amount of people to the maximum extent current resources and technology will allow. It insists on relative peace, calm, stability and order within society in order to achieve this, and if it doesn't get it, it mercilessly punishes its people for their mistakes (as it is doing so today).

Ergo, the more people study economics, all the goals and aims religion was designed to achieve (or perhaps I should qualify it by saying, the NOBLE goals and aims) can be achieved without resorting to fairy tales of hell, burning bushes, killing infidels, gays and whatever outmoded hogwash is out there.

The question is whether we will force our children to study economics, finance and personal financial management as much as we force them to study catechism, or in some parts of the world, force them to learn the economic merits of an engineering degree over blowing themselves up.

Degree Mills

"Do you want an exciting career in the field of medical transcriptioning?"

"Do you want to be on the cutting edge of criminal justice?"

"How about an exciting career in travel and hospitality?"

"Then School XYZ is the school for you!"

"Earn your degree in just 16 months and you'll be on your way to a better you!"

This is the typical commercial for the typical 2 year college you will see during daytime TV. And the reason you see it during day time TV is because the target audience is not you nor me, but basically the welfare bum deadbeats who don't have a job and are looking for a way out of their miserable lives.

Now understand we are smart enough to know such a thing sounds like a scam. But to the average deadbeat watching her soaps or the typical loser turning off the video games long enough to watch TV instead so he can eat, this actually sounds like a feasible opportunity and thus 2 year colleges are born.

But allow me to tell you a couple stories about my days teaching at some of these institutions of "higher learning" so that;

1. You know never to go there.
2. You can tell some of your less fortunate friends never to go there
3. These schools may go bankrupt.

So pour yourself a martini, find a comfy chair, kick back and relax as I regale you with my tales of teaching in 2 year colleges.

I first started teaching at this "business" school where the "campus" was a rented out, brown, 1970's style office building located in the inner suburbs of St. Paul/Minneapolis. The school didn't even rent out the entire building, but let that be a lesson to you kids, highly ranked schools lease out their HQ in suburbanite strip malls.

I intuitively knew this wasn't going to be Harvard, but it was a nice part time job and I got to teach my passion; economics - so I didn't much care.

However troubles immediately started to occur.

The first sign of trouble came when I issued the first quiz, of which 85% of the students failed. It wasn't an issue of the quiz being difficult or hard. It wasn't an issue of me being a mean teacher. The quiz was of an average difficulty and any student paying attention would have passed it. However, upon grading the quizzes I realized just what a low caliber of students I was dealing with and made the egregious error of deciding not to LOWER the standards to them, but to have them RISE to my standards and thereby teach them something.

Complaints flooded into my boss about the test being too difficult, they didn't have enough time to study, "by god I have two children and can't study this much" etc. etc. And sure enough, at the age of 27, I was called into the office.

My boss explained to me that we are here to challenge the students, but not too much. That my test was unfair and I should consider tailoring it more to their skill level. Of course with hindsight I now see what the charlatan of a dean was telling me; "Dumb it down because we're fleecing these kids for their money for a worthless degree and if you rock the boat we'll lose some of them." But he couldn't come outright and say that, ergo why he was feeding me a line of bull.

The next quiz I dumbed down, and this time a whopping 30% of the students passed. Naturally there was the same cacophony of complaints which resulted me landing in the dean's office once again. This process continued until I had more or less realized that not only were the students dead set against learning or trying to feign some semblance of being a scholar as well as the complete lack of back up from management to hold some level of standards to these kids. And so, choosing the path of least resistance, I decided I would not only make the quizzes and tests insanely easier, but skew the grading curve so greatly it would put affirmative action to shame.

To avoid any more criticism that I didn't test the students on what we studied I made them make their own "study guide" for the tests. This consistent of each student writing a multiple choice question on a piece of paper, me taking all those questions and photocopying them into a guide for each student. We would review the questions and the correct answers, and then I would take the EXACT SAME PHOTOCOPIED questions, photocopy them again, insert 4-5 questions of my own and then give it back to the students as the official test.

Even then, with no more than 4-5 question of my own to give those who deserved an A and A, I would still get students to flunk the test. So idiotic and genuinely stupid, or perhaps galactically lazy, were these students, they couldn't pass a test where they had the answers the day before.

Regardless, the majority of the students did pass, but with less than 40% of them earning A's.

Of course the concept of "earning" A's was a joke. Only 2-3 students per class really "earned" an A. But the grading curve was so skewed (at the request of the dean to make sure everybody passed) that the math more or less bumped people who would have really earned a C into the A+ category.

This behooved on my part true pity for the few students I did have that did indeed earn A's. They would study hard and effectively waste their time because all they would have to do is the bare minimum to pass and still get an A.

However, insisting on some kind of level of integrity, if I had to bump some degenerate loser's 12% score to the 70% necessary to pass, then I would bump everybody's score up by 58%. Not to mention the never ending requests from students to do some kind of "extra credit" to pass, I would have to present the same opportunity to every student, of which of course the straight A students would avail themselves of and earn even more unnecessary points. This resulted in some very interesting final scores.

Of the possible 100 points you could have earned in the class the top student had a final score of 170.

She had busted he ass off to earn nearly twice the amount of points she needed simply because that was the work/study ethic she had. The runner up had 150%. I insisted that neither of them study much for the next class I taught which was statistics and instead enjoy their next semester.

Tests and quizzes were just one problem I ran into in the schools. The second one was papers.

Foolish and idealistic, I thought it would be a great idea to have the students write an economics report on a country of their choosing to test their economic and analytical ability. Each student was to pick a country of their choosing and then write a FIVE PAGE DOUBLE SPACED PAPER on that country. This was no Herculean task. Matter of fact, I think I've already written more in this post in the past 10 minutes. Regardless, the hellish bitching and moaning and complaining did not stop.

"I don't have a computer."

"I don't have a printer."

"I don't have access to either."

"Why does it have to be 5 pages?"

"What's the font size."

More effort bitching and whining went into fighting against the paper than actually writing the effing thing.

With much ballyhoo and BS, inevitably I did get them into the computer lab and as the deadline approached, the vast majority of my students were frantically writing as they had procrastinated to that very last day.

Truthfully though, the majority of them did get their papers in on time and with them in hand began a painful task I was completely unaware of.

The first paper I read was on South Korea. The student had written:

"South Korea's economy is a modern industrialized nation, diversified into manufacturing, technology and services. It paradoxically compares..."

And right there I knew something was up.

So well written was that first sentence, I knew there was no way my student could have written it.

Sure enough I went to the Google and found he had just copied and pasted the report from the CIA's World Factbook.

The next paper was on Finland;

"Finland's economy is a mixed free market/socialist economy with the government providing its populace with ..."

Already, too well written. Google. CIA World Fact Book. Plagiarized.

I continued to google search various phrases and sentences that seemed too well crafted for the ability of my students and found out that out of 92 students, 89 had plagiarized.

The next day I ripped into them. I lectured them about how plagiarism was completely unacceptable, they would all get F's and blah blah blah, they weren't listening. And sure enough I got called into the principle's office.

The "dean" then lectured me about how I was overly harsh on the students and that they "didn't know" they weren't supposed to plagiarize. He then went on to read complaints he took in a survey from my students about my performance, one of which was a complaint about this ever so slight speech impediment I have (I cough due to allergies more frequently than the average person). I was to also let all the students write a new paper. I was dumbfounded.

I was to apologize to these students for their plagiarism. Only in a 2 year degree mill.

It was here that I realized that if I was going to keep my job I was just going to have to play ball and pass these kids no matter what. But the trick was to show them still who was boss because by this time they thought they owned me and had won. Never mind their degree would be worthless. Never mind with that kind of attitude they would get fired in half a second. In their little minds they "won" and now life was just going to bend over for them, if not the dean would always be able to save them and would bend life over for them.

But I would get my revenge. For the next class in the next semester was statistics.

Now you must understand that at this school there were multiple "majors" and they would keep the majors together so as to breed comradery. The majors were computer science, accounting, "travel and hospitality," and "health care." Naturally, the computer science and accounting students had a high mathematical aptitude and therefore would not only do better, but advance through the class faster. Therefore after 4 weeks they were already twice as far as their "travel and hospitality" counterparts.

Thinking there was nothing wrong and learning to make the class insanely easy, I thought there were going to be no more complaints. And sure enough there was;

The computer science and accounting students were complaining because they had done twice the work in the same amount of time. The dean then said I can't teach two different classes and they must be standardized across all majors.

This presented a problem to me in that there was no way in hell the travel and hospitality majors would ever be able to accomplish what the other students were doing. Thus I had to slow them down while travel and hospitality caught up. Thus, one of my greatest creations ever;

The Halo Statistics Project.

To grant the travel and hospitality majors enough time to get their fat, imbecilic lazy asses enough time to catch up, I decided that the accounting and computer programming majors would conduct a statistical experiment playing Halo. We linked 4 X-Boxes together, each person (including yours truly) would have a statistics sheet, and as we played various games we would record various statistics;

# of deaths
# of kills
# of assists
Time Alive
etc.

This would then give us enough empirical data to have a field day with to calculate things such as standard deviation, mean kill and calculate very important things such as;

"If you have 18 deaths in Halo, what percentile are you in, in the sub game "Slayer Pro?"

"What is the correlation coefficient between assists and the use of a bazooka."

For the next two weeks we played Halo while the rest of the students caught up.

Naturally, of course there were complaints. The travel and hospitality majors found out the other students were playing Halo. And when asked why they couldn't play Halo, I said, "well you're two weeks behind the other students so I have to find a way for you to catch up and this way we will have empirical data to use in future projects and experiments."

It did not go over well. By this time my repoire with the students had deteriorated so much there was nothing I could do. Teacher's cars were getting keyed, I was regularly called names and insulted by students. It was a "college" but it was more like teaching in a ghetto high school. The students were completely unaware of any possibility it was their fault they were failing or were so inconceivably stupid other students had to resort to "Halo Statistics" for them to play catch up.

Of course, by this time, I had given up on any kind of desire to teach these kids. I made it possible for those who wanted to learn, to learn, but instead of treating my job as an educator, I treated it as a baby sitter. And fresh in my mind the complaints filed about me being a idiot and a jerk and having that "stupid cough thing" as well as being forced by the dean to apologize to these daytime-tv-watching morons, I had one final trick up my sleeve.

The students by this time knew enough about simple statistics that the concepts of the bell distribution curve and how standard deviation can estimate what percent of the population you rank in were within their ability to calculate. But, since I was a concerned teacher, the question was "what kind of calculation can we do or test to make this personal and interesting to my beloved students?" And then it hit me;

IQ.

There was a web site, where if you had the time, you could take a rather thorough IQ test and get your IQ. It wasn't official or anything, but it would serve the purposes of my little statistics experiment. The students would go online, take their IQ test and then calculate what percent of the population they ranked in, in terms of their IQ.

The students were all excited about it. Of course they were the smartest students in the world and the world and meanies like me were just out to get them. They were almost supremely confident they would score high and no doubt some of them were tentatively planning on showing me their IQ to "show me."

So off they went to the computer lab, 45 minutes they came back with their score and I then showed them the method using a mean of 100 to find out what percent of the population they ranked in.

And as more and more of them looked up their percentile on the little percentile sheets their shoulders slouched. Their faces shocked. The travel and hospitality majors, you could tell, were double checking their math because they couldn't believe they were that stupid. Many faced the paradox of having to ask me to help them because on one hand they couldn't believe they scored that low, but they didn't want me to see their IQ (which I insisted be kept confidential). One girl started crying and another student who never shut up and found it a vital necessity to constantly talk in class, actually shut up. We found one student was "officially" retarded (though he wasn't, he just didn't try) while another was ecstatic to find out she was in the top 30%, until I pointed out she subtracted wrong when calculating her standard deviation and she was in fact in the bottom 30%. The class was somber, silent and depressed. Oh sure, there were the genuine straight A students who were happy and arguably finally vindicated that they were smart, arguably MENSA material, but the rest of them got a harsh delivering blow from the real world. There was their real grading curve.

In the end I went on to teach at another 2 year college, this time with the wisdom knowing not to try to teach the kids anything, but to entertain them. Pass them along, give them their B- and everybody's happy. And it is here that the lesson of degree mills and junior college must be learned.

There is no point in going to these schools unless they are accredited and you are intending on moving on to get your 4 year degree. Many states and local governments have 2 year colleges and they're great. They are typically part of the state university system, they are accredited and they are a VITAL AND GREAT opportunity to those who may not have the means to afford a 4 year college or perhaps was just goofing off during high school and now realized the merits of education. However, there are other 2 year "institutions" out there that are nothing more than degree mills. Non-accredited, typically private companies that are just that; companies.

They don't care if you get a good education. They're not really there to help you. And they certainly do not care if you get a job or not.

They're just there to take your money.

MGTOW vs WGTOW

Susan Walsh has an **interesting piece up at her little cabin in the Hookuposphere**. It highlights an article by Katie Bolick about how single women, who are now in their 30's and 40's, are embracing their singlehood, and coming to grips they may never marry, striking out on going their own way.

Read it first, before continuing on.

You **read it** yet?

You **have?**???

OK, here we go.

I like the article and very much agree with everything that's been said because it is essentially "WGTOW." Women of a certain age are starting to realize their perceptions and strategies were not quite accurate or effective when it came to choosing an appropriate suitor, and now that they are no longer the "hot little thing" they were when Milli Vanilli was popular, they are forced to accept reality and abide by it. It's a healthy decision to realize you are on this planet this one time and you better make the best of it, and so to see a movement akin to MGTOW with women, I can and do tip my hat to them.

There's just a couple problems with the whole premise, and permit me to be blunt (not that you thought I was going to be anything but).

One, I don't believe it. Sorry, just don't. Normally I cite empirical data or statistics, but I have none. All I have is the totality of personal and anecdotal experience I've accumulated over the years to realize that women, especially in their 30's and 40's, AND ESPECIALLY IF THEY DON'T HAVE KIDS, become MORE desperate. Yes they'll tell themselves 30 is the new 20. And yes, they'll cite people like "Meg Ryan" or "Jennifer Aniston" who are still "hot" in their 40's. And yes, they'll read US or People magazine and watch reruns of "Tank Girl." But in the end, I don't believe women, like men in the MGTOW movement, believe it for one second. I believe it is their rationalization hamsters merely plagiarizing the MGTOW movement.

Two, while the two are analogous (MGTOW and WGTOW), the analogy ends in the origins of both movements. The origins of MGTOW hearkens back to when these men were in their early teens. Nerd or jock. Player or uber-beta. Virgin or porn star. All men have had to suffer the games, psychoses, drama, and just plain BS associated with dating and courting women/girls since puberty. Some men, with a low threshold for psychological pain or abuse (or as I like to call it "self-respect"), just give up. They make a conscious economic decision weighing the costs and benefits of continuing to pursue the opposite sex and came to the decision not to chase any more. To hop on their motorcycles, get the snippity snip, minimize their expenses and head out into the vast plains of life and maximize the time they have on this planet for their own benefit before they died.

This "process" or "epiphany" is different from the origins of WGTOW or how women decide going their own way is the best option. Most men go their own way in their prime. It's a conscious choice. It wasn't forced upon them. They purposely and consciously chose to quit because it was the wisest choice. Whereas with WGTOW, it's a situation that seems forced upon them. They wake up one day, at the age of 37, realize the past 7 years was not as fruitful as it was from 1990-1997 and are faced with the reality nobody cares about Winona Ryder anymore. They only care about Megan Fox. They never analyzed or assessed the ROI of their efforts on attracting a male. They never looked back and said, "Gee, I'm going to die here in a short 40 years, I better quit pissing away my time at the bars and go hiking in Glacier National Park." They just took the time to finally turn around and see men stopped chasing them back in Bush's first administration.

They then claim, "Oh yeah, me too! Fish-bicycle! I'm going my own way!" Sadly, because it's their only option. This, does not a deeply thoughtful (or intellectually honest) epiphany make.

Three, which is related to two, is an issue of human psychology. Specifically, hard wiring.

I truly believe when a man comes to the decision to go his own way, the romantic/social/dating/whatever environment was so hostile it overrode his hard-wired programming to chase women. This is NOT a light statement. Because if your external environment was so hostile, to the point it overrides your genetic programming, that's a pretty hostile environment. I also contend the environment is so hostile, it literally damages your hard-wiring, or perhaps your brain sabotages it on purpose so that you can continue on with a reasonably normal and enjoyable life before you die. You girls perhaps have ran into the "dark, but quiet" man who you theorize was hurt by some woman in the past and you wish to show him there's reason to live and love once again? Yeah, that's the guy I'm talking about.

Sadly, it's already too late. His wiring has been irreparably damaged. He's no longer capable of love or romance, he's in a sense a fully functional automoton, capable of all human functions bar romance and love. Try as you might, he can't be put back together. He is "damaged goods." It's a battery that is dead and just won't turn over. In short, it wasn't a choice for him. His heart or mentality was permanently "broken" and shan't ever be put back together again.

But this cannot be said for the WGTOW movement. I'm sure womens' hearts have been "broken" and this isn't to say you haven't fallen in love before, blah blah blah. But you have not been driven to the brink where your genetic programming and hard-wiring is damaged or impaired. You haven't been driven to the point where you actually are forced to think of your mortality and how you've been living your life and deciding it is genuinely better to go at it on your own and pack it in before you die, completely taken men out of the picture.

Why?

Well, truthfully (and here we go with that blunt stuff again), ON THE WHOLE (admitting there are exceptions) women have had it pretty good in this country when it comes to quality and caliber of men. They were just WAAAAAAAAAAAAAAAAAAAAAAAAAAAY too picky (or perhaps preoccupied with playing little funny torturous mind games) when it came to men. I know and acknowledge there are women who have been genuinely abused.

But I'm not talking about them.

I'm talking about the other 98.5% of women in American who watched too much 90210, Oprah or what have you and whose expectations were outlandishly high.

These girls/women have not gone through anywhere NEAR the psychological torture necessary to irreparably damage their hard-wiring to just POOF, give up on men and GENUINELY go their own way.

Four, it's an issue of timing. Given a limitless time horizon, yes, I 100% accept and agree that women would go their own way. But their environment has not been that hostile LONG ENOUGH to essentially break their spirit and their hard-wiring. Men have been at this since they were essentially 13 or 14. You add 20 years of that kind of hostile environment of mind games, being stood up, drama, suicide threats, sh!t tests, flightiness, flakiness, divorce, blah blah blah, and he'll burn out. So by the time he's in his 30's, he's done, he's impaired, he's on his motorcycle and you just see a tailpipe obscured by a puff of exhaust.

Women don't start that training or suffer anything approaching that kind of a hostile environment until they're maybe 30 or 35. And given how society and media constantly artificially pump up their egos, the true learning can be delayed until they're 40 (because, as you know, Oprah said 40 is the new 30. And there's this cougar fad. And Katie Couric is on the news. And did you see Aston Kutchner! He's married to Demi Moore...oops...wait ;).

So if I'm to believe this, Katie Bolick and other 30 something women, in a mere short 2-4 years, have suffered enough of a hostile courting environment that it destroyed their genetic programming and hard-wiring?

Sorry, I don't buy it dear. It takes A LOT of pain, agony, suffering and a relentless, never ending massive assault of nuclear-powered psychological BS to destroy your hard-wiring. Men, frankly, have never launched such a long, vicious, vile or sustained assault on women in this country, leading me to once again believe it is the plagiarizing rationalization hamster.

Of course, there is a silver lining to all this. And that is equilibrium.

As an economist I am a big believer in equilibrium. It is a constant and natural state in all aspects of physics, economics and humanity. It cannot be denied or defied. It is a fact. Because, well, if any system (the universe, the economy, humanity, etc) were NOT to be in equilibrium, it would blow up or destroy itself (which in itself is achieving equilibrium - ahhhhh!). But my deep philosophical hookey pookey aside, the point is you WILL most definitely get to suffer enough to the point your hard wiring is impaired. You will most definitely get to earn your stripes and the right to claim GENUINE WGTOW status. Because, banter about it all you want, a large enough population of the single men out there, ESPECIALLY in their 30's-50's have sooooo been put through the ringer, you'll never have the chance you did to potentially woo them into matrimony back when they were 20 and reasonably functional, healthy and capable in terms of romance and love. Your options are now limited to damaged goods. You have no choice now.

So it's not like you won't be going your own way. Don't worry, another 15-20 years wandering in the harsh desert you've essentially created for yourselves and you'll rank right up there with the rest of us. And besides, it's guaranteed. You'll have the honor of turning highly functional automotons like us when you're 55! You will become 100$ USDA certified WGOTW's.

All I ask is you please don't fake it in the meantime.

Accusing Men of Immaturity Because They Don't Wish to Marry

I tire of these stories because the question of "where have the good men gone" has been answered time and time again, it's just I presume the women don't like the answer they're getting and therefore keep asking it hoping somehow they will get an answer they like (even though it won't be true).

So in a spirit of kind-heartedness I will help out the lost WSJ reporter and hopefully end this needless discussion once and for all (which I probably won't because it won't be the "correct" answer women are looking for.)

Here is an excerpt from the article;

Among pre adults, women are the first sex. They graduate from college in greater numbers and they have higher GPA's. As most professors tell it, they also have more confidence and drive. Those strengths carry women through their 20's when they are more likely than men to be in grad school and making strides in the workplace. In a number of cities they are even out-earning their brothers and boyfriends. Still for these women, one key questions won't go away – "where have all the good men gone?"

I shall make it bullet-pointy to be succinct and save us time (though, there are a lot of bullet points to make)

- One, the now never ending common refrain that women now earn the majority of degrees. For the 348th-freaking time *it's because you major in easier/worthless subjects*. THat's why you earn the majority of degrees, but still make only 76% of what men do. Ironically **the reporter has her "masters in English"** because even though you've been speaking it for your entire life, you still need to get an advanced degree in it so you speak it "real good."

- She highlights women's advances in education as proof they are "more mature." Which is the largest erroneous premise of the article. Women are not more mature than men. Just because men play video games and drink and fart and belch, does not mean we are less mature. Maybe by the "female" definition we are, but if we'd follow that we'd all be a bunch of betas no girl would want to date. Being mature is supporting ourselves - not rushing out to propose to a girl and start making babies. Just because we can support ourselves on less money than you can, does not make us less mature. Matter of fact, it makes us MORE mature because we are being fiscally responsible living in dumps we can afford instead of insisting on living in Uptown and buying fancy clothes and cars and appletini's we can't afford.

- Did you hear of this "divorce fad" going around? Apparently it was started by the baby boomers and CONTINUES TODAY. Not to mention a lot of the 20 something men who aren't "mature" enough to get married tomorrow REMEMBER THEIR PARENTS GETTING DIVORCED AND ARE A LITTLE GUN SHY

- Did you hear about this "divorce fad" going around? Apparently the rate of divorce didn't drop with Gen X or Gen Y either.

- Did you hear of this "divorce fad" going around? Apparently men get to pay out the majority of the time be it alimony or child support.

- Did you hear about this "divorce fad" going around? Apparently 65% of the time it's women who initiate divorce.

- Feminism and feminists are not sexy. When you say, "well I consider myself a feminist, but don't mind staying at home and being a good wife" all the guy heard was "well I consider myself a feminist blah blah blah blah blah." The term has been tainted by its "profession" to represent something that is not pro-woman at all. DO NOT CLAIM TO BE ONE. It will send the men running.

- Kids cost around $500,000 each to raise. given employment prospects we can't afford that. Much rather buy a boat or frankly work all that much less.

- Hey, you hear about this federal budget deficit and debt? Apparently we elected this guy "Barack Obama" and a bunch of democrats into office who are now mortgaging the future. This means our expenses in the future will be higher. Well, of course us "foolish, immature, pooping, farting boys" were too "immature" to vote for him like you wise women, but then again we're too busy flinging poo at each other to ponder the future macro-economic ramifications of a collapsing dollar.

- Hey, you hear about this social security medicare thing? Apparently enough "smart wise women" disproportionately kept voting for democrats to essentially have those immature 20 something men pay for the livelihood for these aging people. This added expense on our futures make's it that much harder economically to commit to a wife and children.

- Hey, you hear about this "welfare state" "medicaid" thing?

Apparently enough "smart wise women" disproportionately over the years voted in enough democrats to essentially replace the role of fathers with government programs making fathers not only unnecessary, but an increasingly risky and unrewarding proposition, not to mention, making it easier for women to just up and leave their husbands, because well, "they needed to find themselves" and the government will take care of the kids while they go pursue their EPL fantasy.

- Hey, if I'm not going to be a father, then what incentive to I have to "grow up?"

- Hey, did you hear about this "welfare state" thing? Apparently because we've now outsourced bringing up children to the government and have to create government jobs for all the "sociology majors" and "education majors" and "communications majors" our tax bill will go through the roof. Oh! Wait!!! No it doesn't! I forgot! I'm a guy! I can live on very little, work a crappy job, work part time, live in a crappy apartment with my buds and STILL have enough disposable income to play video games and buy booze.

- Sex in the City? Not sexy. Tell them you watch "Hogan's Heroes" instead.

Then we have much more succinct, non-socio-political explanations;

- The drama and BS men have to suffer from 14-25ish or so drives them into the arms of X-Box 360, the chums and booze.

- The risk/return of known factors such as friendship, a cheap living, fishing, booze, video games, and just the plan damn freedom that comes with it, HEAVILY outweighs any potential returns we'd get from spending time pursuing women.

- There is no risk of having a dog, a gaming console, friends or a poker game. There is a risk of having a wife and a child.

- Girls, in general, are completely unaware of the fact that men are 1/2 the equation. No consideration is given as to what men might want in a relationship (read her article again)

- In general, men and their traditional roles have become deprecated and are no longer needed for society. Therefore some may commit suicide, but most will opt to enjoy a simpler, easier self-serving life while we're here.

So to summarize all the bullet points:

In short you have made a life of bachelortude and singledom more attractive an option (economically, socially and romantically) than marrying you.

You may not "like" that answer. It may even make you angry. But it is the truth.

So can we now please stop it with the "where have all the good men gone" schtick?

Thank you, and as always, enjoy the decline.

It's Not Your Fault

I call my buddy Alejandro to see what he was doing yesterday. He's wasn't doing much and since he's from Mexico, I thought he might find it novel to partake in an American pastime;

Shooting assault rifles.

He had never shot a gun before so I brought my little arsenal with and we headed out to the range.

En route to the range, I asked him what he had been doing with all his free time, because unfortunately he, along with 2,500 other engineers got laid off at one of the larger employers in town. He said he was looking for another job, talking to recruiters, applying, etc., but then he said something that made me quite angry. Not at him, but in general;

"I'm also going to this workshop where they try to help us out with dealing with the stress and the shame that comes with getting laid off."

The "shame?" I thought to myself. Why would he have shame when 2,499 other people got laid off? Fear of not being able to pay your bills, I could understand. Annoyance due to the fact you would now have to restrain your budget and not afford certain luxuries, OK. But shame? Why would you feel shame?

Sadly, it's a story I had heard before. Not more than 2 weeks previously another friend of mine was laid off. A computer programmer. He was telling me how he couldn't bear to hang out with us, his friends, because he was too ashamed he had been laid off. He was in a 2 month depression, holed up in his house, before he got another job (and found the pride to start hanging out with us again).

Another friend of mine just last Thursday was laid off, and though nowhere near as distraught was certainly down and depressed about it. I was keeping somewhat close tabs on her particular employment situation as her boss would constantly berate her for not meeting sales goals, ignoring the fact the economy was in a recession and that sales across the company were down. But despite the psychopathology of her boss, she still felt a little bit of shame.

So let me lay it out for all of you out there who are getting laid off once and for all;

It's not your fault.

Pure and simple, it's not your fault.

I'm not saying this to make you feel better. I'm not saying this to get you in the "cheer up camperoos! The sun always comes up tomorrow. And you should be happy little people, because if you're not perpetually happy, then you have psychological issues and need prosaic!" brainwashed-modern-day-American-mandatory-perpetual-happiness-sort-of-way.

No, I'm saying it because it's true.

It's not your fault.

The reason it isn't your fault is multifold.

One, we're in a recession.

Oh, I know your boss may have berated you and harped on you and told you, you weren't cutting it. But don't kid yourself, the reason for this added pressure is because his boss was pressuring him to boost sales because the regional manager was being pressured by his boss to cut losses, because the president and CEO has noticed the stock price tanking and isn't going to get his bonus this year. And the reason the stock price is tanking is because we're in a recession. A recession, I might add, management should have known was coming years ago and should have prepared for it, but are so incompetent and late in dealing with it, they now have to have massive lay offs.

This is what you must understand from a macro-economic perspective. When GDP contracts at 3.8%, it doesn't matter how good of an employee you are, demand for your firm's product, and thus labor goes down. The company cannot keep you on, not because you're not pulling your own weight, but because there just isn't demand for your labor. If anything, management should be criticized for hiring so many people in the first place, only to lay off again in 6 months when the economic indicators suggested a recession was on the way. It really is something to view as "nothing personal."

The second thing I wish to point out is the childish, assholeic (which is a word I just made up, but is the only way to describe it) behavior some managers have where they lack the maturity to be forthright with their employees and instead insist on blaming the problems of the macro-economy ON THEIR EMPLOYEES!

This enrages me because you have a person in a position of power, a position of authority, falsely blaming their staff for the problems of the company. The reason they do this again is that management is responsible for maneuvering the company through choppy economic waters. Management is responsible for making the decisions, developing the policies and implementing the strategies to deal with the outside environment. And since they are so inept and incompetent that their policies don't work, they don't have the intellectual honesty to admit it was THEIR decisions and THEIR fault that led the company to the dire straits it currently now faces. Ergo, since their bloated egos can't handle it, they blame their staff.

I hear endless stories of my friends being flogged to produce more sales, to make more loans, to sell more cars, despite this being the worst economy since the Volcker Recession. And if they don't, well then it's not the economy's fault, it's their fault and they should feel ashamed as the door hits them on the ass on their way out. To blame an economic crisis currently estimated to cost $2 trillion not on the sub prime deadbeats and corrupt banking system, but because my friend didn't sell enough couches is not only laughable, but hypocritical and typical of management today. Perhaps we should blame the chef of the Exxon Valdez for it running into a reef and not the drunk captain.

The third and final thing I insist you must understand is that your "supervisors" are NOT your SUPERIORS. And I think this takes a little more psychological thinking than normal.

Just because somebody is your boss or is older than you does not make them BETTER than you. Oh sure, back in the day that may have held, but today it absolutely does not.

When historians look back at this recession it is going to be a shameful period for the Baby Boomers for they are the ones who were more or less at the helm of this financial disaster. This is not to foist all blame on them, as there is certainly no limit to the amount of idiotic, disgusting, entitlement mentality driven Gen-X'ers who more or less make up a plurality of the sub prime dead beats and thus are also to blame, but at the helm of all the financial institutions, regulatory institutions, governments and corporations were the Baby Boomers. And they were asleep.

Be they bankers who disregarded any semblance of risk management in an attempt to enrich themselves through commissions, be they middle or senior managers who blindly flogged their staff to boost sales to make bonus at the expense of the integrity of the firm, be they auto manufacturing firms who had not the pair of cajones required to face down the union and basically admit to the reality "we can't afford to keep paying you this much," or be they the politicians and government leaders who instituted policies that channeled trillions to sub prime deadbeats all to buy votes from the degenerates of this country, in all cases sanity, logic, integrity and real leadership were forfeited for short term gain. The decisions being made by the leaders of these institutions were so horribly wrong, misguided and short sighted it is impossible to blame the ground troops over the officers for losing this war.

Of course to blame your elders or supervisors requires some bold and arrogant thinking. You are basically saying, "I, a younger, not-as-experienced, INDIVIDUAL claim to know more than the older, wiser and more experienced MASSES." But all one has to do is look at the empirical data. If the bosses, supervisors, leaders, governors, regulators and elders were right, would we be in this financial debacle? If they were competent, would we need trillion dollar bailouts? If the heads of these firms, the "elite" of Wall Street and other banks, we so god damned gifted, would they require taxpayer money? If they knew what they were doing and were thusly entitled to the rank of "supervisor" or "manager" or "boss" or "executive" would the company be in the red with its stock price tanking, along with the rest of the stock market, impoverishing us with the destruction of our 401k?

Once you understand this, then you will realize why you should have no shame. And not only why you should have no shame, but why you should have pride in getting let go by one of these Titanically-doomed wrecks.

In the meantime do yourself a favor and pour yourself a Fat Dachshund (1 part vodka, 1 part white creme de cocoa, one part baileys). You've earned it.

Dancing Etiquette for Married Women

I got a multi-tiered question that in order to respond fully requires a post in itself.

The question was what was the proper etiquette for married women who want to dance but their husbands don't want to.

In general, albeit dancing is ensconced in a very general environment that would lead towards dating, dancing itself is not an action of flirting or romance. In other words it can be totally platonic and just a fun activity no different than playing volleyball. Of course it certainly has the potential to lead towards some kind of romance, but if Joe Schmoe asks Jane Schmoe at bar x to dance (ballroom) then yeah, they guy might have an interest, but he isn't proposing marriage.

This is arguably one of the largest complaints men have when women are sitting on the edge of their seats, bouncing up and down to a great salsa or swing band at the edge of the dance floor and then when somebody comes up and asks them to dance, they giggle and laugh and point at their friends and tell them "no, you dance with him!" "No! *giggle, giggle* YOU dance with him!"

It isn't a proposal of marriage.

It isn't a sexual proposition.

It isn't even asking if he could buy you a drink because that would cost money.

He's asking for a dance, so married or not, it's pretty safe.

Now that being said, I cannot think of a more adroit and classy way to meet a girl besides dancing. So naturally most men will approach dancing as primarily a means to have fun, but a close second to meet a girl.

This is where the married women have to do one simple thing;

Wear your wedding ring.

A slightly skilled dancer will even have the savvy to feel that large hunk of rock on your left hand, saving you the embarrassment of asking you out. So as long as you're married and have that ring, you're not going to run into any trouble, at least on the ballroom scene.

Now where married women run into trouble is when THEY TAKE OFF THE RING or play a game some female friends of mine called "Testing Our

Market Value."

To simplify things (a lot) women want attention, men want sex. And whereas it's socially poo-pooed to go out and just ask for sex, to get attention is perfectly acceptable. This creates a conundrum, especially for married women who are not getting enough love or attention back at home. They some how feel the need to go out and doll themselves up and "test their market value" and get attention, ie- sit at a bar and see how many men buy them drinks as they're all dolled up and *oops* did they happen to "forget" to wear their wedding ring?

No doubt there are enough veteran males in my readership who could regale you with tales of going to a club/bar/party, meeting a really nice gal WITHOUT A RING and only after spending 4 hours getting to know this one girl, finding out she was married. This is not only deceitful, but it's disrespectful as the woman has not only led the guy on, but wasted his time which he might as otherwise used to meet an available (and might I add, more secure) woman.

This happens more often than you might think and to a severity of more than you might imagine.

The Captain had one experience where a drop dead gorgeous woman was dancing with him with long sleeve gloves (couldn't tell if she was married). I asked her if there was a ring under the gloves and she said yes - ergo "thanks for the dance, no harm done."

On the other extreme was the drop dead gorgeous redheaded economist he met in his dance class and dated for about 2 months. As you can imagine after two months, several dates, her having red hair AND being an economist, the young Captain was smitten. That was of course until we were salsa dancing late one night and whilst on the dance floor the poor ole Captain's hand got lacerated by huge chunk of diamond he hadn't noticed her wearing before. After changing his dance grip he had the shocking realization that she was married this entire time and just forgot to take her ring off.

Regardless the whole point is whether it's an hour or two months, don't be a tease. If you want to dance, go out and dance and wear your wedding ring. I find nothing wrong with dressing up a little fancy. But if you're going to slut yourself up and take off the ring and "test your market value" and lead a guy on so you can get your fill of attention-jollies at his expense, that's where women start to earn a bad reputation and make men long for the likes of Sophia Loren or Audrey Hepburn, or at least join the marriage strike.

"Dame" is NOT Sexist

Dear feminists who have no skill and make their living by criminalizing normal behavior as since you have no real skill, you are otherwise unemployable and need to shake people down.

The term "dame" is not a derogatory remark. It is used by old fashioned classy men to describe old fashioned classy women.

If you are so foolish as to lecture me or any one else about the "improper" use of this term, then you can enjoy the life you've chosen of shaking people down for made up crimes which is nothing more than a parasitic existence, as long as you know FULL WELL YOU WILL SACRIFICE A REAL LIFE WITH A REAL GUY AND ANY SEMBLANCE OF REAL LOVE OR AT LEAST FRIENDSHIP.

Jesus Freaking A. Christ.

How do you people live life?

Seriously. Do you stay awake at night trying to find reasons to be insulted? What kind of a life is that? Is it you have no social abilities, no qualities or traits that attract members of the opposite sex, or heck, just no qualities and traits that make people want to be your friend that you have to engage in such childish and pathetic behavior?

DAME?

DAME?

South Pacific had a song. It was heralding dames.

Humphrey Bogart used the term frequently and in high regard.

Men in WWII just wanted and spilled blood for dames.

And it's every American males God given right to use the term "dame."

And all you schleps can do is bitch and whine about it when a guy says TO SOME OTHER WOMAN WHO ISN"T YOU, "you're a cute dame?"

Go to hell.

Although, something tells me you're so screwed up you're already in your own personal hell.

In the meantime, I officially decree all men shall continue to use the word "dame" if only to compliment the true classy women who are smart enough to appreciate the endearing moniker and to piss off those that are so childish and pathetic that they truly deserve to be pissed off.

I can't believe I have to write about this stuff.

My Pot Rack Story

Let me tell you my pot rack story and then I'm heading out to teach dance class for the day.

I was about 24 or 25, I can't remember which. I was a younger guy and had met this older guy, all of 29, who was also into finance and economics. I looked up to him as he was also conservative, much more successful than I was and kind of tolerated my younger, cocky ass.

Through the course of the next year we became good friends. We'd all go out swing dancing, we talk shop, he was a runner and so was I, all in all a great guy and everybody loved his company.

Then he found himself a girl.

She was a neurotic grad student, getting her doctorate in psychology not to go into practice, of course, but to go and re-teach what she learned 2 years previous to presumably girls in her exact same situation. Obsessed with her looks she was constantly working out, eating sticks and twigs, forcing my buddy to do the same and basically sank her teeth into this guy immediately. He lasted about a whopping 3 months before she moved into his house and then the metamorphosis began.

I saw my friend go from a carefree bachelor guy, to a guy who was otherwise spoken for, to a guy who was committed, to a guy who was condemned. And whereas previously I could call him up and say,

"Hey, John, let's go for a run."

Or

"Hey, John, let's all go out dancing and scope out some chicks."

Or

"Hey, John, let's get the crew together and go see a movie."

I found myself progressively running into "scheduling conflicts" he had that prevented him from going out with his old chums.

The end came on a Saturday evening. It wasn't late. It wasn't too early and I called him up. I said, "Hey, John, let's go down to the Dubliner and get a beer."

The Dubliner being an Irish joint literally 3 blocks from his house.

Over the phone he said, "I don't know, it's Saturday night and I'm pretty busy."

"Busy!?" I said, "What do you mean busy?! Come on, it's 3 blocks from your house, it'll take all of 30 minutes to have a beer. Let's go."

"Hang on, let me ask my fiancé (he liked to call her his fiancé)"

So in the background I hear his lower toned male voice mumbling, asking his beloved if he could go out and get a beer, "Murmur murmur murmur murmur?"

And in return I heard her Beaker-eqsue (from the Muppets) high pitch voice respond;

"Neener neerner neener neneer neen?"

Then I heard my friend say,

"The Captain."

And then in vehement response the girl saying;

"THE CAPTAIN! NEENER NEENER NEENER NEENER NEERNER NEEEEEEE!!!!"

Soon he came back on the phone and said, "I'm sorry, we're hanging a pot rack tonight."

I sat there thinking to myself, "Wooooow. This guy is completely 100% castrated."

I said, "Pot rack? A pot rack? Can you postpone the great hanging of the pot rack?"

"No, we've been meaning to hang this for a while, and you know how long these projects take."

I decided it was futile to try to get him to go and get a beer. I also concluded it was pointless to even try to maintain a friendship anymore.

I never knew what happened to them thereafter. They moved somewhere and that was the last I heard of them, but this taught me a very valuable lesson;

Friends are not there to bide the time away until you find somebody to marry, by which you dispose of your friends like you do used toilet paper. Your friends are arguably more important than your spouse as they hang out with you for you and all your faults and don't give a damn what you do or how much money you make and never lay aim or have ulterior motives in hanging out with you. They are the most pure and decent people you will ever run into which can only be rivaled by the loyalty and friendship provided by dogs. And to shed them like you would an old skin once a cute piece of tail walks by is a testament not to their disposability but to your personal caliber.

Now I know that women are just as prone to do this as men, my story is only about a guy, but regardless of sex, it angers me how people just drop their friends once they find, not even somebody they're going to marry, but somebody they just become romantically involved with. And sure as Obama destroying the US economy, once they dump your sorry ass, who do you go crawling back to? Your friends.

Ergo, I think a "repatriation of friends" tax should be in order. Not necessarily some kind of monetary tax, but like a celebrity roasting or hazing where you make the traitor beg and plead for re-acceptance back into the fold of friends. Where you make your buddy profess to the guys why you and the guys were infinitely better than the girl he ran off with who took him for half, left him with a kid that wasn't his and made off with his house. Or the girlfriends make the girl admit that dating the loser who took her money to buy drugs, ended up getting another girl pregnant and racked up $40,000 in credit card debt was indeed the most boneheaded move she could have ever possibly made. I would also go so far as to enforce a level of "indentured servitude" upon them where they have to go and buy the beer, they have to be sober cab and they have to help friends move for a period of a year to earn their way back into the system.

Of course, this is all dreaming and poppycock, but when I am king. Ohhhhhhh, when I am king. There are going to be some really new and weird laws being made.

America's Collapse Causing Depression in Males

I often sign off with my signature "enjoy the decline."

The purpose of the sign-off is to emphasize that the decline of America is really unstoppable and that you might as well enjoy the decline while you're here on Earth. Don't produce anything, don't work hard, just live off of the carcass that is the US, and yes, you must take that mentality because it's reality.

For example I refuse to make more than $30,000 a year (if i can help it) and ensure that I take at least one month of vacation in a remote destination with 3 weekend vacations a year to split up the horrible Minnesota winters. Why do I refuse to do this? Because life is short and any money that I make beyond a certain point is taxed into oblivion and all I end up doing is becoming a host to the economic parasites of this formerly great nation. Additionally, it ain't like there's a lot of jobs out there anyway. Regardless, since I will die inevitably, I am packing in as much fun as I possibly can and avoiding working as much as possible.

Of course there is a drawback to this approach - it's anti-male.

Not "excelling" or "doing your best" and just "loafing off" is quite literally against the psychological hard-wiring men have. To sit and do nothing, to NOT have a career, to not (over the long run) advance and progress is the single worst thing for a man's psychology. It will ruin a man, at least a man with morals. And to tell men to just simply "enjoy the decline" EVEN THOUGH THAT IS THE ONLY OPTION THEY REALLY HAVE, still sometimes doesn't work.

How do I know this?

I am a male.

I am the creator of "enjoy the decline."

And even though I am fully aware that there is nothing that can be done, and was at the forefront of realizing this epiphany, I still suffer the same fate as my good friend **Save Capitalism**, I suffer the occasional bout of depression.

Now as he writes, he is not trying to beleaguer you guys with his problems, and neither am I. However, he does bring up a good point and I wish to amplify it. The collapse of the world's formerly greatest nation will and already is having a negative and disproportionate effect on men. It's one of the rare statements and claims I'll make WITHOUT researching for hard data to prove it and will solely rely on anecdotal evidence. The collapse of the US is foisting depression on men.

Craig, a good buddy of mine, was formerly the most driven, hard working entrepreneur you'd ever meet. Now, with the economy more or less destroying his business, and no hope in sight, he's depressed, he's sad, he no longer cares to try anymore and he asks me "why the hell did I bust my ass off." He's now thinking about driving truck out in the Williston oil fields (until of course environmentalists protest and lobby) and I'm half tempted to join him. He feels guilt for not being able to provide for his wife as much as he'd like.

Another buddy of mine, Richard, has the natural spirit of an entreprenuer, but every venture he tries never grows sprouts. Not because of the lack demand or lack of brilliance, but because of a lack of disposable income on the part of would be customers. Any ideas he has at his current place of employment are quickly disregarded on account he is a mere 27 years old, and thus he is relegated to stagnation. He is arguably just as knowledgeable on economics as I am, and KNOWS he has to enjoy the decline, but in the end whenst we share cigars there's still the lack of hope and spirit there might be a future.

Dave, a friend of mine in Chicago got his MBA AND LAW DEGREE has not the connections or ass kissing skills to find stable employment in Chicago. He only stays alive to "observe what's going to happen" because he's got nothing else to do and has taken a truly macabre approach to life.

There's of course me, your beloved Captain. I KNOW you have to enjoy the decline. I am intricately familiar with how hopeless and powerless individuals are against the ignorance and spoiledrottenbratedness of the masses of "Americans" if you can even call them that. I KNOW to forfeit labor for leisure and I KNOW I have no choice. BUt sure enough, I listen to some Rush Limbaugh or Joe Soucheray and before you know it I'm at the liquor store buying bottle of Rumpleminze. I get angry. I get pissed. I get enraged. I get near a debilitating level of depression. I force myself to run. I force myself to work out. But it only helps temporarily as the endorphins wear off from a 7 mile run in about 2 hours. In the end I buy a bottle of booze to put my brain out of its misery from running every possible economic scenario in its head, all of which end in demise. Perhaps buying booze and getting drunk is "enjoying the decline," but it's nothing more than an escape and a lot of nights the only way to force myself to sleep.

The larger point is that no matter how much a man "conscientiously" knows what the reality of the situation is and how hopeless it is, he is hard-wired to care regardless about his and his loved-ones' futures. He is wired to care about the future of his country, especially if it is a good one.

He cares about reality and justice prevailing. And above all else, a man cannot help but be depressed when he sees greatness destroyed by parasites and ignorant spoiled children for what essentially ends up being "no damn good reason at all." And this creates a problem.

Suicide is up. Alcohol consumption is up. And more men will be killing themselves in the future as they can no longer reconcile an "Enjoy the Decline" philosophy with their male hard-wiring to care (and I don't know this for a fact, I'm guessing, so prove me wrong). But where this is particularly going to affect America and makes this a particularly disturbing trend is that it won't be the degenerate males that are offing themselves.

It won't be the druggie, hippie, OD-ing types like Kirk Cocaine or Jim Moronson or Janis Joplin and other degenerates of society. It's going to be John Jones, engineer who can't find a job. Bob Bobson, computer programmer who can't find a job. Steve Stevenson, mechanical engineer who lost his job, couldn't find another one, couldn't support his family, and got divorced. Philbert Philbertson who is too young to receive a SS check, but never had the economic opportunity to earn enough for retirement. Craig Craigson, entreprenuer, who in any other economic times would have founded a successful company that employed Bob, Steve and John. It will be the productive males that made American what it was (and would have continued to maintain America as it was meant to be) that will be no longer participating. It will be the sole solution to America's economic problems that are either offing themselves or are depressed to the point of paralysis and indifference, rendering them an ineffective force and denying America any genuine hope of a future.

Now a lot of people will immediately dismiss my premise that these "stupid males" are somehow the backbone of the country and how dare you dismiss the contributions of women and blah blah blah. You will also notice how they will completely ignore my pointing out there will soon be a "crisis" of male suicide in the US (certainly a "crisis" by the standards people on the left use to define minor problems in society as a "crisis"). But this post is not for them. It's for the dwindling population of genuine, old school American men who, like Save Capitalism, like Craig, like Richard, and even like myself, have a hard time "enjoying the decline." So permit me some wisdom that will hopefully bring some solace to your lives.

First let me point out and reiterate that one of the most important things you can do to achieve a happy life is realize what you do and **do not** control. It is simple logic that you should not get excited, let alone spend one single calorie of energy "worrying" about things that you cannot control.

Can you overcome millions of idiotic youth brainwashed to vote for socialism? No.

Can you overcome millions of desperate women who vote for a president based on his "pecks?" No.

Can you overcome the trillions of words of indoctrination women receive from "women's magazines" or "Oprah" or prime time TV or EPL crap? No.

Can you overcome the millions of men who forewent their manly calling and instead became Prius driving white knights and are more than willing to sell out men as a whole to get the attention of women? No.

Can you overcome the incomprehensible level of ignorance the average American has when it comes to economics, and quite frankly, doesn't know the difference between a million, a billion and a trillion and are thusly COMPLETELY unaware of the severity of the financial crisis? No.

The ONLY thing you end up doing is wear yourself out and shorten your life expectancy.

So let go of what you can't control and instead of listening to Rush Limbaugh, turn on the jazz station and pour yourself a Rumpleminze.

Second, life, no matter how bad or at a disadvantage you may be, is still life. What else are you going to do? Like my friend Dave, a bad life is much like a bad movie. So, what? Your only other option is to watching NOTHING. "Blackness" to quote Robert Downey Jr. Additionally, if it gets so bad to the point suicide is the answer, then you have what I like to call "God Freedom." "God Freedom" meaning that if you really don't care if you live or not, act like God. Rob a bank. Go sky diving. Borrow as much money as you can from a bank and blow it all on Vegas or whatever you want with no intention of paying it back. Complete a bucket list before you kick off.

Third, no guilt. No matter what no guilt. Along with kicking around the idea of writing a book titled, "Enjoy the Decline," I want to write a post about how, with the government now accounting for 40% of GDP, that it is PERFECTLY fine to accept government handouts and live off the dole. It is more or less impossible now to completely support yourself 100% and be a real man. I have to this day done so and in my youth used to think it was a shame to accept government money. Nowadays you are insane if you think you can get by without government money. Let go and relax and enjoy some of the socialism forced upon you by the idiots of society. You again really have no choice.

Fourth, understand the type of men like you and me are the ones who are biologically, Darwinistically and genetically suited to survive. We are minimalists. We can get by with crappy cars, crappy clothes, and some bare level of food and water. Have you seen our adversaries?

They cannot live without a;

McMansion
Sugar Daddy bank account
Food stamps
Government housing
Welfare
Daddy's credit card
Medicaid
Medicare

and a whole litany of other income transfers.

Can you imagine your typical American suburbanite princess wife surviving if the scheit hits the fan and her spending account dries up?

Can you imagine the ghettos of society without their monthly welfare checks coming in?

Can you imagine the spoiled brat liberal arts students-come-law-students-come-professional protestor trying to survive if electricity is shut off?

It may not be a wonderful society...matter of fact society will have collapsed if there's no electricity, but who do you think is going to be in charge? Tanner McEffeminite-Hyphennamed kid and his sociology degree? Bob McBobson collecting his welfare check and never bothered to learn a useful skill living in government housing? Or those "stupid" "minimalist" males who bought guns and ammo and know how to field dress a deer and know how to repair cars and build structures and run plumbing?

Understand, that if the WORST case scenario comes about, then WE are the ones who are going to do best because we can at least deal with it and don't need a McMansion con Lexus or government subsidized living.

Fifth, and this is the hardest part, you need to train your brain to accept 1-4. This is hard because I'm now asking you to go against your hard-wiring. Millions of years of evolution and genetics have programmed you BEYOND conscientious thought to react a certain way. Hormones and chemicals are released into your brain no matter how much FACT your brain knows and WILL make you feel a certain way. But there is hope.

If you're like me and millions of other men in the manosphere, or just plain society, you've overcome something more powerful than having a psychological or genetically embedded interest in the advancement of society. You've overcome something more powerful and more visceral to your genetic code than your "man code" of self-supportation, independence and freedom. You've overcome your natural, Darwinistic desire for women.

Not that you've abandoned women or sex. Heavens no! We still love women and sex. You were just able to not have it ruin or rule your life like you did when you were 18. At the age of 18 you were, like all of us, a slobbering...well...slob-beast, trying your darndest (even though you had NO CLUE HOW) to attract members of the opposite sex. You were lost, you were clueless, you were above all else miserable. Of course overtime you started realizing that no matter how much effort you put into the system, it didn't increase your chances. Matter of fact, you probably realized the LESS you tried, the BETTER you did (thus the element of "game" which is a whole other matter). Additionally, the epiphanal realization that you are finite and are going to die, put more value on for-sure things like video games and buds. In short, you were able to temper your natural Darwinistic desires for the em-betterment of yourself. And just like you were able to temper your natural Darwinistic desires for women, you must also temper your natural Darwinistic desires for a successful society.

Of course the natural follow up question would be;

"OK, so what do we have to live for? We don't have a progressing, advancing economy, women we have abandoned, I can't find a job, I have no career, there's no hope whatsoever in the future, what is left?"

And the answer is simply, "How about yourself?"

It's greedy.

It's self-serving.

It's anti-male.

But you have no choice. And I want you to incorporate that into your thinking.

YOU HAVE NO CHOICE.

So you might as well relax, pour yourself a bottle of Rumpleminze. Get a motorcycle. Buy that video game you wanted. Order the lobster. Screw your 401k (it's just going to be confiscated anyway), don't invest in any property or any fixed asset that ties you down, date a ton of different women and above all else

enjoy

the

decline.

Advice for My Younger Cappy Cap Brothers

WARNING - This post contains somewhat adult commentary/situations so if you have youth around or are easily offended I'd suggest not reading further.

I often forget what I have been through and this I don't think is coincidence. I think the mind, to maintain its sanity tries to purge or at least subconsciously avoid you having to think about things in the past that are so depressing, if not debilitating, that you have gone through that you would not be able to function or would be severely depressed if you remembered them in full and in all of their gory detail. However, at the same time, you have to view these trials and tribulations throughout life as learning experiences and if you are to be any kind of honorable "elder" you will pass on what you learned through your successes and mistakes so that the future generations may have a more productive and successful life than you. Ergo, I think it is time for a lesson for the younger male cappy caps out there who read this blog and who I often forget do make up a considerable percentage of my readership. So permit me this lesson as I think it will be of great help and benefit to the younger men out there.

Story 1

There was a time in the Captain's youth when he was comely enough to court two ladies at the same time. Well, actually the Captain was comely enough in his youth for this to be a regular event and not always were there two girls, but perhaps maybe even 3, or 4...I think even one time 5. In any case this ONE time (in band camp) he was courting two girls. Both started off as awesome candidates for long term courting potential. But then one of them stood up the Captain, canceling their date at the last minute. The Captain, not worried because of his diversified portfolio continued on his merry life and continued dating the other girl. However, the first candidate then asked him out again, to which the Captain agreed, only to have the date be canceled at the last minute. This continued on until one final time, they had a date and the girl (you guessed it) called the Captain and said she was too sick to go out. The Captain, undeterred by her cancellation, hopped in his Captain Capitalismobile and headed for the evening. However, whilst he was filling up his car with gas, he saw right before his eyes, the "very sick girl" who was "too ill to go out that night" drive past him in her car enroute to the city.

It was here the Captain decided that he was no longer going to bother with this one girl and instead decided to dedicate himself to the other girl who by this time had NEVER stood him up, NEVER lied to him and NEVER played any childish, middle school girl games with him. After getting gas he went to his favorite neighborhood bar where he saw "Amy" who was a friend of the "very sick" girl who was currently heading towards Minneapolis. She asked the Captain,

"So Captain, how's it going with Girl X?"

I replied, "Not too well. I've decided I will not longer court her and instead will dedicate myself to Girl Y."

Amy, visibly disturbed said, "What???!!! Girl X was ready to commit to you! She got rid of her boyfriend in California (to which was new news to the Captain) and was ready to date you!"

To which the Captain replied,

"Nope, I don't care. She stood me up too many times, she lied to me about being sick and I don't know about this California guy, but Girl Y is reliable, has never lied to me and actually treats me nice and good. I don't have time for childish games and if Girl X wanted to go out with me, then tough cookies, she just blew away her chances."

The Captain then finished his drink, paid his tab, went home and fell asleep. And I had every right to do so WITHOUT WORRY, for you see, when men dump women or just "stop dating" them, we don't have to worry about any kind of revenge or "consequence." We just STOP CALLING. It's one of the great advantages of being a man. We just stop chasing. The girl keeps running never ever thinking it was even a remote possibility the man would stop chasing her, and we just go home, pour a whiskey and light up a cigar and we never see the girl again.

Or so I thought.

The next morning I get a distraught call.

"Captain!??!?!"

Half awake I said, "Yeah?"

"It's Girl X! We have to talk!"

Now at this point in time, I didn't see what possible point there would be in talking. We never "dated" officially and went on several dates, interspersed with her canceling and standing me up 2 times for every 1 date we went on. You could have certainly NEVER claimed we were boyfriend and girlfriend, not to mention with Mr. California whom she was presumably seeing (a convenient 2,500 miles away), ergo I thought this odd that we had to "have a talk."

Now by this time, I will admit, I wasn't a rookie. By this time I was more or less a fully trained Jedi knight and basically said, "Heh, yeah, sure, I'll give you a call sometime."

Sensing my indifference and complete lack of desire to call her, "NO, I'M SERIOUS, WE HAVE TO TALK!!!"

I said, "No, we don't. I'll call you when I feel like it."

"Well you better call me!"

I said, "Yeah, sure."

And hung up.

Almost immediately after hanging up I figured that sooner or later I would have to have "the talk" with the girl, even though we were never dating. It was only putting off the inevitable, so I decided that I would call her, endure the pointless and baseless argument she would tender forth, rely on plain, simple, adult logic to explain why I would not be "dating" her any more and be done with it. Thus I called her back, said, yes, I'd be willing to talk and to have her come over.

She came over, tight lipped and I could almost sensed she was going to give me "what I deserved." We went downstairs where she then began to yell at me and lecture me about how dare I just break up with her, and she thought I was different and that I was one of the few guys who "got it" and blah blah blah. I tried to make some points or explain things to her, but I quickly observed anything I said was summarily ignored as she continued on her tirade. She was going on and on, but then said something rather unique;

"Oh, and I know about Girl Y."

Apparently, Amy had spilled the beans.

"Oh, and you know what's sad? You just like her because she treats you nice and cooks for you and everything."

And that was the most precious statement of all the argument.

"You just like her because SHE TREATS YOU NICE AND COOKS FOR YOU and everything."

Right now I can hear men saying global-wide, "well, duh!?"

No, we like the women that treat us like shit and never cook or do anything nice for us. THose are the ones we go after.

It was from here on that I knew this girl was delusional and psychotic and there was no point in entertaining the notions of an adult conversation with an adult resolution. She gave me my opportunity as she continued on with a litany of things "wrong" with me;

"You know that one time I wouldn't sleep with you!?"

Having a hard time trying to nail that night down I said, "Uh, no, what night?"

"The night you wanted to have sex and I wouldn't let you. I said I didn't think it was what was best?!"

Remembering it slightly I said, "Uh, yeah, I think so."

"Yeah, well that was just because I knew you were a player, Captain. I knew you were a player and I was going to see if you could handle a girl rejecting you!"

Sensing her kind of weird, self-made sense of self-control I said in the most straight faced and stone cold demeanor (because I was that serious),

"Well Girl X, you don't ever have to worry about that again, because I never want to sleep with you again."

Now, you must understand that this girl was a "party girl" from California. She was a car model for GM. And if memory serves me correctly, she may have even been in one of them modern day pin up calendars. Regardless, the whole point was that she was overly physically attractive. And never, in her entire approaching-30 years of life, had a guy turned her down or ever told her they would not sleep with her. Never, had a guy been immune to her single (and arguably) only quality; her looks.

The blow she delivered was weak, but not weak enough to not leave a slight black eye. Regardless, what was more shocking to me was not so much being punched in the face, but a woman who was 29 punched me at the age of 31 because I just didn't want to go out with her.

Story 2

Many years ago in the Captain's youth, he was deemed "a good guy." So "good of a guy" he was deemed by his friends, one of his friends decided to set him up with one of her girlfriends "Ms. Taiwan." Ms. Taiwan was a drop dead gorgeous girl. Her previous boyfriend who was a Minnesota Viking or maybe a MInnesota Timberwolf (I can't remember) was a "jerk" and our mutual friend wanted to set us up. She lived in a private estate in north St. Paul with her parents who were directly related to some of the head honchos in the Kuomintang Party of Taiwan. Cumulatively the parents had a net worth of over $1 billion and when the Captain went to pick up Ms Taiwan in his 1985 Cutlass Supreme (with out the muffler), they not only asked him to park the car three blocks down from their house so as not to bring shame to their family, but also got to endure a conversation about why he wasn't of Chinese/Taiwanese descent (even though he tried, MULTIPLE TIMES to explain he was a mix of Irish, German, and Jew and ALL OF THIS WAS BEYOND HIS CONTROL). One would think the anti-Irishgermanjew sentiment of the parents would be enough to drive him away, but no, their daughter did a splendid job of that by herself.

The Captain knew something was already amiss when on their SECOND DATE Ms. Taiwan answered the door in a naughty catholic school girl outfit. Certainly, the first date had gone alright, but nothing to warrant the outfit on the second date, and though just as male as any other guy, this willingness to don an outfit was making a worrying twingling sensation in the back of the Captain's head. However, the twingling sensation would soon be validated. For as they went forth on the third date and your beloved Captain went to get some gas and he went inside to pay. Upon his return to his car the girl was sitting in a pouting like fashion. Not noticing it too much, the Captain continued on his date and continued to drive.

Now if you want to look this up on Google Satellite to see how the next 20 minutes of this date went start at the intersection of Louisiana and Texas in St. Louis Park and plot directions to Hwy 280 and 35W.

By 394 and Louisiana the Captain noticed the girl was upset. Not thinking there was anything the Captain could have done to possibly upset this girl he said, "What's wrong?"

To which Ms. Taiwan responded, "If you don't know, then the hell if I'm telling you."

Again, not a fully trained Jedi knight, but enough of a guy to know I didn't do anything wrong, I had a hard time validating that statement by playing "20 questions."

By the intersection of Hwy 100 and 394 I had said, "I'm not going to play 20 questions, what is it?"

This then triggered screaming and accusations and yelling and crying from 100 and 394 to...

280 AND 35W

Nearly 14 miles of non-stop bitching and crying and sobbing and name calling and drama and other things that could all be categorized in the category of "shit" which culminated into....

A suicide threat on the bridge over 280 and 35W. She was going to jump out of the car at 65 MPH and if she survived would jump off the bridge.

I was, I think, all of 23 years old.

Oh, and by the way, guess what she was mad about?

That I didn't OFFER TO BUY HER A SODA when I went in to pay for gas!!!!

Story 3

The Captain had met a quite attractive, but above all else, a quite moxie-fied girl named say, "Julie." She was 25, she was drop dead gorgeous and not only did she want to learn how to dance she was also in training for a marathon (the Captain is an avid runner). Naturally we started dating, dancing and running, but soon problems would be found out by the fourth date. For by the fourth date, that's the date where you are more or less obliged to kiss. If you don't, then you are just friends, and there's nothing wrong with that, it's just a little late in the game to not be kissing.

Twas the end of our fourth date, we had gone salsa dancing and when invited to come into the Captain's Pad she agreed. I threw in Father Goose which is one of my all-time favorite movies, she laid down on the couch, I poured her a glass of wine and we then watch the movie as we spooned. We were tired and didn't make it through much of the movie, but she was already nestling her nose in the back of my neck. Thinking this was a for sure fire thing WITHOUT EVEN KISSING HER, I asked her if she wanted to go to bed. She said, "yes."

We got to bed, her still rubbing her nose in the back of my neck and when I went in for a kiss...

She stopped

Sat up

Looked surprised

and said,

"WHAT ARE YOU DOING!?"

Completely confused I said, "What do you mean, what am I doing? I'm trying to kiss you!"

To which she responded (are you ready for this?)

"Well, I'm not kissing any man until we're engaged."

If the look on my face could have been photographed at that moment in time it would have been in the Smithsonian.

Obviously I stopped dating her, but within one week she went salsa dancing, had one martini, ended up having her much-anticipated first kiss (and make out session) with an illegal alien who didn't speak English, but not before she gave him her phone number and when he left messages for her broken English and wouldn't stop calling, guess who she called to ask what to do?

I was about 30 or 31 at the time.

Now I could go on. I literally could with a limitless number of stories that are just as shocking and appalling as those mentioned above. But the larger point of all these stories is an important one and one that I wish to get to younger men in America as quickly and as early on in their lives as possible, and it is this;

No, you're not insane, the women are.

Now this may seem like a funny ha ha, half jesting lesson, but it is not. And the reason it is not is because in order to learn this lesson ON YOUR OWN you would have to go through the hell I and all the other 30 something men in America have gone through. And not only that (and this is key) you have to be driven to such insane lengths and endure such insane situations that you have NO CHOICE but to make the arrogant assumption that there might not be something wrong with you, but rather something wrong with society. This is an arrogant assumption because when is it the "individual" is right and "society" is wrong? But I'm here to tell you that this is just such the case.

If you are a younger man in the US and you cannot believe or comprehend just the sheer magnitude of idiocy you have to deal with when dating, understand it is NOT you, it is society. And the reason I bring up this overall and very important point is because you do not deserve to endure the hell you have to go through from puberty on thinking somehow you are the one to blame for the insanity. There comes a point in time where you just have too much experience and empirical evidence where you have to look back and say, "OK, am I really that insane? Have I really goofed up? What on god's green earth did i do to deserve to have that girl threaten to kill herself? What did I do so that girl would not kiss me until we were engaged? What did I do to have that girl stand me up?"

You didn't do anything. It's just the way girls are.

Now I know I will catch much flak for this post, but I don't care. I'm sick of good honorable men getting stood up, lied to, cheated on or just plain mind-effed with because literal "girls" think its funny to stand men up. I'm sick of seeing boys or young men grow up under an environment that turns them into cynical full grown men who abandon marriage or courtship altogether because girls wanted to play little middle school girl games or re-enact scenes they've seen from 90210 for 2 decades. And I'm dirt tired of seeing men, not much younger than myself, go through their teens and 20's utterly confused, and worse, somehow thinking there's something wrong with them, when there's nobody older than them saying, "Hey kid, here's the reality of the situation. Here's the ropes. Sorry, we didn't make the rules, but at least you know it's not your fault. There's nothing wrong with you."

I also fully intend to put a stop to clueless mothers telling their younger sons, "Well YOU must be looking in the wrong places. There must be something wrong with YOU that you are attracting these types of girls."

And replace it with the concept that maybe all there is to select in the population is Britney Spears and a limitless sea of sociology majors.

Regardless, as in tune with the original theme of this post, permit me my young, aspiring male (and female, because some of these rules would apply to you too) junior, deputy and aspiring economists a couple rules or tidbits of wisdom that will help make your younger years easier to deal with and perhaps save you a couple bucks and hours along the way;

1. Life is short, you're going to die, quit trying to pick up chicks at bars. Bars/nightclubs are where stupid people go because they have no conversation skills and need to rely on their looks to get them buy. Girls in particular just go there to get free drinks (I did a survey on this on my economics students and that was the number one reason girls go to bars, not for you, for your propensity to buy them drinks). Instead pick up a hobby or activity that YOU want to do. You will find similarly minded girls and without the loud bass BOOM BOOM BOOM, chances are she'll be smart enough to converse with you.

2. Learn to ballroom/swing/salsa dance. You don't have time to rely on one liners or meeting Suzie Jones in class or to have your friends get off their lazy asses and set you up. Dancing is a great and polite means by which to meet a girl. For every hour you spend learning dance you will save yourself literally 10 hours at a bar with the same amount of success. And NO, it doesn't matter if you "like" to dance, it's your job to do it.

3. At the first sign of trouble, ditch the girl. You look out for number one, YOU. You, especially if you are going to school and working, don't have time for it. If a girl acts weird, or perhaps a better way of putting it is her behavior is "hypocritical" bail. Immediately. You don't have time for games. I'm sure curiosity gets you, like "Why is she acting weird" but it has been my experience you will never find out "why" and the question will be evaded (also, the "why" tends to be another guy, so don't compete, again you don't have the time, you have you to work on).

4. Akin to three, one strike and you're out. I had a buddy Tony, who said something very wise. When he was stood up or a girl didn't call him back his mother would come up with theories as to why. "Well, maybe she got hit by a truck. Maybe the electricity went out in her neighborhood. Maybe

she tripped and hit her head and forgot she had a date." But inevitably, Tony said, it all boiled down to that the girl just plain didn't want to go out with you. Think about it, if you had an interview for a job you really wanted, or you really wanted to go on a date with a girl, if you couldn't make it, you would call. If she really wanted to go out with you, she would call. She didn't so quit wasting your time. Which leads us to...

5. Ball in Court Theory - Consider calling or e-mailing or "texting" (what you young punk kids do nowadays) a basketball or a ping pong ball. If you throw or hit the ball to the opponent the ball is in their court. You can't hit it back until they hit it back to you. Don't be an idiot and call/e-mail them if you already did so once. That's it. If they don't call you back, don't call them back. You'll look like an idiot just like you would swinging at a ping pong ball that isn't there.

6. Date Math Girls - Math girls not only tend to be more employable, but I've never had a engineering major/engineer stand me up. Not once. Women that are in the sciences are always on time and are least likely to lie about their availability (a major reason why the majority of girls I dated in college were Asian, they were all in engineering, computer science, physics, etc.). Business majors, HA! Those are your future power hungry HR directors. Give me a geek girl any day.

7. Ask your self "What is my opportunity cost?" - I look back at it and my best times in college and my twenties were NOT with girls. They were with my friends (be they guys or girls). Rock climbing, video games, drinking, you name it. They are always there, they are always willing to hang out and you are GUARANTEED to have a good time. Consider your expected rate of return on a Friday night; Go clubbing where you have a 2% chance of getting a girl's number and a 10% chance of it being a right one and a 10% chance of her actually going out with you (.0002 chance of you going on the date) or play some video games while drinking beer with your friends 100% chance.

8. Do not chase, they will chase you. If there is an important rule, this is it. Life is too short chasing after people. You have to do your own thing that you enjoy and live life and meet the people along the way. The frat boy at the bar with his cap on backwards with the Ambercrombie and Fitch. Yeah, not getting as much play as the guy playing ultimate frisbee with his

friends who heads up a tornado chasing expedition and knows how to dance. And the reason why is the A&B boy is a conformist. Girls can get those a dime a dozen. If you're out doing your own thing, girls will be attracted to that. Better yet, girls that like the stuff you do will be attracted to that so you don't have to endure listening to her speculate on "American Idol" or "Obama's pecks" but rather she will be like, "Hell yes, let's go to Glacier National and get freaking on a glacier!" Oh, she's not going to show up on your doorstep that instant, but it won't matter. YOu'll be happy doing what you want to do. And for god's sake, playing an acoustic guitar is NOT a hobby.

9. Religious girls. If you're religious. Good for you. If you're not, stay away from them. And I'm not talking the girls that say, "Well I'm Catholic" but haven't been to church in 3 years, I mean girls that go to Christian colleges and won't court any non-Christian guys. God comes first, dad comes second, and somewhere around 573rd place next to "clean toe fungus" is "find and date cool guy." Ranked 1,435,984th is "kiss cool guy." Save yourself the time, it isn't worth it.

10. Go to school until you're 27. There is no point in looking for a partner to set up a family until you're AT LEAST 27, so you might as well get your masters or doctorate. Girls (as well as boys) will not mature until that time. You want to get married before that, enjoy divorce. I would make it 35, but by that time everybody has a kid so start looking, there is the occasional girl that has her act together before that time, but like I said, you have more important things to do like college, besides which, she'll make herself known.

11. Do not tolerate any drama or soap opera stuff. It's weird, but I almost sense a lot of girls, especially when they're younger get more of a kick off of drama than anything approaching a normally functioning relationship. They lay what are called "land mines" which are nothing but traps to give them an excuse to get mad at you (see you didn't buy me a soda). You think they're not common, oh but they are.

12. Sex is not negotiable. I can understand if you are religious and wish to adhere to your principles and I do genuinely salute you. For the remainder of us men, sex is not negotiable. The girl either has sex or not. And if she doesn't that's fine, nothing wrong with it, but don't think you're going to

somehow "convince" her. All you're going to do is waste your time. If you want sex, find a girl that is willing to have sex. And if you can't find one, guess what? You have more important stuff to do any way (see hobbies and college).

13. Never tolerate being stood up. And there really isn't anything you can do about this one in the sense that if you're stood up, you have no choice but to be stood up. But you can protect against it. Always have plans with the guys. Always have something else to do. There was a rule I came up with called the 505025 rule, the founding of which was based on the empirical experience I had where 50% of the time the girl would say yes to a date, but only 50% of the time she would actually show up for the date, resulting in a 25% real chance of a date. In actuality it was more like 70/10/7, but the point is even if the girl says yes, chances are you're not going out, especially in your late teens and early 20's. ASSUME you're not, make other plans and if the girl actually pulls through, consider it a bonus.

14. Buy the **damn book!** You youth cannot afford to be jerking around with worthless degrees. Focus your efforts and resources WISELY and early on, on productive pursuits.

Now there is infinitely more precise bullet points i could give you, but the overall point is to have not only self-respect, but to draw the lines and standards by which who you are or are not going to date. Self-respect because young men waste so much time trying to date girls who frankly are not worth it (and this time could be spent bettering oneself) and also to establish rules and lines so as not to be taken advantage of. The key thing is to not worry if you are having troubles or are immeasurably frustrated by the insanity going on. All guys are. But if you focus on yourself and enjoy YOUR life you can not only endure the 20's and early 30's, but improve yourself immeasurably, and maybe even find that nice girl who has a job and (as Girl X liked to disdain) "has the audacity to treat you nice."

Sacrilege!

Parks for Kids

Let me tell you about "Super Sucker."

Super Sucker was a game me and my siblings came up with that we'd play in the basement of the house during winter. The game entailed grabbing toilet plungers and one of them 50 cent el cheapo balls you can pick up at the grocery store. My brother and sister and I would then don capes made from whatever cloth material we could find and the goal would be kind of a tag like game where we'd whack the ball with the toilet plungers at each other. It was a great game because you could hit that ball as hard as possible at your siblings, beaning them right in the head. We'd run around with our capes flying with no particular rules or structure to the game aside from hitting that ball with the plunger as hard as possible. And when not in possession of the ball, we'd taunt our sibling who had the ball by plunging the plunger on the cement floor of the basement - "PA-THWOP PA-THWOP PA-THWOP." Occasionally we'd hit a line drive right at the drier which would make a loud reverberating "BAUWAWAWAMMMMM" sound, reliably followed by our step dad yelling from upstairs to keep it quiet. That basement, despite it being January, got so hot we were dripping sweat.

Another game we'd play was "Hit." Jayme our neighbor would come over and ask me and my brother if we'd want to play "Hit." All Hit was, was a simplified version of baseball as there was not always enough kids to play baseball in the neighborhood. There would be the hitter and two fielders as the hitter would self-pitch the ball to himself and crank it out as far as it could go. We then upgraded to "Super Hit" where we replaced the baseball with a golf ball and summarily pissed off the neighbors as golf balls have a tendency to fly a little farther and hit cars more frequently than baseballs off an aluminum bat.

A friend of mine played "Hogan's Heroes," a game where his dad would come out, armed only with a flash light and the kids would then have to somehow sneak past him, crossing from the neighbor's yard to the east to the neighbor's yard to the west. If the dad spotted them with the flashlight "Colonel Klink" caught them and would have to be sent back to Stalag 13...only to try to escape again!

The common trait in all these games is that all of them required very little, if not, nothing in terms of capital investment. Super sucker required 3 toilet plungers (our step dad, upon finding out we were using the REAL toilet plunger said, *"Oh, for Christ's sake, you're playing with used one!!!????"* which capitulated him to buy 3 brand spanking new plungers, oh they were shinny), "Hit" required a bat, a ball and some gloves, and "Hogan's Heroes" required a flashlight. And though, there was not a lot of capital investment in these games, these games were the funnest and most memorable games of our childhoods.

No doubt we all had these games. Some a bit more conventional than others. Sure, "Kick the Can" was a popular one or "Bloody Murderer" was another, neither quite as fun as "Super Sucker," but regardless, all these games were the best freaking games on the face of the planet and all you really required was other people and a mere nano-ounce (pun duly noted) of creativity.

Which brings me to my point today; "Parks for Kids"

Well, it's not really "Parks for Kids" because I can't remember the precise title they gave themselves, but I heard a public service announcement on the now dying AM 1500 that there's this political group or campaign "trying to fight the obesity epidemic" and they want you to donate money or vote for more funding for parks for kids.

And the reason I bring this up is because this is a huge testament to just how pathetic we've become as a society that we now have to have government financed parks to help facilitate "fun" for kids.

It also starkly reminds me of just how quickly people forget what it was like to be a kid. I don't know about you, but truthfully, I never stopped being Calvin from Calvin and Hobbes. I still like to go sledding. I still would SO play a game of Super Sucker. I like watching my Saturday morning cartoons. And I still demand to play video games. About the only REAL difference between my life as a child and my life now is that I smoke and drink and chase after skirts. Alas it seems this fun has to be ordained or organized by government and MUST take place in a "park."

In any case, the larger point is the hypocrisy or inanity in demanding we "pay" for more "parks" to help fight the obesity epidemic.

For one, if you looked at where kids expend the most calories of energy it isn't at the park. It's in their neighborhood where they run and jump and play games like "Hogan's Heroes" or "Hit."

Two, "parks" are SOOOO typical of public schools where the government tries to convince kids with lame and ineffectual campaigns that no kid really believes;

"Hey Kids, it's "cool" to play on the play ground and in the park. Pete the Park Puma says "roar! playing in parks is fun!"

Smoking it's the same thing;

"Hey kids, Phillip the Frog says 'Don't smoke. Ribbit. Smoking is dumb!"

Alas, just like every other government campaign, it isn't working. I see TONS of parks, TONS of baseball diamonds, tons of beautiful volleyball sand courts, all empty, all abandoned. And the only reason I don't avail myself of those empty baseball diamonds is because I can't get enough of my lame ass adult friends to play kickball with me.

But, three, is this outright lie there isn't enough parks. Come on, I see parks all over the place. What kid doesn't have a park within walking distance (and by walking distance I mean that in 1983 terms meaning 5 miles), besides which WHAT KID PLAYS IN A PARK?

And this gets to the heart of the hypocrisy.

NO KID PLAYS IN A PARK.

Kids play with other kids and will make their environment, no matter what it is, the park. They will create and concoct various and unlimited games in whatever environment they have. And when the government or some nerdy, hypocritical non-profit organization, headed up by adults who forgot what it was like to be a kid, give them these sterile, fake, fabricated areas called "parks" no kid is going to use them.

Alas, this drive to "create more parks" is really one of two things;

1. A crusade to give worthless adults something to do with their worthless lives to make them feel like they're making a difference even though they're not.

2. Another excuse to extract money from the productive members of society to the non-productive. Lord know where the "donations" go. To help some middle aged woman repay her student loans for her psychology degree? To some guy who, despite being 48 still wears a pony tail and sits on the "parks and recreation board" because he couldn't land a real job and still lives off his parents' inheritance? Whatever the case, the children (as is typically the case...ahem...cough cough...TEACHERS UNION) are never considered.

In the meantime kids, do what Uncle Cappy Cap says and go buy yourselves some toilet plungers or have dad go buy himself a flashlight.

Best of Cappy Cap - A Tutorial on Obamanomics

Figured this would be a good repeat from over 2 years ago;

As the market ebbs and flows 400 points here, 500 points there, I am often asked by friends:

"When is the market going to bottom?"

And I find it interesting that people are even buying right now, because as far as I'm concerned there's absolutely no reason to buy stocks until after the presidential election. When I tell my friends this, they say,

"Well why wait till then? Couldn't stock prices have gone up by then and you missed out of a great buying opportunity?"

Which indicates to me we all need a basic lesson in "Barack Economics."

You see, there are two things that drive the price of a stock; the profits the corporation makes and the capital gain one receives when they sell the stock.

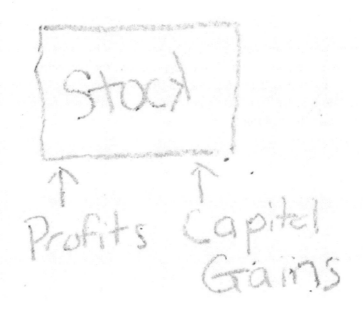

First, let's start with profits. Profits are nothing more than what a company or corporation has left over when it pays for all of its expenses. Profits typically make people happy because that's how we not only enrich ourselves, but, frankly, live.

But hold on there now! You don't get to keep all of those profits. No no no. You see, since you own part of a corporation, the corporation has to pay on average a 40% tax rate in the US (though the effective rate for some is around 32%). This is taken out of your profits (pre-tax profits) before sending them along to you.

Sales
- Expenses
= "Pre-tax" Profits
- 40% corp tax

= Profits to shareholder

But with Obamanomuks this tax rate will go up. Nobody knows for sure how much, but 50%, 70%, maybe even 90%. Regardless, when it's all said and done, there won't be a lot of your profits left;

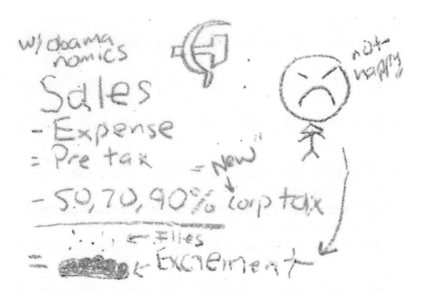

What profits do remain, however, can be passed along to you in the form of dividends.

But, UH OH!!! That was a transaction, and even though you own part of the corporation, since it is a separate legal entity, you get to pay taxes on the DIVIDENDS, typically between 5-15%. This is called "double taxation." It may not make you happy, but it makes lots of government freeloaders happy.

Post tax profit
– Dividend TAX
(5–15%)
= What U really get

I know you may be upset that you get to pay taxes twice, but with the cutting edge of Barackian Economics, you will get to pay an even higher dividend tax! Don't worry, according to Joe Biden it's patriotic to pay more in taxes leaving you with even less.

w Barakonomuxs
Post tax profit
– "New" Dividend Tax
of 72%

Well how does this affect the stock market and stock prices? Well, it's very simple. Although if you go to any major corporation's web site and they make it seem like pursuing green policies is what gives them value, in reality they're just doing that so you are foolish enough to buy their products without guilt. No, the truth is what really gives stocks value is the underlying profits those firm generate. You see, if a firm doesn't make a profit, why would anybody forfeit their money to invest in it? I don't invest in stocks so they can sell green products or be socially responsible. I invest in a corporation so it makes money. And the less money I see after all the expenses and taxes are taken out, the less value that firm has to me and thus the lower the stock price.

But profits are not the only thing that drive the value of the stock (well, technically they are, but we won't go into that right now). There is also a "capital gains" ie-how much money you make when you sell the stock. Say you buy a stock for $10, and it goes up to $100. Why, that's an impressive profit of $90, and you are happy!

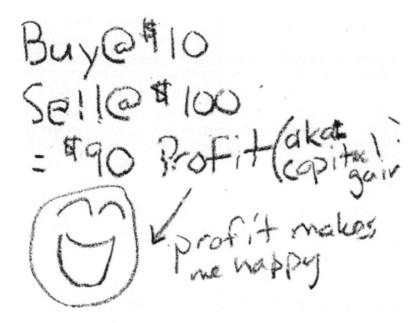

But hold on there little buckaroo! Uncle Sam wants some of that and you get to pay a capital gains "tax" on it. This tax can be anywhere from 0-35%.

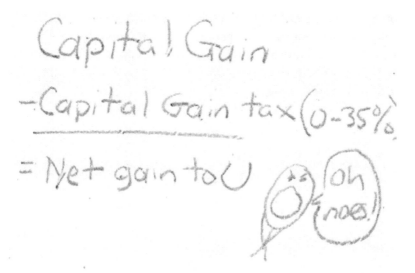

But with Obamanomuks this rate will go up even more, leaving you with even less.

w/O bamonomuks %
Capital Gain
-"New" Capital Gain tax (80%)
= Excrement

The relationship between the amount you get to keep and the value of the stock is the same. If you get to keep more, then the value of the stock is worth more and therefore prices go up. But if capital gains are increased, then the value of those stocks go down.

↓ Profit from ⟷ ↓ Value Cap. Gain? of Stock ↘ ↗ Lower Stock Price

"But isn't it the rich that only own stock? And shouldn't we hate the rich by the fact they're rich, even though they may have actually worked for it and have never done anything to us?"

Although a common misconception, it's not just the rich that own stock in the US. Most everybody in the US, rich, poor, short or tall, own stock in one way or another. Most commonly this is done through our 401k, 403b and other retirement programs. We buy mutual funds which are nothing more than groups of stock which we hold in these retirement accounts. Also, pensions pay for your retirement by investing in stocks and mutual funds. So if you have a pension or you have a retirement program, YOU OWN STOCK!

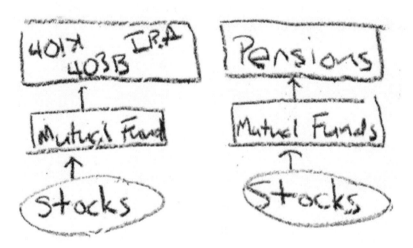

Ergo, it is profits that drive the value of stocks which in turn determines the wealth of the people of the entire nation.

But with Obamanomuks there will be no profit, and therefore no stocks, and therefore no retirement.

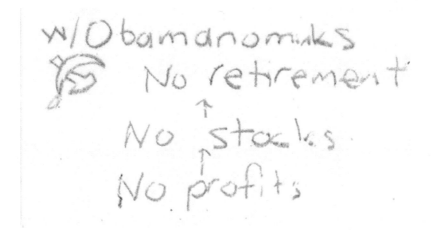

All you'll be left with is;

And that's why the Captain is waiting to see if Barack Obama and the democrats take a supermajority in Washington before he invests his money in the stock market.

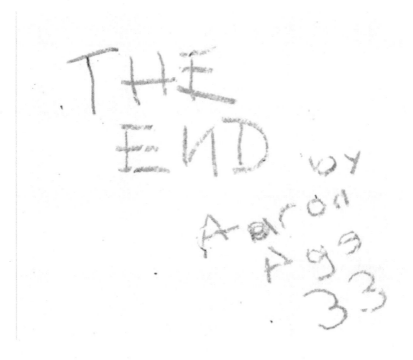

Why I Had a Vasectomy

It angers me or at least annoys me when, presumably I am a free man and am allowed to live my life as I choose, I get lectured or this visceral, almost instinctive response from people when I tell them I had a vasectomy.

"WHAT!? Are you crazy? Why would you do that!"

"Well what's wrong with you? Why don't you want kids?

Some go so far as to even call it "selfish" that I don't want to endure the 18 year pain and agony that is known as a child.

But despite the obvious benefits to never having children, these benefits do not seem so obvious to the masses. And therefore as a benefit to the masses (not to mention to get these pro-children zealots off my ass) I have decided to explain, in detail why I decided not to have children so you may see there is actual rhyme and reason to such a decision and that you may really want to seriously think about it yourself.

First off there is the cost of a child. Forget it. Depending on the figures you use, a kid can run anywhere from $200,000 on the cheap to $500,000 on the average. I made a post once about the ROI of a vasectomy and basically you don't have to worry about paying for your retirement if you don't have kids. Amortized over 18 years (22 if you pay for college) you get an annualized rate of return (or technically savings) of around 47%. But forget investing it in the stock market, just think about the opportunity costs of that $500,000. A house, a boat, a car. All bought and paid for if you just refuse to have children. And if you think about that house, boat and car, isn't that why you're already an indentured slave anyway? What if you already had your house paid off by the age of 40? Retirement wouldn't be such a worry now would it? So I don't want to hear about people saying, "it's only money and you can't hug money." No, but I sure can hug a boat or a Pontiac Solstice.

Second is the issue of time. Time is empirically and economically the same thing as money, but that assumes you can choose to work. You don't have a choice when it comes to children. You have to allocate time to them. So when you are done working for 10 hours with a 2 hour commute, guess what, that kid is still going to need attention. You essentially have not only committed your personal financial resources, you've really and literally have committed yourself to becoming a slave for 18 years. And guess what? Every time you have another one, the sentence is renewed. Sorry, I get one shot at this life and it isn't going to be baby sitting a child, or multiple children. It's going to be doing what I want to do. And no that isn't being "selfish."

The reason it isn't being selfish is (third) the fact I know I would be a bad father. In knowing I don't want to have children, I spare any would be children from what would be guaranteed to be a horrible upbringing. THIS IS INFINITELY MORE COMPASSIONATE THAN SOMEBODY WHO HAS A CHILD, FINDS THE CHILD INCONVENIENT AND THEN SENDS IT TO DAY CARE OR HIRES A NANNY TO TAKE CARE OF IT. This is INFINITELY MORE COMPASSIONATE THAN THE THOUSANDS OF PEOPLE TODAY WHO HAVE CHILDREN BECAUSE THEY "WANT A CHILD" JUST LIKE THEY "WANT AN SUV" OR A "EUROPEAN TRIP." AND THIS IS CERTAINLY INFINITELY MORE COMPASSIONATE AND CARRYING THAN HAVING A CHILD TO COLLECT ANOTHER WELFARE CHECK ALA OCTOMOM. Call me selfish all you want, I at least care enough about children to know that unless I would be home with them or my wife would, then I shouldn't even bring them into this world.

Fourth, along the same lines of caring enough about a child to not have one is the issue of slavery. Oh sure slavery is illegal, but I'm sorry, have you seen the entitlement spending commitments this country has burdened future generations with? That $1.4 trillion deficit the government ran? Yeah, that's just a mere fraction of the estimated $10 trillion in new debt future generations will be saddled with by the "compassionate and caring" socialists in the government. And social security and medicare? You see the commitments on those programs? What worsens it is that I adamantly refuse to have my child grow up to become anything but a productive member of society, which only guarantees he'll be a battery or host for future parasites whose parents were not so adamant about instilling an honorable work ethic, if not brainwashed them that the "man" was out to get them and they were disadvantaged and poor and were entitled to sit on their asses and achieve nothing while, essentially making my child a slave for them.

Forget it. Again, my unborn child does not deserve that and will never have to face that.

Fifth, I see this more and more in Minnesota. The legal risks of having children. You can't spank them, you can't discipline them no matter how much of a beating they need. No they need "time outs." They need "stern words." I can see it now. I will be prohibited from effectively disciplining my child which will result in a mini-Kim Jong Ill dictator who, with the help of the public schools brainwashing him, will turn me in for false charges of child abuse or (give it 10 years) failing to recycle. I'll be as effective as the UN.

Finally, and this is what I don't get, is the lifestyle. What is so damn wrong with wanting to have a lifestyle of no children? Look, 6 billion people on the planet and 50 billion before them have done what we've always done and that is;

have children.

Well yipdeefreakingding.

Having children is NOT a new experience. It's NOT unique. And if people would stop and think about it for one genuine second and ask "Hey, I only get one shot at this life. What do I want to achieve?" I think more and more people would start to realize they are finite and get only one shot at this life and would start to agree more and more with me. I'm about to take a month long vacation. I get to sleep in till 10 AM everyday. I get to keep my house in whatever order I want. I get to go fossil hunting and shan't leave this planet until I go dustdevil chasing in Australia. I get to salsa dance every night. I get to do whatever I want, whenever I want and even at this early age have already achieved and lived more than most people twice my age.

And the reason why is that children, no matter how lovely or loved, still handicap your ability to go and live this life as contrasted if you were without them.

Now I know people do have children and do genuinely love them and do genuinely appreciate them and would have it no other way. But for god's sake, can society at least accept or acknowledge there are damn good reasons NOT to have children? Can society at least respect another individual's wish not to have a child? And for the love of all that is chocolates and ice cream can you people with "baby-rabies" that find it your place to lecture others about not having children back off? Besides which, we all know why you insist everybody have children just like you.

Misery loves company.

Why You Can't Argue With a Liberal

Let me explain something that you must understand, for I see it frustrating my conservative, libertarians and capitalist friends;

It is pointless to argue with liberals and leftists.

I don't mean this in a broad-insulting-stroke-of-the-brush sort of way. I mean that in a sincere, realistic way.

It is pointless to argue with liberals and leftists.

And here is the reason why;

When you argue with them, you are not arguing facts or statistics, you are arguing against a religion. Understand that conservatism, capitalism, and liberty are all founded in empirical evidence that has proven, time and time again, that when a people are free and you do not tax them to death, they will thrive and succeed. Limitless examples throughout history show this, not to mention terrabytes of economic data will support this as well.

Capitalism is the BEST economic system, hands down, period, if for any other reason it is the only system based in reality.

However, leftists ideology, whatever the strain, is not based in reality. It is based in a belief. Specifically, a belief that they WANT to believe in. There is no empirical evidence. There is no rational thought or intellectual honesty or rigor involved. It is simply something for the masses to opiate themselves on and feel good about it. ie- it socialism, leftism, liberalism IS

A RELIGION.

Now two points that must be made of this;

1. You can't argue with fundamentalists, not matter what their stripe. Religious right christians that insist sex is bad and gays are evil. Radical muslims that want to blow you up because, well, you're not a radical muslim. Extreme fringes of Jews who won't fly on planes on Fridays (or whatever day it is, I'm not terribly familiar with the Jewish religion). Regardless, trying to convince a leftist that lower taxes and a small government is best for society is like trying to convince a christian that dinosaurs did indeed exist MILLIONS of years ago and that carbon dating is a correct technique. It goes against their religion.

Yes, they have no basis. Yes, they ignore the empirical evidence. But that is the whole point of a religion. You ignore reality because you CHOOSE to believe in what you WANT to believe in.

2. The hypocrisy of it all. I want to know the number of global warming zealots that mock christians and religious people in general. No seriously, think about that. How many leftists who believe in this global warming RELIGION in the same breath then slam on religious people. The brush could be plied to leftists in general. How many socialists scoff or mock people for believing in something that has no empirical evidence to support it yet at the same time swallow the socialist religion whole?

Thus, my friends, there is only one thing to do. And that is let reality do your arguing for you. You can't win, because they won't believe you. It is more important to them to adhere and subscribe to their religion of socialism than it is to adhere to anything as noble and honorable as the truth. Therefore you're just wasting your breath.

But just like the radical muslim who might have second thoughts about blowing himself up, or the 75 year old christian, spinster virgin who passed up on plenty of honorable men to be alone with her cats and her bible reality will inevitably dawn on them. They will look at their single, infinitesimally finite life they were given and realized they ruined it. They pissed the only thing they had away. Think about it for a second. Don't you think the burnt out hippie who is now approaching 65 years old who still wears the pony tail and can point at nothing but, "sticking it to the man" back in '68 as his largest single achievement? How about the millions of aged Russian communists who were all for the Bolshevikian revolution? Boy, wasn't the past 90 years of their lives fun and fruitful? What will the modern legions of socialists, leftists and communists achieve in their lives? You do realize that the majority of young people voted to have Obama make them indentured slaves (ergo why "young" is latin for "stupid as all hell.")? How successful do you think these socialist zealots are going to be in their lives pursuing a "dream" that is really a nightmare?

But you see, that's the only thing that will convince them otherwise. It's not going to be you. It's not going to be the charming Captain with all of his charts and graphs. It's not even going to be people who have lived and suffered under communism.

No, what will inevitably prove you right will be the leftists getting what they want and realizing they've pissed their lives away.

And that is the best revenge one can have.

Deondra

This one is for a poor kid I just met, Ferdinand.

I entered college at the age of 18 weighing 147 pounds.

By the time I was 19 years of age I had dropped down to 118.

And the reason for this precipitous loss in weight was two-fold.

One, I was dirt poor with no financial support from my parents, nor the government, and thusly could not afford any kind of fast food, let alone groceries, and therefore LOST the freshman 15 instead of gained it.

Two, I worked as campus security where, among other things, our job was to patrol the campus on foot or on bike where the AVERAGE night you would put 50 miles on your bike or 10 miles on foot.

Now I'm leaving A LOT of stuff out, but in short this period of time was hands down, without compare, the worst days in my life. I worked full time, went to school full time and frankly barely attended any parties, let alone had much of a social life outside of work, because the financial and academic rigors of college demanded it. Ergo, why I have no pity whatsoever when I hear spoiled brats complain about the costs of college while daddy financed them a brand new car or takes care of their credit card bills and practically all other living expenses, EXCEPT tuition.

Regardless, though all of college could generally be described as a 3.5 year abyss, the pits of the pits, the darkest depths of the abyss was my first Christmas break.

I didn't know if I was going to make it or not. I was just one trimester (the U had "trimesters" back then) into college then and all I had known was sleep depravation and poverty. But add to this hellish existence two more complications and it became unbearable;

1. Loneliness. I couldn't afford to go back home for Christmas break, and home was only 1.5 hours away. I had to sign up for as many shifts and OT as I could, or I otherwise would not have been able to afford the next trimester of tuition. And while I was happy to have the work, instead of a full force of security, they scaled back operations to "the Dirty Dozen" the 12 or 13 or so security guards that would pick up the rest of the shifts while the rest of the guards went home for Christmas break. And sure you'd see each other occasionally checking in or out of HQ, but you'd patrol by yourself for 12 hours, over a veritable lifeless arctic tundra, go to a deserted dorm, and do it all over again, day in, day out for the next month.

2. Cold. Minnesota is cold. And though nothing personal or emotional, it wears on you psychologically, especially if you're patrolling out in subzero temperatures on hour 22 of a 32 hour shift over the Washington Avenue bridge on Christmas eve (and no, I am not making this up). It doesn't get warm. It's always cold. But the campus needed parking lot and bridge patrols and so you would do push ups to stay warm, pad your boots with paper towels from the bathrooms to stave off the frost bite and come up with stupid poems to stave off the insanity.

However, there was one bit of hope. There was one shimmer of light I had in this otherwise dreary, bitterly cold nightmarish existence;

Deondra.

Deondra was a freshman just like me. And though I had no time for social activities or the pursuit of cute girls, Deondra was that one weird girl that pursued me. Not aggressively, but as I was just sitting there in the cafeteria she just came up and asked if she could sit there. Kind of shocked I said "sure" and thus begat a friendly conversation which led to a couple dates.

It was already late into fall and my work schedule was such that not much of a heated romance could form, but by the time winter break rolled around and the campus emptied itself, there was really nothing or nobody else for socializing. Sure I had friends at work, but we were nothing but sleep-deprived, hypothermic zombies that would greet each other in between work and sleep shifts. But there was that one nice, kind girl. The one who was kind enough to go out on a couple dates and even drive me to the grocery store so I could get groceries.

Well it was the middle of December, the campus was deserted, and I received a call from Deondra. She was wondering how I was doing and what I had going on for Christmas. I said,

"Well I have to work Christmas Eve into Christmas Day, then wake up again around 8PM so I can start my shift at 9PM."

She said, "Aren't you going home?"

I said, "No, I can't, I have to work. Besides, I don't have a car, so I couldn't go even if I wanted to."

Feeling pity for me she said, "Well, why don't you come over to my folks house for Christmas dinner in Apple Valley?"

The smile on my face was like seeing a beautiful nurse in a WWII battlefield hospital. I was already physically and psychologically depleted and the company on Christmas day, not to mention a home made, warm meal was the best Christmas gift one could ask for.

I said "Sure, that would be great."

And she said, "Well I'll pick you up at 5PM and then drop you back off at the police department at 9PM just in time for work."

I said, "Thanks, I really appreciate it."

My Christmas Eve shift was somehow not as cold as the previous ones (even though if I recall correctly that night it had dropped to -10 degrees). The patrols were not as dreary and the entire night I got to look forward to and dream about the food and this really sweet nice girl that was going to have me over for dinner. Matter of fact, this is the type of girl you would probably want to hold onto and get serious with. Beautiful, educated, and kind. I let those thoughts carry me through until you could see the sun start to lighten up the eastern sky as 7AM approached and most families in the nation started opening their Christmas gifts (unless of course you're one of those cheating Catholics that can't wait until the 25th and open theirs on the 24th!)

I trudged back to my deserted dorm, too tired to take a shower, crawled into my bed in full uniform, set the alarm for 430PM and fell asleep immediately, though no doubt with a smile on my face.

The alarm on my Ironman digital watch woke me up. I got up like most kids did 10 hours previously, giddy and excited. Hopped in the shower, put on a nice shirt and some slacks, packed my uniform and my winter gear, until I realized I hadn't gotten Deondra any kind of gift. I looked around frantically as well as equally hopelessly because what possible gift would an impoverished college freshman have in his dorm that would make for any kind of Christmas gift? I figured the best I could do was write a funny, light hearted poem thanking her for her kindness, but with the 10 minutes I had to go before she picked me up, the poem was nothing to be proud off. Regardless, I took it, still debating whether I would even give it to her or not and rushed downstairs.

There I sat in the lobby, nobody there except the desk clerk working on some papers. Deadly silent as the snow was falling as I looked out the window, sitting there with my backpack and a folded up piece of paper with the poem on it. It was getting dark, still a little bit of light left, I looked at my watch and it was 5PM.

I set my watch fast just for instances like these to make sure I was on time. Still had a couple minutes to go, so I figured she would pull up momentarily and let my thoughts drift about what kind of food would be at her house.

Turkey? Chicken? Steak? Some potatoes. Ooo! I could get a doggy bag and be able to eat a good meal on my overnight shift. I could totally gorge myself and get that first home made meal in 3 months.

I looked at my watch. 5:03.

Hmmm... Must have run into traffic. Snow probably slowing down traffic.

5:10.

Wow, traffic must really be bad...even for Christmas day...I hope she's alright.

5:15

I decided to go call her house (because we didn't have cell phones back then) to see if she was on her way. Went to the desk to use their phone. It rang and rang and rang and I got her voicemail.

"Hey Deondra, it's me, just wondering if you're on your way or not."

5:25

Decided to try calling again. Still no answer, just her voicemail.

And at 1730 hours on December 25th, 1993 your rookie, idealistic, naïve Captain had a pivotal epiphany that would set him down the path that in part made him he is the man he is today.

"I don't think she's coming."

It's kind of like Afro Samurai, if you've ever seen it. Samuel Jackson does the voice for an imaginary sidekick Afro Samurai has and more or less acts as his id-subconscious. And the entire movie this hallucination talks to Afro, giving him advice, if not, more so picking on him.

It was the same thing. Not that I was hallucinating and there was some alterego version of me, but in my head I started having a conversation with myself.

"Why wouldn't she show up?

What did I do wrong?

How could somebody do something like this?"

And other stupid questions naïve, 18 year old American boys will ask themselves on the precipice of the hell they have no idea that they're about to enter called "conventional American dating."

Now needless to say that Christmas night was certainly one of the darkest, badest ones in my life (and I've had plenty). I have rarely had such anger and hatred. I don't even remember the night being cold or dreary or painful. I don't even remember getting tired. But I do remember coming to a very important conclusion that most men do not have the benefit of realizing until they're much older.

"I don't have time for this shit."

Now, this is long ago in the past, but that does not mean the lesson should not be passed on or that we should not learn something from it. And as I see men younger than me, confused and dazed as to what they did wrong, and girls wondering why men seem to become aloof and indifferent to marriage or engaging in things such as a "marriage strike" allow me to help those of you younger aspiring, junior, deputy and otherwise economists out there by making some lessons crystal clear;

Boys/Men – When you are younger, say 14 to 25 or so, you have to realize you are not dating adults. You are dating children. I don't know why, but my experience has told me sometimes girls at this age prefer to play games more than do anything approaching engaging in a real dating or courting relationship. In a sick and twisted way, they prefer to string you along and play games and find it fun. I don't even think they realize that you are a human being too, and it takes on more of a roll where it's like a cat toying with a wounded mouse. I don't know why. I don't have empirical proof of it. It's only been my anecdotal experiences that have led me to this conclusion.

Regardless, the whole point is that IT IS UNACCEPTABLE TO BE STOOD UP FOR A DATE PERIOD. There is nothing wrong with you if you get stood up, but rather there is something wrong with them. And if there's one thing I wish I could convey to the younger men out there it's that it's NOT YOUR FAULT. You cannot take it out on you as did I and millions of other men have. And while it is hard to be indifferent or aloof to a girl standing you up, you must view it in terms of "Is a girl who stands men up for s's and g's the type of girl I want to date?" You will come to the same conclusion I did;

"I don't have time for this shit."

Conversely, it is just as evil and bad to stand girls up. Don't do it. Think about what you've been put through and then think about how you felt and know you've caused the same pain in a girl, who is probably equally innocent.

Girls/Women – DO NOT STAND UP A GUY EVER. You want to be the 40 year old with no husband, but a nice collection of cats and a lonely hate-filled life? Well sweetheart, you're well on your way. Men are not bobbles to toy around with and re-enact your favorite episodes of Dawson's Creek or 90210 on. Many women ask "where are all the good guys?" Well, ask yourself the question how many you stood up, how many you played games with, or how many you just didn't treat respectfully and there's your answer.

Not that it will make you feel any better Ferdinand, but all the veterans have been there before.

The MBA Bubble Continues

A **friend of mine** sent this to me.

And what I get a kick out of is **not** the fact they can't find jobs or that once again your beloved Captain has done his job as an economist and predicted things accurately again. I get a kick out of how they don't know if this is "normal" to be out of a job this long. Telling me they have NOT had the basics of economics taught to them (or some slanted, indoctrinist's view of economics was foisted upon them).

Ergo, I believe it is high time for another "Economic Lesson of the Day" by the Captain.

Now, everybody who is graduating would like jobs. And I know you may have been taught jobs come from Barack Obama's Magical Farting Unicorns and we'll just borrow a trillion dollars in some Keynesian thing and then the "pump will be primed" and then there will be a multiplier effect and then boom! Jobs!

But, I'm sorry kiddies. That's not how it works.

You see, you've been misled. The way I can tell is that (1) people in the general population think the government somehow has something to do with creating jobs. they say the "government must do SOMETHING" and (2) MB-freaking-A's can't even explain why they don't have jobs.

Both of which suggest to me you're working from an erroneous premise and that is that somehow the government is where jobs come from.

I've been meaning to make a post titled "The Great Liberal Economic Oort Cloud" (GLEOC) where liberals (and others) typically believe jobs come from government. The reason for the Oort Cloud metaphor is because they don't really know HOW jobs are created by government, but just assume that's where jobs come from. In reality, it is simply people being too intellectually lazy to think the economics of job creation through. They believe the government with its trillions of dollars and businesses and laws and lawyers and all these "really smart professional people" make this nice big "economic Oort cloud" and farts out jobs. It's not their concern how jobs are really created, it's all really too complicated for them to understand. Thank god we have Barack Obama and really smart Ivy Leaguers heading up the GLEOC!

But allow me to pose another theory (which isn't really a theory, it's reality). The Symbiotic Parasite Host Relationship Model (SPHRM).

You see, if you think about it, without an economy, without a people, without businesses, there is no need for government. If you have nothing to govern, then governments would not exist. Ergo, the GLEOC model is flawed because it puts the cart before the horse. If you believe in the GLEOC, then governments existed and people arose in response.

Obviously it's the reverse. With people, with a society, with an economy comes the need for it to be governed.

Therefore it is the government that lives off of the people and the economy.

Now, this FACT makes government a parasitic organization. It NEEDS a host. If there is no economy or society, there is no way a government can form on top of it. And this is not to say that government is bad or that were are using the word "parasitic" in the pejorative. It is needed and ergo why the relationship between the government and the economy is (or at least should be) symbiotic.

Symbiosis aside, the key thing is the SPHRM is correct in that it puts the horse before the cart. Therefore if you want job creation, guess what?

Yep, I'm sorry, that means you have to grow the private sector.

See, there is no public sector if there is no private sector because the private sector is the host the public sector needs. But if you look at how public sector has been crowding out the private sector you are seeing a parasite that has gone form just 3% the size of the host to now 40% (the chart below just shows federal spending, not state).

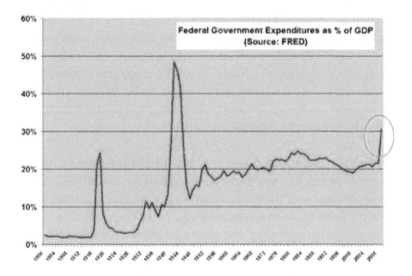

The host is frankly going into shock and dying.

Now, I know in college you were told by academians and government paid bureaucrats that you could all major in Puppies and Flowers and all get government jobs as "social workers" or "teachers" or "community organizers" or "government consultants" or become **professors like them**, but unfortunately that is following the GLEOC model. And the GLEOC model is not sustainable.

If you want jobs you have to grow the private sector. Which means doing things like;

1. ELIMINATING (not cut) ELIMINATING corporate taxes and BANNING THEM FOREVER
2. ELIMINATING (not cut) any form of capital gains or dividend taxes
3. Simplify the tax code.
4. Put limits on how large the parasite can grow as a percent of the economy
5. Scale down the size of the parasite itself so that the host may grow again

Of course (and this is where I spend most of my time now thinking and philosophizing about economics because this is really where the crux of this whole economics/political dynamic is being fought) what it funny is you've all been brainwashed from high school on to more or less hate the private sector. You hate "evil corporations." You hate "evil Corporate America." You hate "big oil." You're more than willing to vote more and more regulations to strangle the host. "Hey, let's all go green because it's cool!" "Yeaaa! Corporate Social Responsibility is the NEW MBA TREND!" You are all more or less programmed to be part of the parasite (or at least support the parasite) at the expense of the host.

And as I've been pushing the frontier of this particular philosophy out further, I've realized (sadly) you're so brainwashed no amount of reason, logic or plain ole facts and statistics are going to convince you otherwise. In other words, I've explained to you why you don't have jobs. I've explained to you how to get jobs. But you're so intellectually dishonest and weak your ego cannot sustain the fact you've been duped by previous generations. And since pride is now going to get in the way of truth, thereby condemning the host (and parasite might I add) to death, for me and my SPHRM-subscribing colleagues there's only one thing left to do;

Enjoy the Decline!

Why You Have Bad Government

This is arguably going to be the most important post of my entire blog, so please pay attention.

The below chart is confusing.

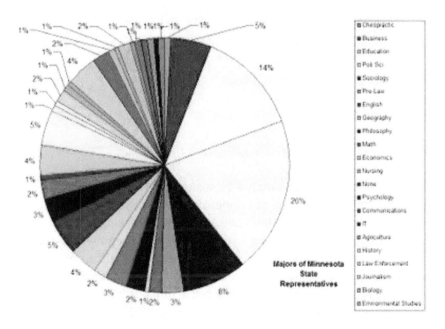

The reason it is confusing is because there are many different types of majors that it is hard to see any kind of trend or relationship. But if I simplify it into the chart below;

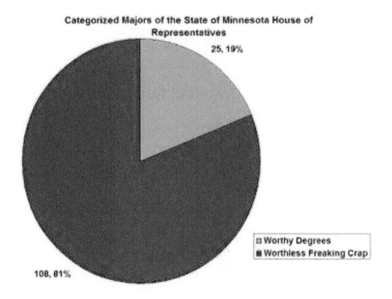

Categorized Majors of the State of Minnesota House of Representatives

25, 19%

□ Worthy Degrees
■ Worthless Freaking Crap

108, 81%

Now you start to see where I'm going with this.

The two charts above are simply a breakdown of the House of Representatives in the state of Minnesota by major. I further simplified the chart into "Worthy Degrees" and "Worthless Freaking Crap." And for the sake of informing my readers I defined "Worthy Degrees" as degrees that would actually have some kind of net positive benefit to society and "Worthless Freaking Crap" as **degrees rich spoiled kids pursue as a hobby with no real intention of ever finding a real job**, but just an excuse to go and chase tail for 4 - 6 years during your twenties. They break down thusly;

Worthy degrees;

Math
Nursing
Agriculture
Engineering
Biology
Economics
POLICE Science/Criminology

Votech
Physics
IT

Worthless degrees;

Business
Education
Poli Sci
Sociology
Pre-Law
English
Geography
Philosophy
Psychology
Communications
History
Journalism
Environmental Studies
Music/Arts
Foreign Language
General Studies
Rhetoric
Broadcasting
Home and Community Services
Metropolitan and Urban Studies
Fashion Merchandising

(*note, "business majors" were considered worthless as they were either general business, HR, or marketing, none of which are real degrees. Interestingly enough NO ACCOUNTING majors were listed...which goes a long way in explaining why the budget is always out of balance).

Now the reason I bring this up and point this out is that while it is as clear as day to me why we have incompetent government and incompetent legislatures across this nation, it seems to be the ever elusive question as to "Why can't we just have competent government? Why do we have such bad government."

So allow me to tender you a "theory" (which I already know to be law and will bet my life on it) as to why, not just here in Minnesota, we have incompetent morons in government, but why across the entire nation, as well as the entire western world we all suffer an unacceptable level of incompetent government.

UNDERSTAND that the VAST majority of people who go into government do not originally set out to do so. THey are a by-product of their own laziness and abhorrence to engage in real work or engage in any meaningful activity that will result in REAL, TANGIBLE PRODUCTION for society.

THIS MANIFESTS ITSELF when they are young and have to choose what kind of career they are going to pursue.

NOW UNDERSTAND that the past roughly 2-3 generations have benefited from the massive fruits of capitalism that have made it possible that you really don't HAVE to work if you don't want to. Your parents are rich enough to carry you through, and though you may not be a veritable trust fund baby, you can essentially major in fluff and get by if you so desire. This results in the decision, by what is essentially 18 year old children to major in a subject that is NOT in their best long term career interests, but something that is more of a luxury or hobby and suits their childish, short term desires (on a related note see **this**).

THE SINGLE MOST DETERMINING VARIABLE AS TO WHAT THESE LAZY SPOILED CHILDREN CHOOSE AS A MAJOR IS MATHEMATICS. The MORE math a major has, the LESS likely these lazy slobs are to pick it as a major. Ergo, they are not majoring in a discipline or study that actually will produce something of worth to society, they choose to major in a hobby that requires little to no math simply because math is difficult.

Now, in due time, those with real degrees and real disciplines will go out and find REAL work that will produce real goods and services society desires. Oh, sure I know, the sociology major will tell you they contribute to society by helping the poor. And the environmentalist major will tell you he's saving the planet. But the empirical evidence, known as MONEY, tells you something different. Sure, the effeminate "global studies" major will tell you he's saving the planet, but he spends all of his money on his I-

Pod, cell phone and Prius, ALL OF WHICH WAS CONCEIVED, DESIGNED and BUILT BY THE REAL MEN (also known as "engineers.") Regardless, the point is those with worthless freaking el-crapo degrees will find no obvious employment and are thus relegated to a few employment options.

Some will become euphemistically named "Barristas" at coffee shops.

Some will actually do something of economic value and flip burgers.

Others will just marry and engineer and work part time as a "social worker."

And a disproportionate amount of them will enter public education.

But there is one other venue of employment for these talentless and worthless souls and that is government.

Now understand, not everybody can run for government. The natural laws of economics will ensure that those foolish enough to major in "English" IN A COUNTRY WHERE IT'S THE NATIONAL FREAKING LANGUAGE will inevitably become unemployed (though very verbose). However, if you have rich parents or well connected parents, you now have the funds to run for public office.

Allow me to point out just a couple bits of anecdotal evidence.

Humphrey. I know Hubert H was the original Humphrey, but hey, look at Jr. Why, daddy's little boy is so damn bored, he guesses he'll just run for public office.

Mark Dayton. Awwww. The little Heir to the Dayton's empire is bored. Good thing Grand Daddy stored away $22 million for you. Go buy yourself a senate seat!

Nancy Pelosi. Daddy's little girl. And when I say "Daddy" I mean the former mayor of Baltimore (that urban utopia). Do you really think she had to pay her way through college to get that political "science" degree. Wow, for an "independent woman" she really depending on a rich dad and a rich husband. And I don't think she started in the mail room to work up that wealth.

Al Gore. Wasn't his daddy a senator?

And just to show you I'm not slamming on just democrats, this criticism EQUALLY is laid on Repulicans as well;

George W. Bush. Well Jesus, H Christ, we'll prove to the nation we're not a group of elitists! We'll nominate THE SON OF A PREVIOUS FREAKING PRESIDENT!

It is here that those who are by all accounts and standards morons can run for elected office, which practically guarantees that you will have BAD GOVERNMENT.

And the reason is simple;

1. Rich people are shielded from the everyday struggles and strife that normal, even poor people face and therefore cannot sympathize. However, even more important is

2. They NEVER HAD TO FACE REALITY. THEY HAVE NO CLUE WHAT THE REAL WORLD IS. And therefore cannot make effective decisions or policies because it is based in the utopian idealism afforded to them by the parents and not the harsh real world the remaining 95% of the population live in.

A very common criticism by talk radio show hosts such as Jason Lewis and Rush Limbaugh is that NONE OF THESE GUYS EVER HAD TO MAKE A PAYROLL. Barack Obama, for all his cuteness and nice pecks and pretty words and pet unicorns, never worked a real job in his life. His mom paid for everything. He never had to strive. He has as much in common with the poor on the south side of Chicago as Jesse Jackson does. The same applies to the Humphries, the Bushes, the Pelosi's and practically every publicly elected official out there.

THEY DON'T LIVE IN REALITY BECAUSE THEIR PARENTS MONEY SHIELDS THEM FROM IT.

Furthermore, AND THIS IS KEY SO YOU UNDERSTAND, they do not choose to go into public office for anything as "noble" as "public service."

They go into it for themselves.

They are bored.

They are otherwise unemployable.

And (you MUST UNDERSTAND THIS) they are better that you. They aren't going to dirty their fingers working manual labor.

They aren't going to work the third shift as a security guard to make ends meet.

They aren't going to change diapers in hopsice care.

Why, "they have a college degree in philosophy. Why, that work is for the underclasses. Certianly not an "educated, elightened" person like me!"

They go into public office FIRST AND FOREMOST for themselves and NOTHING as noble as public service.

In short they are politicians, they are NOT statesmen. They put themselves first and will tell you whatever you want to here to keep them in office.

This is why you have bad government. Because NONE of these politicians want to do what's good for the state or the nation. They just want to do what's going to keep them in office and away from REAL work for as long as possible. This is why you get idiots parroting things like;

"Hope and change."

and

"We'll bail you out of this mortgage crisis."

and

"Don't worry, we can print off money and everything will be alright."

Of course, the real problem isn't the politicians. You will always have scammers and scumbags who wish to live off the population without providing anything else in return. The real problem is the American population. Such a spoiled, uneducated, uninformed, ignorant bunchs of brats. 300 million people who'd rather watch "American Idol" or see some moron swing a wood stick at a sphere and then run around a diamond while their entire country and livehlihood is stolen from underneathe their noses. Veritable children who borrow more money than they could ever hope to pay back and then blame their ensuing financial woes on a presidential administration. Genuine, USDA 100% certified dumbasses who vote for candidates because they say pretty words and promise them cake, bread and circuses, while completely oblivious to the impending financial disaster of social security and medicare which will make this housing "debacle" look like a joke.

Sadly there is nothing that can be done about it, because how do you defeat ignorance on such a grand scale. The only thing that will defeat it is when the children who are now currently in government run this country into the ground so fast and so destructively that we're no longer able to feed ourselves and will have to entertain euthenasia as a viable means by which to keep the economy from truly collapsing.

In the meantime, I hope you enjoy your cute little hobby majoring in **"Rhetoric,"** **"Metro and Urban Studies,"** and **"Home and Community Service"** (all of which were REAL majors "earned" by current house of representative members). Yeah, THAT will get us out of the recession!

Best of Captain Capitalism - Jim Still Wears His Ring

My buddy John hasn't bought a new shirt in about 20 years. And the reason he hasn't bought a new shirt in 20 years is because he buys used shirts at the Disabled Vietnam Vet store.

His logic is irrefutable;

"I don't care to find a wife. I don't go out to bars or clubs. So why spend $20 on a new shirt that will just go out of style in a year when I can buy a used shirt for $1 and help out the disabled vets?"

But his logic also applies to other wares and services, especially when you don't care to go to boomchicaboom bars and just want a beer or just want a burger.

God bless the VFW and American Legion.

For if there are establishments that stand to gain from a recession, it will be the American Legion and the VFW.

I've started frequenting the VFW's and American Legion's in the area simply because of three reasons;

1. I don't "go out" anymore "trying to meet girls" and therefore have no reason to pay $9 for a martini.

2. You can not only get a martini, but a burger, fries, a soda and tip for $9 at an American Legion or VFW.

3. I'd rather give my $9 to the vets than some young preppy putz on daddy's dime who thinks they're going to make it big by setting up a bar and charging $10 for a martini in down town. Additionally the conversation and company of veterans is insanely more intellectual and less painful than trying to converse with Bambi the cosmetology major about who should be voted off Teen Idol.

And that's why I like Jim.

I met Jim at the American Legion in town. He was an older guy, WWII vet and dapperly dressed for his age. We got to talking and I noticed after five minutes of conversation that he had a wedding ring on. The problem was it didn't add up. It was approaching midnight and he was at a bar sipping away at some kind of bourbon talking to my skinny Irish ass. Where was his wife?

Unfortunately I knew the answer, but thought an old guy like him might like to talk about it.

"Where's your wife?"

He paused and with no change or inflection in his tone said, "She's dead."

"How long ago?" I asked.

"Three years." he said.

I didn't want to make a comment about him still wearing his ring. Not that I wanted him to "go out and find another girl" or that "he should get over it and move on." Quite the contrary. If I would have said anything it would have been, "Hey, I respect that you're still wearing that ring and being loyal to your wife, even after her death." But I didn't deem my political observation necessary. Based on how many drinks he had, I figured he was bidding his time and numbing the pain until he could see her again.

That being said, I'll be damned if I don't applaud him here and now. For I could never figure out, for my self anyway, if I got married and my wife were to die, how I could re-marry. Maybe I'm too idealistic. Maybe I've watched too many American movies where the good guys win and there's some semblance of justice or honor. But if I lost my wife, I don't think, let alone see how I could marry another gal. No disrespect to all you other gals out there, but that concept of marrying "the one" (not to get all chicky on you guys) means "the one."

And I tip my hat to Jim for having such a lovely wife that he could accept no substitute.

And So Ends Another Season

I was at my bar last night with Natasha and a Russian friend of mine and in the other room was a crowd of 20 and 30 somethings with their eyes glued to the TV screen. The reason their eyes were glued to the TV screen is because a group of men had decided to go out onto a field, one of which was throwing a spherical object repeatedly over a plate like object.

However, the reason for the intrigue, was that not only was it a group of men in a field throwing a sphere, but there was this OTHER group of men, one of which had a stick and was standing over the plate like object. And not only was he standing over the plate like object, HE WAS TRYING TO SWING THE STICK AT THE SPHERICAL OBJECT after which he would run around in a circle should the stick come in contact with the sphere.

It seemed the two groups of men would then occasionally switch positions, where the other group would swing stick and the other team throw the sphere.

However, the most interesting observation was that of the 20 and 30 something men in the other room at the bar. For apparently on TV the group of men in the white clothes didn't swing the stick or throw the sphere as good as the men in the gray clothes. And thus they were "defeated" and walked off the field sadly while the men in the gray clothes jumped up and down and engaged in very big hug. And this "defeat" elicited the oddest response from all the people in the room;

depression
sadness
and
anger.

I found it odd, that group of guys swinging sticks and throwing spheres in a place far far away would have this affect on other people who, quite literally, HAD NOTHING TO DO WITH THE MEN ON THE FIELD. How a group of men playing a game could actually affect the mood, happiness and lifetime fulfillment of other people who were 100% inconsequential to the stick-swinging and sphere throwing. But there it was, empirical proof right in front of me, people were actually affected by OTHER PEOPLE'S stick swinging and sphere throwing.

It left me to believe that the people who not only glued their eyes to the screen, but their happiness to the ability of complete strangers to swing a stick and throw a sphere were psychotic. Complete morons who pinned their hopes and happiness on something completely outside their control. How else would you describe this phenomenon?

Were their lives so pointless and meaningless and void of purpose that THIS is the best they could come up with? To sit and watch OTHER men throw spheres and swing sticks? And to get excited or depressed based on which colored-shirt men swung the stick really good and threw the sphere really fast? Could they not spend time with family and friends? Could they not play X-Box or some other video game? Could they (and here was a REALLY radical thought I had) GET THEIR OWN FREAKING STICKS AND SPHERES and engage in their VERY OWN game of sticks and spheres?

Natasha even said she heard that some of these people actually spend 5 HOURS OF THEIR FINITE LIVES driving to fields, whlie they pay $200 EACH PERSON to watch the stick swinging and sphere throwing. Then they spend another hour and a half in traffic as if it were rush hour on the way back. Some even go so far as to pay $20 for parking near the field AND $10 for a hotdog which are served at the fields. My Russian friend said he heard that stick swinging and sphere throwing was SO important to some societies that the government would pay for the fields where these activities occurred.

Worse still was just how many of these simple-minded automotons would still be obsessed over stick swinging and sphere throwing...WHEN THERE WAS NO FREAKING STICK SWINGING OR SPHERE THROWING OCCURRING.

Apparently before the sticks are swung and the spheres are thrown there are "pre-stick-swinging-sphere-throwing" shows where other idiots speculate on whether or not certain men will swing sticks and whether or not spheres will be thrown. This results in shows that are horribly boring to anybody with the slightest bit of sense;

"Well Jim, what do you think Joe is going to do?"

"Well, I'm not sure Steve, but I think Joe is going to try and swing the stick."

"You think he's going to try to swing it really hard?"

"Yes, Steve, I think Joe will try to swing the stick really hard."

And by god, guess what? Joe DOES swing the stick really hard!

My goodness, who saw that coming?! Thank god we have Steve and Jim to predict such things.

Of course, you'd think with the "Pre-Stick-Swinging-Sphere-Throwing" show, the masses would be satiated.

Oh no.

You see, then comes the "Post-Sticking-Swinging-Sphere-Throwing" show where a whole new set of idiots tell you what just happened even though you were there to see it.

"Well, it looks like Joe swung the stick really hard."

"You're right Phil, Joe swung the stick really hard. I also noticed how Mark threw the sphere really fast."

"Wow, great analysis Tim! Mark DID throw the sphere really fast!"

This then entertains the 20 something and 30 somethings for another hour.

Regardless, it was a very sad revelation I had. That so many people had so little going on in their lives that this was one of the more important aspects of their lives. Let alone they seemed relatively indifferent about things that actually did impact their lives.

Federal deficit is at an all-time high?

Naw. Not relevant.

Your children are now enslaved with all the debt we saddled them with?

Meh, couldn't care less.

Unemployment is at 10%.

Pfa, who cares.

Oh, but "Joe Schmoe" swung the stick really good and hit the sphere really far?

"OH WOW! WOO HOO!!!! YEAAAAA!!!! THAT'S MY MAN!!!! YOU SHOW 'EM JOE!!!! YEAH FOR JOE SCHMOE!!!!!"

Ah, what could possibly go wrong with a society with priorities such as this?

Explaining "Rent Seeking" to Joe Soucheray

Garage Logic, as some of you know, is one of my favorite radio shows to listen to. Joe Soucheray is no doubt incredibly busy and so, on the rare occasion, I send an e-mail or a letter to the show, it usually is lost in the pile or never read. Not out of spite, but sheer time-saving, I decided not to really write into radio shows or call, simply because you rarely get on and by the time you do, the platform has moved on, it's a waste of time. But I slipped recently after Joe was talking about the behavior of "Mysterians" because all he was describing was "rent seeking." I wrote a letter, but then caught myself and realized, it isn't worth driving to the post office.

However, I do believe that in order to understand leftist ideology and psychology, we all could use a lesson in rent seeking and what it is. Therefore, I post the letter, that was never sent, below;

Dear Joe,

I've been listening to your show for about 5 years now however when you speak about The Mystery I think you do not realize you are explaining an economic phenomenon that you are unaware of called "rent seeking" and hopefully in my explaining this to you, you may be able to solve The Mystery.

"Rent seeking" is a form of economic behavior where a person or an entity wishes to extract compensation or wealth for essentially doing nothing, or in short, getting paid to produce nothing of worth. A text book example would be the US mafia in the 1930's offering "protection" for various shop owners when in reality it was nothing but extortion. Regardless, the

example still holds. The mafia acts like it is offering a service (protection) and receives compensation for this "protection" even though no real service or good has been produced.

Today you do not have such flagrant examples of "rent seeking," but they do exist and are largely the primary sources of employment for your "Mysterians" and goes a long way in explaining The Mystery. The primary and most common example you cite on your show would be your mysterian politicians who are on constant crusades to enact various legislation that limits the freedoms of Americans under the guise of protection. Most of your liberal (and for the most part, conservative) politicians do nothing productive nor produce anything of worth. Therefore to make it look like they are actually working they have to seek out "crusades" or fabricate "crises" so they may keep their jobs as politicians. Fresh in my memory is the ban on candy cigarettes in St. Paul. This does nothing to help society. There was no crisis, there was no problem. And therefore there was not one cent of production in enacting this law, but you still pay these elected officials to do such nonsensical things.

Another example of rent seeking would be your professional protestors or activists. These people do not produce anything of value, but regardless, be it through ACORN or some other non-profit organization, they are still paid to essentially produce nothing of value. The kid working at Burger King is producing more for this nation than a professional activist from Macalester.

Lawyers that sue companies for fraudulent claims is another example of rent seeking. One can claim that a lawyer is providing a service for a plaintiff or a defendant, but in the end, the lawyer produced nothing. He or she simply took money from a company that actually did produce something of value. The finance industry is another. An investment bank repackaging mortgages into CDO's or ABS's creates no additional value in doing so. It is merely taking a commission to repackage production that is already existing.

Whatever the instance of rent seeking may be, the key to understanding rent seeking and how it relates to The Mystery is that people who engage in rent seeking put themselves ahead of society. And not only do they put themselves ahead of society, they must engage in an "act" or a "farce" as if they are doing some kind of real work so as not to destroy their egos and permit them an excuse to deny they are actually just living off of society. Therefore you will never see a Mysterian just sit there on government assistance for that would be too much of a blow to their pride. But at the same time you will never see them work hard to become an engineer, a doctor, a pharmacist, etc., because the schooling required is too difficult. Therefore you see the majority of your Mysterians employed in very rent seeking industries;

Education – very few people who work in education actually educate children. Most are in administration and counseling and literally do nothing to advance the education of the children. Even those that do, based on international PISA scores, do a poor job overall.

Politics/government – with no competition from the private sector there is no urgency to work hard or be efficient let alone productive. You just tell people what they want to hear and never bother studying what laws (or perhaps lack of laws) would be best for society and still collect a check. Barack Obama is a perfect example of a life-time rent seeker who has done nothing (bar write a book) productive yet still collects a check.

Colleges – There is no limit to professors in worthless subjects such as sociology, women's studies, anthropology, communications, journalism, etc., that require no rigorous study, yet still provide employment (usually financed in part by government money). You could pay taxes to get a road or more defense, but instead your money goes to one of the "prematurely gray-haired woman" you talk about to espouse theories of philosophy to her students that will never result in a penny of worth or production.

Non-profits – Non-profits are big rent seekers because their goal is first and foremost NOT to solve a problem, but to employ people to act like they are solving a problem. I would even claim some non-profits purposely avoid solving the problem because that would be the end of the cash stream for them to do nothing. The UN is a perfect example of the world's largest non-profit that has achieved nothing yet has been compensated to the amounts of many billions of dollars.

There are other industries, but I assume you get the idea of what types of industries would employ Mysterians.

Why you have a "mystery" or why Mysterian's behavior does not make sense is because it is contrary to reality. It is hypocritical. They need a job and some kind of employment not just for money, but for pride. But since the reality is that they are producing nothing, when they are criticized or this reality is pointed out, they then come up with the most inane and irrational explanations and excuses because their entire life existence, their entire purpose of being is being called into question.

"Don't tell me we don't have any money" is a perfect example of Garage Logicians calling out these rent seekers on their hypocrisy. Americans spend more money on their education system (per pupil) than any other country in the world. Yet they constantly need more money. Their illogical excuse is that it is for the children and how dare you cut off funding for children. In reality they are just cowards for hiding behind children to keep their unnecessary jobs.

The "Flower Pot Gang" is another example. Basically middle aged women who were rich enough to afford to run for public office because they were bored. Nancy Pelosi is another example who was nothing but the daughter of Baltimore's mayor. And Mark Dayton is a perfect example of a bored "trust fund baby" who has nothing to do but run for public office even though he is not qualified and has no real skills. These people did not run for office because of some noble intent to become a statesman, they ran because they were bored, had the money, wanted an easy job and needed something to point to in their lives as being an accomplishment. And when you question their policies or their qualifications, you get bland, vague, indirect answers that never really answer direct questions because you are getting too close to the truth; they put themselves ahead of the people they represent, they do NOTHING and they don't want to be exposed.

Therefore I think if you look at these rent seekers as merely people looking for an easy job, whose egos and personalities cannot handle the fact they are not producing anything of worth, and they find no problems putting themselves ahead of society you might be able to understand the Mysterian's behavior better as well as the Mystery overall.

Good luck

GDP Growth vs. Government Spending

GDP growth is chaotic.

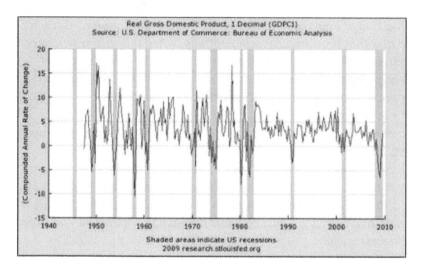

Therefore to see if there's any kind of trend you need to average it out over longer periods of time. I did this on a 10 and 20 year trailing average, where I simply took the past 10 and 20 years worth of economic growth and averaged it out into a "rolling average."

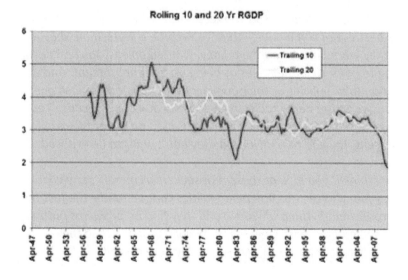

I like to call this figure, especially the 20 year rolling average RGDP growth, "Generational RGDP Growth" because the 20 years spans a generation, economic booms and busts included, and shows their overall economic productive capacity over those years.

Now what I'm going to do is very simple, because that's what economics is. It's very simple (plus i don't want to confuse any leftists and socialists).

I took Generational RGDP growth and compared it to government spending (state and federal) as a percent of GDP. And wonders upon wonder, guess what? The relationship is inverted.

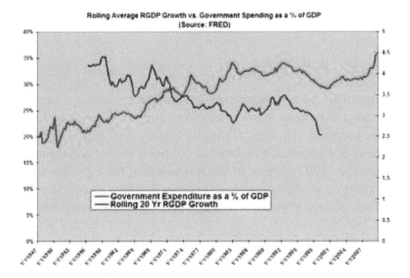

What this means is that as government spending has gone up, economic growth has gone down.

This simple chart has many economic ramifications, most of my readers already intuitively understand. But, for those of you who vote for your presidents based on their pecs, let me spell it out for you.

1. This is why the stimulus and by large Keynesian economics won't work. Understand the government DOES NOT PRODUCE ANYTHING. It does NOT PRODUCE WEALTH. It doesn't make X-Boxes. It doesn't make food. It merely TRANSFERS WEALTH FROM ONE GROUP OF PEOPLE TO ANOTHER. Now there are some genuine services that the government provides that

helps society and does show up on GDP. BUT STIMULUS MONEY TO ART INSTITUTES, ACADEMIA AND WHATEVER OTHER FLOWERS AND PUPPIES POPPYCOCK HAVE YOU DOES NOT PRODUCE ANYTHING. The reason why is that even if an Obama-fanatic sculptor produces a worthless and sinfully ugly government piece of art for the local building, the money used to pay him came from somebody else, ergo a net production increase of ZERO.

2. The government is less efficient than the private sector.

Do you want growth?

Do you want jobs?

Do you want food on the table?

Then you better let the people have the majority of the money and not put it into the government. History has shown you this via this chart. Your eyes are not deceiving you. Look at the chart again. And no, I'm not Michael Mann or Phil Jones. The data has not been tainted and comes directly from the FRED Database at the St. Louis Fed. You can recreate this very same chart on your own, whereas I cannot recreate the hockey stick chart, so if you believe in global warming, you better damn well believe this chart.

3. No, majoring in sociology or planning on becoming a government worker will not help this situation.

See, I know what a lot of you are thinking. "I want to help people because it sounds like an easier job than engineering...errr....I mean, because I am noble and moral. Ergo I will go and work for the government as a social worker, a professor or run for public office."

The problem is none of these jobs PRODUCE ANYTHING THE POPULATION NEEDS NOR REALLY WANTS. And as a **higher and higher percentage of the population goes and majors in worthless subjects in the hopes of a cushy job that doesn't produce anything**, but merely transfers wealth, you can expect GDP to drop further.

4. If growth keeps dropping, then where precisely are you people going to come up with the money to pay for...

social security
medicare
nationalized health care
the Obama-corps
the stimulus
education
government financed day care

not to mention the extra money we'll need to pay back the national debt?

You see, the governments combined (state, local and federal) already spend about 45% of GDP, leaving only 55% left to be taxed (difference in revenue vs. spending duly noted), how much more do you think the economy will take before people just stop working altogether?

Is everybody supposed to work in government?

Who, might I ask, is going to produce the I-Pod you want?

Who, might I ask, is going to produce the Wii you want?

Who, might I ask, is going to produce the computer networking system so you can e-mail your friends, let alone put the food on your table?

Or are we supposed to be like the Pelosi's, the Bush's and the Gore's. Generation after generation of losers who never worked a real job in the private sector?

Of course, I know all of my regular readers understand this. My regular readers get this simple logic. Not to mention before they form opinions, they get the facts first. Not form opinions and then find facts.

But good lord, to the 60% of the population who voted for Obama, when does reality sink in? What does it take to get you people to grow the hell up, drop it with your naive, college-age thinking and idealism, and intellectually and honestly admit you have no FREAKING clue how the real world and economy works. LET ALONE take the time to study the federal effing budget and do some simple mathematical calculations much like you would your own personal finances to see if any of this socialism BS is even affordable, let alone feasible. Let alone (and this group really confuses me) for those of you with children, start to stop and really think about what you're doing to your childrens' financial future? When do you wake up?

Alas, what can I do aside from make a record of it here on this blog so that a thousand years from now historians will look back and say, *"Wow, look how insane the population was. There was this one guy over here that saw it coming, but the rest of them were all doped up on REality TV, Obama's pecks, bread and circuses, they couldn't even understand how everybody working as a social worker and nobody farming the fields would result in a collapse of society!"*

I'll be long dead by that time, and I'm supremely confident I'll be proven right, but in the meantime, good lord, why would anybody invest in America?

The Economic "Fail" of the Century

As some of you are aware, the price of oil has become somewhat pricey in recent months. It's now around $100 and we get to pay approaching $4 a gallon in gas.

(chart removed)

Accusations will be made. Big oil will be blamed. Investigations launched. But in the end it is the unstoppable forces of economics and the declining currency of a declining nation that will win in the end of the day and you will continue to have to pay $4 a gallon in gas...maybe $5 or $6 when summer rolls around.

Now we can blame the turmoil in the middle east (correctly) for the increase in prices. You can blame the declining dollar (correctly) for the increase in prices as well. And yes, I will even allow those on the unthinking and galactically ignorant left to go to their knee-jerk position of blaming "big oil" (incorrectly) for the increase in prices. But it will all be for naught because the debate is moot. There is no reason to argue about oil. And I shall explain why with some more of my super awesome economic genius.

IN REALITY (and I say this with all seriousness) gas should be trading at about 40 cents a gallon. And if I were president and had both houses of congress it would be at 40 cents a gallon. It would trade at 40 cents a gallon NOT because we would enact price controls, but the MARKET rate would be 40 cents a gallon.

Now, would this be because I would drill baby drill?

No.

Would this be because I would invade the middle east for their oil recreating an oil-rich empire?

No.

Would it be because I would subsidize alternative fuels to the point gas would have to be 40 cents a gallon?

No.

It would be because I would gather up all the business "leaders" in the US and we'd get them into a little room and I would ask them one simple question;

"Why in frick's name are you requiring people to commute to work when today's technology makes it pointless?"

I have **brought up this point before**, but at the time I was not a student of computer networks or IT like I am today, and was informed that for security reasons, among other reasons, businesses do not like it when people work from home. But after a year of studying computer networking I am here to inform you that it is not only technologically possible, it is no riskier (bar human behavior) to have people working remotely. Telecommuting from your home is no riskier (with the appropriate measures taken) than working at an office, if for any other reason, you are technically still telecommuting while in the office, using the exact same routers and servers.

Of course, the question is "why don't we telecommute then?" and this is the largest most gigantic economic fail the US has ever made.

In short we passed up on the latest economic revolution because we are no longer American and no longer dare to dream.

If you look through history there have been various economic "revolutions" that have advanced and improved humans' lives greatly.

The agrarian revolution basically wiped out hunger.

The industrial revolution brought us electricity, transport and limitless goods and services making out lives that much easier.

The technology or "information" revolution made communications immediate.

And a by-product of the revolution allowed for the next great economic revolution, the "telecommuting revolution."

The only problem is, nobody in the US cared to avail themselves of it.

Oh, India certainly has, taking significant business from the US' IT sector. So has China and Ireland.

But no, not us. You must have us confused with the Rockefellers and Vanderbilts and the Carnigies and those other stupid "old" and "industrious" Americans. No, not us. We're modern Americans. We don't dare dream of never having to drive to work again. That's just not in our blood. No, we much prefer to sit 2 hours a day in bumper to bumper traffic while we hole up in some beige, tan cubicle and do mind-numbing tasks. That's the American dream!

This is the real reason why you are paying $4 in gas. This is the real reason why we have to spend billions on infrastructure that is unnecessary and unneeded. This is why there are thousands of deaths a year more than there has to be on roads. And this is a major reason why your families are stressed, torn or sometimes just plain destroyed. Because the American people failed to avail themselves of this most recent economic revolution because we just don't have the audacity to do so anymore.

Of course, there is another option.

You could do what I do.

Let me explain.

I get a call occasionally from a recruiting company called "Robert Half International." They have an office in DT Minneapolis. Their main finance/banking guy "Doug" knows who I am and knows that for the most part no bank in the area would hire me because of my **super awesome book that predicted the housing crash** (because why would you want to hire THAT guy? I mean who would want to hire the guy who PREDICTED THE BUBBLE?) In any case, when I do get a call from them, I know;

1. It's some rookie new hire who doesn't know I'm verbotten in the Minnesota banking industry
2. I'm not going to get the job (**again because of my super awesome book you should all read**).

So when it comes time for him to set up a "meeting to get to know you" I can more or less decree whatever I want because there's no way I'm getting the job in the first place.

Rookie - "Can you come downtown to meet me?"

Me - "No, how about you come to my local bar in my town. I usually start drinking around 1PM."

or

Rookie - "We have a position open in the vibrant DOWNTOWN AREA! You'll get to be where all the action is."

Me - "Will they pay me $20,000 extra per year to deal with the commute and give me an underground parking space in the building I'd be working in?"

Rookie - "Well (shocked), no...um, I don't think so."

Me - "Can I telecommute?"

Rookie - "Well,...um, I could ask but I highly doubt it."

Me - "Can I set my own hours to avoid rush hour?"

Rookie - "Ummmm...I think they would prefer you be there 8-5PM."

Me - "Eh, forget then, not interested."

In other words, desperate as the employment situation may be, why do you accept commuting? Why do you not demand the right to telecommute?

Sure, it's a bold move and sure there's plenty of other people out there willing to become the corporate slave who would just "love" to commute, but if the entirety of the US labor market would simply get a little self-respect and say, "eh, I'm not commuting" what could they do?

Then again, maybe I'm just crazy. Maybe people like to commute and waste years of their lives, missing out on seeing their children and spending time with their families. Maybe they like spending trillions of dollars on gas over the years. I mean, what better to spend your money on that gas, right? And who doesn't love the increased chance of divorce because "you're never home?" And did I mention all the icky yucky gross economic growth that would occur because of extra disposable income?

Yeah, we wouldn't dare take advantage of this latest revolution.

Fort Bachelortude

As the recessionary woes plague the nation your beloved Captain, now on permanent Galt vacation, has had the time to observe a couple trends or phenomenons occurring. Most notably the young man who now sleeps on my couch on account he is a friend and he is in a time of need because, well, his wife is an insufferable pain in the ass. This has resulted in my abode becoming what I like to call "Fort Bachelortude" - an oasis for bachelors as they battle against life's daily onslaughts.

Go to the neighboring town of mine and you will see two other bachelors forming a brother fort on account one of them is a pilot (whose industry is not known for long term, stable employment) and needs just a place to sleep and a stall to shower in. The owner of the house (a bachelor) does not have a wife nor kinder and therefore has an extra room by which he can rent out for very cheap to the pilot bachelor. This is a mutual advantageous relationship in that the room has gone unused and why not generate at least a pittance of rental income while splitting chores.

Of course these are merely anecdotal stories of bachelors shacking up, but enough anecdotes make a trend, and trends make statistical fact, and so allow me a prediction;

The RISE OF THE BACHELOR FORT!

Both the pilot and my romantically beleaguered friend are empirical evidence of two traits of society that are going to drive this "bachelor fort" trend. A trend by which bachelors minimize their expenses, just try to get by as cheaply as possible, and therefore form MANLY coops (because most coops are pretty effeminate) of residency by which to save money.

For example my friend who now resides on my couch is suffering from one of society's trend whereby the entire courtship/romance/marriage or whatever you want to call it industry is completely biased and tilted against men. Divorce courts, child custody, and forget law. Just look at the purified hell a young man must go through in the US when it comes to dating the American Idol worshipping prima modannas. Inevitably a man comes to the realization that he is finite and he is going to die. Does he spend his time slaving away to make daddy's little princess happy? Or does he decide to find a couch, play some video games, smoke some cigars, drive a motorcycle and do what he wants to do? I could go into this in infinite detail and no doubt I will receive many complaints from women, but it doesn't change the fact that courting and marriage for the average American male is so horrendous that it should not be surprising that the trend of men opting to never marry will not just continue but increase.

This trend of course is great for Fort Bachelortude in that without a wife demanding a brand new 3 story suburbanite dream home and children crying and screaming and bringing communicable diseases into the house, the sole, lonely bachelor only needs a couch and a bathroom for his living needs.

The second trend is what my pilot buddy faces - unreliable employment. Not because he is an unreliable employee. Oh no no no. Scott Adams has long ago proved corporate America is to blame for the lack of loyal employees. But because employers, for the most part, are just as incompetent as the employees they love to blame their incompetence and quarterly losses on. The WWII generation is no longer at the helm. It's the baby boomers at the helm, the even-more-entitlement-mentality-driven Gen X'ers seeping into middle management, and the even-more-entitled-than-that Millineals at the entry level. And you people wonder why there's 10% unemployment and no private sector growth.

Regardless, this poses a quandary for your conventional bachelor. Simply;

THERE'S NO JOBS!

You also combine that with the fact that this latest recession has disproportionately affected men more than women to the point it's called the "mancession" it leaves a populus of bachelors out there looking to minimize expenses as much as possible. This drives American men NOT to go back home and live with mom at the age of 40 (like many of our southern European counterparts do), but rather shack up with other impoverished bachelors to pool resources and share expenses.

Now at first, most people would look at this and say, "My god, what a bad thing. How could this be happening?" But permit me a couple observations.

First, bachelors, if they're real tough, traditional American men, do not have their lives nor base their lives on their homestead. Their lives are defined by what they do OUTSIDE of their place of sleep. Ergo, a single male WHO HAS NO KIDS, does not call home "where he rests his head" but rather "home" is his network of friends, his hobbies and what defines him as a man. And whlie in our ignorant youth some of us may have thought a house in the suburbs with a June Cleaver wife (who was actually pretty hot by the way) was the "goal" as we've aged we've realized there's more to life than just doing what literally billions of people have done before us. And instead of having the majority of our finances tied up paying for a mortgage and family we can't afford, with minimal living expense and a lot of free time (thanks Barack!) we can now actaully pursue interests and hobbies that interest us. This is the key thing to Fort Bachelortude - trading labor for leisure. Since there are no jobs, if we can master the art of cost-minimalization, we can enjoy a higher standard of living at a much lower income in that we have all that much more free time.

Second, Fort Bachelortude is not a frat house. I'm not talking about a bunch of rowdy teenagers, getting drunk, living off of daddy's dime while they major in "business." I'm talking men in their 30's and 40's who can actually shack up without any drama or chaos about who left the puking donkey in the living room. Men who are forced to join Fort Bachelortude are much more mature and make any kind of traditional roommate dramas a thing of the past.

Thirdly, it forces bachelors to rethink what's really important in life. I know women are not going to like this, but men, you are a factor too. And not just any factor, a very important factor. Matter of fact a completely necessary factor in by that default you are 1/2 the factor. Your life and your happiness should come first as long as it does not expense or hurt somebody in the process. I know we've been trained to put family and household ahead of us, but please. That doctrine was established in the 40's and died once conventional feminism took hold. There is a whole world out there for you to explore, and as I mentioned before in point #1, you may be forced through divorce or dumping, combined with economic realities, to not just minimize expenses, but that you will also have a wake up call forced upon you. If you have such minimal resources to pay for your living, what are the most important things for you to spend your money on?

In other words, Fort Bachelortude is not just a means by which you get cheap rent and your landlord buddy gets beer money, it makes you take inventory of your life and ask how do you want to spend it.

Now the ramifications of this trend are very politically incorrect. Men just going and doing what they want? MEN abandoning the courting/dating/marrying market and pursuing hobbies of leisure? Men not walking up the isle and instead just renting a room in the basement of some other heathen bachelor while he plays video games all day???

Sadly (or perhaps maybe happily) yes.

For you see, men don't really have a choice. The economy has been feminized to the point safety is put ahead of any kind of innovation or production. Equality is more important than excellence. And harmony has replaced competition. This is not a welcoming environment to the traditional American male simply because it goes against a male's nature. And when this is the environment a male doesn't go forth and try to produce huge amounts of production or start up a new company or become the next Tony Stark, because...well...why should he? (First, he can't, second, you'd tax him to death) Instead, and this is the real threat to the conventional way American thinks, what if the real men of society, just plain gave up, decided to play video games, decided to minimize expenses, and never work hard again? What if they stopped marrying, working, and instead put their own happiness ahead of everybody else's and simply pursued a life of leisure and hobbies that they wanted? What would be the long term economic consequences if such a large percentage of the labor force just plain gave up or didn't try their best anymore?

I'll let that thought fester in your mind, in the meantime, doors are open at Fort Bachelortude. BYOB.

Bachelor Object Migration

Allow me to explain to you girls the concept of Bachelor Object Migration or BOM.

You see, BOM, is based on the principle that any new object entering a bachelor's life musn't be rushed or accelerated into that bachelor's life. That it has to be acclimated, going through various stages, before it find it's rightful place in the bachelor pad. This can range from any object be it a car or something as simple as food, but again, key is to take your time and make sure that object is neither rushed, nor hurried into the bachelor life.

The first stage of BOM is the **contemplation stage**. In this stage life tells the bachelor, subtly, that he needs something. For example boxer shorts. Life, over the course of time, wears down the bachelor's boxer shorts to the point they have holes, are thread bare and are about to lose all function. And as the bachelor does laundry or goes to the bathroom he notices this in his boxer shorts and comes up with a great epiphany;

"I think I might have to get some new boxer shorts this year."

Now understand that was just the contemplation stage. The bachelor is sensing a need and is contemplating filling it. But it will not manifest itself into action until the **Need Stage**.

The need stage is where the bachelor obviously needs this object. His boxer shorts are in disrepair, he has NO food in the fridge, or is in desperate need of some kind of surgery. But the key defining trait of this stage is where the bachelor realizes he "needs" it, typically notated when the bachelor says to himself;

"Wow, I need to get some new boxer shorts."

Then comes the **procrastination stage**.

Yes, he "needs" it, but would he really be a bachelor if he immediate ran out and got it? That's what girls do. That's what married folk do. They have a need and then they call their spouse and tell them to "pick it up on the way home." Whereas the bachelor has the skills of procrastination. Bachelors are gifted creatures, able to find quick fixes to needs. The bachelor may cut his long pajamas, made of the same boxer material and convert them into boxers. The bachelor may just suffer with the now shredded boxers perhaps hemming them with a bit duct tape. The bachelor, though in desperate need of food will simply go to the bar or substitute it with a substitute food such as beer or whiskey. It is these skills that a bachelor makes.

Sadly, however, even the most gifted bachelors have to inevitably break down and go and buy the objects the need for survival. This is a low point in the bachelor's life in that they now have to "do" something that is outside of work, video games, drinking, scoring with chicks and play. They have to do a "chore" and you can tell when they are at this stage as they are usually depressed. Head hung low and not smiling. Regardless, they man up, grab a pen, and put together a "To Do List." This is the **"To Do List"** Stage of BOM.

Understand the to do list will not just be that one item. Here the bachelor embarks one what is the closest he will come to life planning. And aside from "get new boxer shorts" he will list other things so as not to make his life sound so dull;

1. Get new boxer shorts
2. Buy Ferrari
3. Take over Goldman Sachs by borrowing TARP money
4. Date Jennifer Aniston
5. Fly F-16 Fighter plane
6. Retire in the Bahama's with a harem of honeys managed by Jennifer Aniston
7. Have weekly bikini wrestling to decide who gets to date me that week

With the completed to do list in hand we now move onto the **"purchase stage."**

The purchase stage is where the bachelor is willing and able to buy the object. He has psychologically prepared himself and admitted that it is just a fact of life he needs new boxer shorts, and is the only thing holding him back from achieving his other objectives on his to do list. However, the purchase stage is regulated by one thing; "the right turn."

The bachelor is an efficient creature you must understand. Expending minimal amounts of effort for maximum gain. Ergo when purchasing items, the bachelor will only purchase the items if the store is on the right side of the road thereby requiring a right turn and thereby avoiding a left turn. If you need gas, yes, the "closest" gas station may be a mile away, but if it's on the left side of the road, this requires a left turn. A turn that can last 14 days. Many bachelors as we speak are still stuck behind some SUV driving soccer mom, who hasn't realized the green arrow means go. Ergo, even if the closest gas station is a mile away, because it is on the left side of the road, the bachelor will drive the next 50 miles on fumes to the closest gas station on the RIGHT side of the road. The same applies to boxer shorts or any other purchase that is necessary. The bachelor will not engage in the purchase stage unless the store is on the right side of the road (British bachelors engage in the opposite practice).

The bachelor enters the store, returns with the purchase in hand, throws it into the car which starts our next stage; the **"Leave It in the Car Stage."**

Satisfied he has done the majority of the work, the bachelor now has no guilt or psychological pressure to continue completing the chore. As far as the bachelor is concerned, he has completed his task and can now go about his bachelor activities. Notice the "To Do List" said, "Get boxer shorts." Not "wear new boxer shorts." Triumphantly he returns to his home, smug look on his face, goes into the house, opens a beer and promptly plays Call of Duty 5.

The leave it in the car stage can last anywhere from a week to a year depending on the object. If the object was say, ice cream, and it is December in Minnesota, that ice cream can stay in the trunk of the car, and thus the "leave it in the car stage," for at least 3 months. Sometimes the psychological trauma of having to run an errand and buy something is so devastating, the bachelor purges the experience completely from his mind, forgetting he purchased an object and it is in the car. Not until the bachelor has a date and is forced to clean out the car does he discover object, at which time he heralds great efficiency because it "saved" him the trip to the store he through he still had to take.

Regardless, the boxers, now nothing but strings inevitably prompt the bachelor to bring the object from the car into the house. This is a relatively short lived stage known as the **"move it into the house"** stage. However, the house is nothing more than a really big, immobile car. And like the car the object can stay in the house without ever really being used. Typically it begins this stage by starting on the desk or the floor, a large flat area the bachelor usually tosses stuff for general assortment later, only to be disturbed by the biennial bachelor pad cleaning. This is an important part of the process as the new object or objects, must become acclimated to all the other objects in the bachelor pad. From there it advances to the floor that it's supposed to be on. For example my dresser, and thus the boxers, are on the 2nd floor, requiring a simple toss of the boxers up the flight of stairs where they land near the vicinity of the dresser. As long as they're in the vicinity of where they're supposed to be, in the bachelor's mind that's "put away." Typically females, be they moms, sisters, friends or femme fatales, will protest it is "not put away" "lying there on the floor." This requires the bachelor to explain to them the concept of "put away good enough," which usually results in rolling eyes.

With order now in the bachelor household, now begins the **unpacking/assembling stage**. Some objects such as boxers you unpack. Others, such as entertainment systems you assemble. Again, here you do not want to rush them, unless they are related to the entertainment system or consist of electronics. But for the most part there is no need to unpack them right away. I mean, come on, you WENT to the store, you PURCHASED them, you brought them back HOME, you brought them INTO THE HOUSE, you PUT THEM AWAY GOOD ENOUGH, and now you have to *rush and unpack*? Be a bachelor, leave them in their original wrapping.

And finally comes the **use stage**. After a long and difficult struggle to acquire, transport and put away good enough the objects, now comes the time to actually use them. In total the whole BOM process can take anywhere from 1 week to 1 year, but now the bachelor finally gets to enjoy using the objects. Of course, criticism is laid upon us, primarily by those of the female persuasion, that this is nothing more than procrastination. However, they do not realize the merits of BOM. First, the order and balance of the bachelor pad was not disturbed by rushing in new objects. Who knows what chaos would have ensued if those boxer shorts were haphazardly purchased the day of need and worn the very next? The house could have collapsed or caught on fire. The orderly, deliberate process of BOM prevent that from occurring. Second, the bachelor expended the minimum amount of effort to bring objects into the house. Following the right turn principle and efficient space management through the use of his car, the bachelor has freed up additional time to be spent on video games and football...I mean his "girlfriend." Third, the bachelor maintains order in his household as the BOM process ensures all objects are put away good enough where they belong. And finally, the bachelor ensures a frugal lifestyle, purchasing only what he needs and not racking up credit card bills that he'll inevitably ask daddy to pay for. It are these benefits that make BOM an essential part of bachelorhood management and a vital tool for bachelors everywhere.

To the 30/40 Something Woman Who Wouldn't Leave Me Alone

I heard you the first time.

It was obvious you didn't pick up on my somewhat less than subtle hint.

And therefore I had to endure your frequent commentary, obviously directed my way, which interrupted my dinner.

So let me explain to you why you are 30/40 something and sitting at a bar by yourself and I am 35 sitting at a bar by myself but why I am infinitely more happy.

I came there because I was hungry. I needed food. And since I am an alpha-male bachelor of the highest order (not to mention an outstanding economist) I have outsourced all of my food preparation to third parties, namely restaurants.

The reason I chose this particular restaurant was not because you were there, nor the score of other desperate 30 something women, but because it served four simple purposes;

1. It was open
2. It had good food
3. It also served Rumpleminze
4. It was nearby

These four simple things AND ONLY these four simple things is what made me show up.

I wanted food.

I wanted a drink.

I didn't want to prepare it.

And I wanted to go home.

However, you were there for different reasons.

And it was plainly obvious.

First off, I wore crappy khaki shorts, sandals, a crappy shirt and a cap. It was obvious I did not come there to meet anybody.

You however, still thinking it's 19-freaking-93 and you're still 21 were dolled up in a silver sequene top and black slick slacks. You were on the hunt, purposely looking to find a guy, whereas I was not looking for a girl.

(Oh, and by the way, please don't act indignant that I presupposed you were looking for a man. I'm not a naive, simple, honest 22 year old kid anymore. The truth with that clothing, you were on the hunt.)

However, much like 20 years ago when young men (who you would not doubt today give an appendage for) gave you unwelcomed advances and you poo pooed them away, your unwelcomed advances I had to endure today were incredibly hypocritical. The reason being is that those "unwelcomed" advances you had to "suffer" 20 years ago were no doubt at a bar where you were dressed the part and enticing such advances and no doubt welcoming them whilst acting appalled they occurred not to mention picking up free drinks all along the way.

Today, I was sitting by myself, warfing down food, in crappy clothes giving no such false signals to beget attention or free drinks. I wanted to be left alone, eat my food, yet you continued to harass me.

Second, I ordered a Rumpleminze.

Why?

Because I like Rumpleminze. Strong, ice cold, soothing on the throat. You can enjoy it for a while. Nice patient, enjoyable drink.

You, at the age of 40 something ordered a vodka-freaking-red bull.

Really? Is that what the "kids" are ordering today? Is that what's "hip?" Are you in with the "in crowd?" Perhaps you can find yourself a Vampire/Wolverine Boyfriend or whatever the fad is with the mentally insane teenagers of today.

Third, speaking of kids. How many do you have? Because I see that "single moms" are all the rage. See, I have no kids because instead of thinking of myself the entire time I remembered what it was like to be a kid. And I then came to the incredibly OBVIOUS conclusion that before bringing a kid into this world, maybe I ought to find a reliable, stable, loving wife before I start breeding and bringing innocent souls into this world. That they weren't "toys" or "objects" to have. That they were humans, just like you and me and had feelings, needs, requirements and demands. But I guess I'm just supposed to ignore my natural and visceral disgust for single parenthood in that obviously both parents failed to get it right the first time and I should instead go the politically correct route and cheer on the "nobility" and "courage" of "single parents."

Un-freaking-likely. There's still a victim. It's the children, and unlike when you guys invoke the term "for the children" to advance your own personal aims while cowardly hiding behind the child, I actually mean it in that I actually care about the kid, mine or not. I'm going back to enjoy my Rumpleminze while I avoid divorce if it's all the same with you.

Fourth, physically you got to be kidding me. I run 4-7 miles every other day and lift weights. I watch what I eat and I am in great shape. You look like you watch Oprah 4-7 times a day and occasionally lift your ass from the couch to get more food. I don't care what a bunch of bitter, burnt out 1960's hippie aging feminists said in the drug induced 70's and neither should you. The truth is that no matter what philosophy they lay down and tell you how things "should" be the REALITY is that men like women that are in shape.

I know.

We're evil, sexist, bigoted misogynist poopy-heads.

All of us.

But it ain't going to change and the sooner you learn that, the sooner you ACCEPT that FACT, the sooner you will start to employ strategies and techniques that are actually based in REALITY and have success.

Now, no doubt many of the female readers of this are livid.

No doubt I am evil and a horrible man for daring to lecture this slightly-aged woman about her unwelcomed behavior not to mention point out truths we all know to be true.

But for just once will you girls listen to me? Especially those of you who continue to watch dumbass movies like "Eat Pray Love" thinking somehow it relates to you and will somehow help you. Because if you listen, you will actually get some practical advice that will bring you genuine progress and happiness in your life unlike the tombs of women's magazine articles you've read which has resulted in you ended up where you are today (which is where the annoying woman was this particular night)

You are in your 30's or 40's.

You are not in your 20's.

And whereas men may have been naive and willing to fall over each other just to get a date with you when Clinton was in his first term, that is no longer the case. The game has changed.

Namely it has changed in that the men are no longer playing. They left the field. I don't know how many times I've heard late 30 something female friends of mine say, "You have to play hard to get. You have to get him to chase you."

I ask in return;

"Have you ever looked back to see that NOBODY is chasing?"

This somehow turns out to be some kind of "revolutionary" (not to mention" insulting")thought.

"WHAT!???"

"MEN, NOT CHASING!!!????"

"HOW DARE YOU!!!!"

No, how dare you.

What, you thought men were going to chase forever?

You see, men only have a finite, limited amount of energy for chasing. And you girls in your 20's were masters of exhausting it all.

Giving out your phone number, but then never returning the call.

Agreeing to a date and then canceling at the last minute.

The made up drama and land mines you laid around to keep them on their feet and never sure of where they stood.

And good lord, don't even get me started on all the complications involved with having sex.

It all worked GREAT back in the late teens and 20's, but guess what happened?

Inevitably men got smart. Men got wise. And worst of all, men just plain got some self-respect.

It wasn't an immediate flood on account different men woke up at various ages, but you throw in some divorces, the general disrespect and disregard for men and male behavior in society, and guess what?

20 years later men aren't chasing any more. They left in droves. They flooded OUT of the market.

Don't take it personally, it's not that they don't want to chase "you" any more.

They just don't want to chase period.

The "field" or the "market" has become so hostile, so hopelessly lopsided men increasingly went against their largest biological drive (women) and started enjoying life on their own. And think about that. It's become so hostile, so futile and such a waste of resources MEN HAVE LITERALLY STOPPED CHASING WOMEN.

You think I'm joking?

Why is the average age of marriage jumping?

Why are people having less kids?

And might I ask, do you know any perpetual bachelors out there who just enjoy a good Rumpleminze, some video games, or perhaps some fishing instead of trying to even entertain the idea of suffering a first date?

Do you know any 30-4o something men who regularly "go out clubbing" and "partaaaaay?"

Yeah, those ranks are thinning a bit aren't they? It's not that ALL men are quitting, just the good ones in that they have enough smarts, self-respect and sense to.

Worse still, and please don't shoot the messenger, this is just the plain truth-

Men can and usually date younger. So all those nice college boys that tried to pine for your affection back in the 90's you never called back or dared to mock infront of your girlfriends? Yeah, they're not gunning after you any more (if gunning after anybody at all). You need to chase after some Reaganauts who remember Duran Duran. Enjoy the Rogaine!

The overall point can actually be summarized with a classical supply and demand chart of economics. The "supply" women were willing to supply to the market was somewhat limited and Maureen-Dowdishly stingy (thus a supply curve that is far to the left). And in 1993 young Gen X men, quite obliviously were all desperately trying to get any kind of attention and affection they could (thus a demand curve to the far right). This resulted in an insanely high price the men had to "pay" to get a date (denoted by "P1"). This "price" manifested itself in terms of expensive dates, kindness, willing to show up, asking girls out more, general attention towards women, not to mention suffering being stood up, psychotic episodes, drama, soap opera BS and just general abuse they would endure. Over time though the sheer hell a man had to go through dating deterred him from the market (not to mention, a lot of men found lovely, kind caring women and immeidately grabbed them for themselves and left the dating market forever). This shifted the demand curve to the far left over the course of 15 years. What's interesting, given the "EAt PRay Love" and "Why You Rule and Your Boyfriend Sucks" magazines and the "cougar" fad and feminist indoctination and lord knows whatever other faux-fads the media barraged poor young women with, women were led to believe that they would always be in demand. That they owned the market. That they owned the hottest piece of property in 2006 and that there was no housing bubble. Ergo, almost unbeknownst to most 30-40 something women they never picked up on this dramatic drop in demand and held their supply incredibly low not knowing most of the buyers had left the market for substitute goods (look it up if you're interested in economics). This shift in the demand curve resulted in a huge drop in price from P1 to P2.

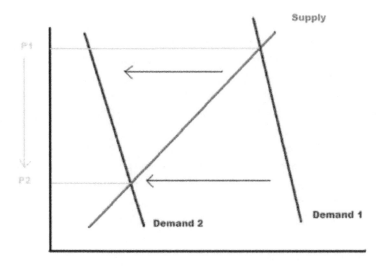

Now the question is (assuming you would inevitably like to get married or start a family or just plain have a guy in your life) how do you deal with this dire "market."

Well, the sad truth is it may be out of your control.

Notice the only thing that changed is demand. Men (the "buyers") left the market, not the women. Additionally it took about 15 years to drive them away, it's certainly going to take longer to get them back. They're more focused on deriving the most utility from the remaining years of their lives. They're not 25 thinking of starting a family, they're 40 and thinking about an LCD projector and Red Dead Redemption and football season and how to make up the lost income they're never going to receive from social security. Therefore you can hit the clubs all you want, but if no men are there, no men are there.

This means about the only course of action you have is to ask men out.

I remember an old female college friend of mine who had a HUGE crush on this guy. She spent an ENTIRE YEAR fretting and worrying about asking him out and tried every trick in the book to get him to ask her out. Hilariously in true male form, he never picked up the hints which compelled her to ask him out.

Did she?

Never did. She CRIED MULTIPLE TIMES PER WEEK instead of just getting it over with and asking him out. Suffered infinitely more and longer than if she had just bleeping asking the guy out.

Sorry ladies, it's the 4th quarter, you're down by 14 points and you do not have the luxury of waiting for the guy to ask you out.

When myself and my other male colleagues were told women were equal back in the 90's we actually took it to heart. We believed it and incorporated into our thought process that women are equal. And guess what, whether you like it or not, today you ARE equal which means you now have equal responsibility, not least of which in our minds back then was asking us out or making your intentions known.

Today it's not even an academic debate. It's reality. Men aren't looking, they're not asking, they're out of the market. Your only option is to take matters into your own hands and pull the trigger yourself.

Sadly, or perhaps not so sadly, the only other option is to give up like most men. I will readily admit it's not just the women that have made the courting world a nightmare (though I will defend till my death they have disproportionately done so). There are members in the males ranks that are entitled to their fair share of blame. And given this you may realize what a lot of men have already and that is life is too short to waste it on a pursuit that will never materialize. You have 82 years of life expectancy. And while you may not like playing video games or fishing, there are certainly other things you can be doing aside from "clubbing" or "looking for a guy" or just plain wasting your finite energy looking/hoping for one.

You may biologically or naturally be against this. You may say, "but I want to find a man and get married and have kids."

Well again, it's an issue of reality. Reality may be that's never going to happen. So do you want to continue wasting life pursuing something that is not going to happen? Or do you want to enjoy it doing things that are within your control, never worrying about men again?

It sounds sad and depressing at first, but when you realize the reality or at least probability of the situation you can move on and enjoy a really good life without men. Millions of men have done the exact same thing, just without women. And the freedom that comes with it to enjoy your life and do your own thing with no regard or attachment to the idea of courtship is actually quite liberating and genuine happiness can be found in such a life.

Besides which, there was only one small difference between myself and the desperate 30 something woman at the bar that explained why I was happy and she was miserable-

She's still looking.

I gave up long ago.

Who do you think has the happier life?

The Economics of Courtship - Part 1 - The Two Tiered Market

I've decided that much of romance, courting, marriage, blah blah blah, seems to confuse a lot of people on both sides of the dating game. And I'm only half-jesting when I say this, but just some basic economics goes a long way in explaining the different phenomena we see in the courting/dating world. And it is because of this, I've decided to write a yet-to-be-determined number of pieces of the economics of courtship in that I've already come up with three and thought it might be worth writing about.

Today's topic is the "Two Tiered Market."

I cannot claim to have been the original observer of this phenomenon, it may have been Roissy, but it I think it was somebody perhaps a little less visceral (if anybody knows, please send the link my way), regardless, it was the observation that women in their late 20's to about their 40's believe or associate sex with marriage. Or, more specifically, that if they have sex with a man, they believe that is a representation or a proxy for his level of interest in marriage.

Now, again, when we delve into the courting world there are no databases, there are no records kept and so it largely goes based on anecdotal evidence and experience, but I would say not ALL women obviously fall for this, but some certainly do. So as a favor to them, not to mention codify this theory, permit me you this graph (I love that phrase);

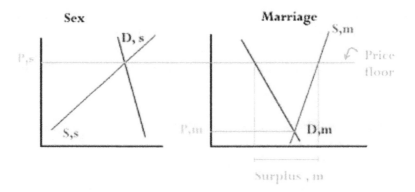

What we have here is a classical supply and demand chart of two markets; the sexual market and the marriage market.

In the first market we have the demand for sex (presumably from men) and the supply of sex (presumably women) - (the roles actually do not matter as to who is the buyer and who is the supplier, you could switch them if you wanted, as long as you are consistent amongst both markets, you will get the same results). In general, men demand sex more than women. Yes, horribly politically incorrect of me, I know. Send the Speech-Police's best sniper after me, in the mean time it does not change the fact that it is true, so my death will avail nothing and no one. In any case, demand is high and relatively inelastic.

Also, in general, women in their late 20's to 40's are more or less over that initial fear or discomfort with sex. They are more comfortable with it, they certainly aren't just going to go willy nilly offering it all over the place, but their supply curve is what I would consider normal (yes, send in the Politically Correct Assassins).

The point where the two meet is the equilibrium point, where if you were paying atttention in high school economics, is the "price" you pay for sex - denoted by P,s. In this metaphorical example it would be dinners men must take women out on, gas, psychological issues, the time dedicated to it, etc. etc.

Now notice the line, P,s, goes across to the other market, the marriage market.

The reason it does this is SOME women think that because a man has sex, that he is now interested in marriage. When in reality they are TWO SEPARATE AND DISTINCTLY DIFFERENT MARKETS. TWO SEPARATE AND DISTINCTLY DIFFERENT "GOODS AND SERVICES" AS THE ECONOMIC TERM IS.

However, in assuming sex=marriage, this brings about an economic phenomenon known as a "price floor." Meaning you cannot charge BELOW a certain price, or "below the floor." This is why P,s is carried over to the marriage market on that green line.

In the marriage market, women also supply marriage. For the ages of late 20's to 40's, women, in general, are more than willing to supply a LOT of marriage. But with this sex-induced psychological floor, they are led to believe that demand is much higher than it actually is (see line D,m to realize that men of equivalent marrying age do not demand marriage ANYWHERE NEAR as much as they demand sex, resulting in a free market price of marriage that is very low, P,m).

Now, because there is an effective price floor, this results in a price that is "too high." At that lofty price very few men are willing to demand or pay for a marriage. Whereas at that very high price, women are MORE THAN WILLING to supply it. This results in what economists call a "surplus"- denoted by the gray "Surplus, m."

A surplus of what? A surplus of women in the marriage market.

This is why I fear for (and have genuine pity for) women who mistake sex for marriage or at least perhaps more realistically, love and affection that may lead to marriage. It may not be seen too frequently in the late 20's as most men at that age are still willing to get married, but no doubt you know of some guy in his 40's who is dating some woman who "just won't commit."

Well, there you go, in economic-charty-goodness no less.

And that's, frankly that. I have nothing more to really add to it, because, well , it's economics. It's kind of cut and dry.

Chicks Dig Guns

I was dating a girl a while ago. Typical late 20 something girl who towed the liberal line and said all the right things and thought the right way. She came into my house for the first time and saw my pistol which I keep on my desk next to my computer. I was in the kitchen when she said in a shocked voice,

"Is this your gun!?"

"Yep." I said.

"Is it real?"

"Yep." I said.

"Well why do you have it?"

"In case I need to shoot the bad guys."

"Well, I'm not comfortable with guns."

"Then don't pick it up. Besides which you don't have to worry about anything. You're not one of the bad guys."

"Well I just don't understand why you would need a gun though."

"As I said before, it's in case I need to shoot the bad guys."

"Well what kind of bad guys are here? I mean have you ever had to use it?"

"Almost once, but otherwise no, thankfully."

The conversation continued on and it was typically typical of somebody who's never thought about guns and just regurgitates the line they're fed vs. somebody who likes to ensure his life and freedom is guaranteed by a little more than some piece of paper located in Washington, D.C. The typical naivete of a person who never suffered strife and was not capable of realizing the merits of owning a gun for protective purposes AND had also never studied history, arguing against somebody who had the slightest bit of common sense and was fully aware of history.

I had finished pouring myself a martini when I walked back into my office and saw her holding the gun. She was holding it in extreme fear, but obviously curiosity had gotten the better of her.
I extended my hand, signaling her to give it to me. Like carrying a bubonic-plague-infested dead mouse by its tail, she handed it over. I dropped the magazine out of the handle, doubled checked to make sure the chamber was empty, flipped it around in palm of my hand so the handle was facing her saying, "Here, knock yourself out. It can't hurt you now."

"It won't go off?"

I shook the magazine in my hand as I turned my attention back to my martini, "Not without this."

And in what had to be no more than 30 seconds, she said, "this is pretty cool! I should get a gun!"

I was rolling my eyes over as I was sipping my martini.

First let me state that chicks like guns.

I don't care who they are. What they tell you. What they say they think they say they believe they think they say.

Chicks

like

guns.

You put one in their hand, get them used to it, and even if they're a peacenik they all of the sudden are no longer irrationally afraid of this piece of metal. And not only are they no longer afraid, they want to try and shoot one. Makes for a great date, or just a good time with friends of the female persuasion, or anybody of any persuasion. I have never known anybody NOT to like firing guns.

Second, it shows you just how shallow some people's political and ideological beliefs are. It would be like going to an atheist, who after 5 minutes of arguing with you about how Christianity is stupid, all of the sudden after holding a bible for 30 seconds wants to go to church. Of course, guns are way more fun than bibles, but you get my point.

Finally, she couldn't help but look in the mirror because of how the gun looked. Do not be confused. A man with a gun is more attractive than a man with out one. Just look at any action flick movie poster and sure enough the hero is carrying a gun. Doesn't have to be a huge M-60 Rambo gun, but James Bond with his little pea-shooter is enough. Why do they put it there? Because Hollywood marketers know a guy with a gun who has to go hunt down the bad guy/s is more attractive than a peacenik who tries to go and talk to the bad guys into hopefully seeing his side of the situation and resolving the conflict peacefully with a little help from the UN and Jimmy Carter.

Therefore Cappy Capites of both the male and female persuasion, IF YOU DON'T HAVE KIDS and DON'T HAVE KIDS WALKING INTO YOUR HOUSE ON A REGULAR BASIS, may I suggest leaving a semi-automatic pistol in a very Peter Gunn sort of way hanging about your abode?

I know gun safety nuts will go into hyperdrive and say, "how dare you leave a loaded gun in your house laying around for untrained people to accidentally grab, pull back the hammer and then accidentally pull the trigger!"

Set that legitimate criticism aside. I'm making a point aside that.

A pistol, laying on your desk or on in the holster hung up on the door is akin to leaving something unique about you that women do indeed notice and will probably find attractive. For example, a nice pair of jeans hanging over the chair (ex-girlfriend told me about that one). A tie hanging on the doorknob. A martini glass on the coffee table. A motorcycle jacket over the chair. A Ty Wilson painting on the wall. A friend of mine even suggested an issue of Playboy laying about (which suggests a bit of bravado and confidence on your part, on account you are not worried about being perceived as a perve). A gun achieves the same, but because of its lefty-MSM-induced "forbidden nature" it's even more so. You are a bad boy. You have a gun. Something that can take a man's life away (or if you're good enough, multiple people).

Combine these bad boy aspects society places on guns with the natural, biological, darwinian implications of gun ownership and you are showing the girl that you take survival, protection and providership seriously. No man (or woman) is going to hurt you or your family. You are not messing around. By leaving that piece of metal on your desk you are not only a bad boy, but a bad boy that will fight. And it is this, no matter what they might say otherwise, is ultimately sexy.

Yes, slightly dangerous, but oh, wait, dangerous is also sexy too.

So to re"Cap" (har har har!)

Gun = bad boy + defender/protector + dangerous + forbidden = Sexy.

Am I wrong here? The formula missing something?

Capitalism Is NOT Why the US Will Fail

Cappy Cap readers should be really appreciative of me. Not because of the awesome economic commentary I make. Not because of the super awesome economic foresight I have. But rather because I screen out the most inane and idiotic comments that would shorten your life expectancy with high blood pressure if you did indeed read them.

Of all of them, however, there is one no more blood boiling than this one;

"CAPITALISM is what is going to destroy the US."

or

"The US will fail because of capitalism."

This is, without a doubt, the most ignorant, intellectually dishonest and patently wrong comment I receive.

Now, I'd like to go into detail in my typical arrogant prose, but since this post is very important, I am instead going to be brief and succinct in the hopes of keeping most people's attention. It really is just too important not to read. The reason why is that when the US economy DOES ultimately collapse, I want it recorded here exactly what kind of economic system was in place before knee-jerk college students just regurgitate what their aging hippie professors tell them.

First, we are no longer a "capitalist" economy. We are a mixed or socialist economy (please don't make posts on technicalities and nuances in the terms - they will be ignored). We have the same public sector spending as Norway (the left's favorite nation - and probably more thanks to BO).

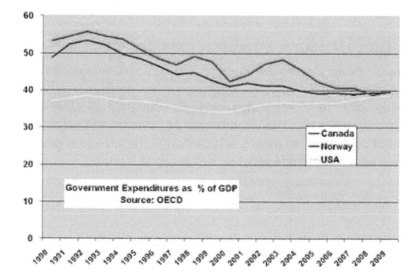

Government Expenditures as % of GDP
Source: OECD

Second, we have the world's second highest corporate tax rates at roughly 40%. An effective rate of 32.5% (I'll give a shinny nickel to a liberal who can explain the difference between the two, instead of just relying on this fact as a talking point when talking about corporate taxes).

Country	Central government corporate income tax rate [2]	Adjusted central government corporate income tax rate [3]	Sub-central government corporate income tax rate [4]	Combined corporate income tax rate [5]
Australia[a]	30.0	30.0		30.00
Austria	25.0	25.0		25.00
Belgium[b]	33.99 (33.0)	33.99		33.99
Canada	19.5	19.5	14.0	33.50
Czech Republic	21.0	21.0		21.00
Denmark	25.0	25.0		25.00
Finland	26.0	26.0		26.00
France[c]	34.43	34.43		34.43
Germany[d]	15.825 (15.0)	15.825	14.35	30.18
Greece	25.0	25.0		25.00
Hungary[e]	20.0 (16.0)	20.0		20.00
Iceland	15.0	15.0		15.00
Ireland	12.5	12.5		12.50
Italy[f]	27.5	27.5		27.50
Japan	30.0	27.98	11.56	39.54
Korea	25.0	25.0	2.5	27.50
Luxembourg	22.88 (22.0)	22.88	7.5	30.38
Mexico	28.0	28.0		28.00
Netherlands[j]	25.5	25.5		25.50
New Zealand[a]	30.0	30.0		30.00
Norway	28.0	28.0		28.00
Poland[o]	19.0	19.0		19.00
Portugal	25.0	25.0	1.5	26.50
Slovak Republic	19.0	19.0		19.00
Spain	30.0	30.0		30.00
Sweden	28.0	28.0		28.00
Switzerland[h]	8.5	6.70	14.47	21.17
Turkey	20.0	20.0		20.00
United Kingdom[a]	28.0	28.0		28.00
United States[i]	35.0	32.7	6.54	39.25

You throw in dividend taxes and you're roughly at a 50% overall tax rate.

Third, understand the US economy and people's standards of living were growing fastest when tax rates (as measured by government spending as a percent of GDP) were the lowest. Standards of living have gone down as the US economy has become socialist;

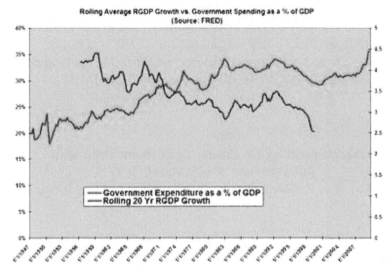

*(*I get a lot of confusion on this chart. The rolling 20 year includes 20 years worth of data. The data point I place in the middle, which is why it seems there is 10 years of data missing on the start and end of the blue line)*

Fourth, understand the majority of government spending is NOT for governance, but rather income transfers, which is the epitome and definition of socialism.

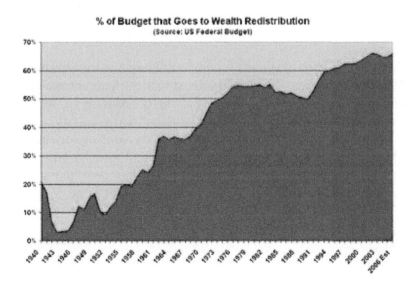

Fifth, understand that it is these income transfers and entitlements into the future that are the primary reasons for our current and future projected deficits and is the primary reason we are facing bankruptcy as a nation. These are DISTINCTLY socialist policies. NOT CAPITALIST.

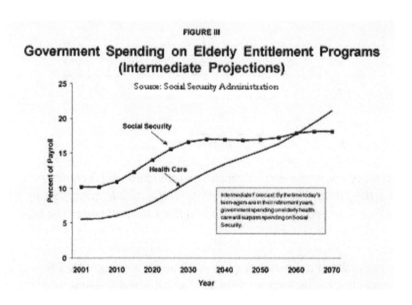

FIGURE III

Government Spending on Elderly Entitlement Programs (Intermediate Projections)

Now there are more statistics, but the above is enough. I cannot make it any clearer and I don't have to because it's not a matter of opinion. It's a fact. It is SOCIALISM that is destroying the United States. NOT capitalism.

Therefore, please, I beg of you idiots who just regurgitate the above inane comment, since you have the right to vote, stop being ignorant and start getting educated on economics. This isn't a "choice." This isn't a "fun little game we're playing." And this isn't some "crusade" where you try to impress the hippie grunge chick at the coffee bar by extolling socialist tripe as you try to pass it on as "virtues." You future is at stake. Your current state of unemployment is a direct result of your own ignorance. And if you'd want any kind of future for your children, let alone yourselves, knock it off with the childish "ranting" and "protesting" and grow up. The country depends on it.

Daddy, Where Do Jobs Come From?

A REPOST OF A CLASSIC IN THAT UNEMPLOYMENT IS STILL AROUND 10% AND I'M GUESSING SOME OF YOU MIGHT LIKE JOBS ABOUT NOW.

Jobs, it seems is becoming a very important issue as we seemed to have shed 5 million of them recently and are on the precipice of the worst recession since 1929. But fear not, for our president elect has a plan and it's quite simple;

"More jobs."

Yes, that's about it, we'll just "create" more jobs.

Now 3rd grade logic would tell you something is wrong. You can't put your finger on it. Maybe you can't full explain it. But you have this twingling sensation in the back of your head that you know something just ain't right. That it ain't as simple as;

"Just creating more jobs."

It's the same kind of twingling sensation you got back in school when you said, "Well why don't we just print off more money."

You intuitively knew something had to be wrong with that solution, but you perhaps couldn't explain why. And thus it's the same thing with Barack's plan to create new jobs.

His idea for this massive infrastructure (and Keynesian) investment gives us all the same twingling sensation in the back of our heads. Why, if it was that simple, to just build roads, bridges and splurge more on education, what were we getting all worried about in the first place? Why are the stock markets so low? Why don't we create jobs right now today? And so, since we all intuitively know it can't be that simple, let me explain why. Let me explain to you where jobs come from.

Jobs come from one thing; demand.

Demand for goods and services currently existing or yet to exist. For example I demand food, a good that already exists. I also demand a hovercar and a clone of Jennifer Anitson, a good and service that have yet to exist. Regardless, if the product or service exists or can be created, and there is demand for it, then there is the potential for jobs to be created.

But demand must be met with supply and here is where the actual jobs are created. In order to supply these goods and services an entrepreneur or a company must hire people to help provide those goods and services. This includes everybody from the head of the company managing the firm to the suppliers, vendors, laborers, admins, marketers, accountants and anybody else required to bring these services to reality. However, there is a key element to make this all happen and that is profit.

Oh yes, that "evil" profit.

For you see, no entrepreneur, nor company, nor corporation is even going to bother going through the trouble of setting up the venture in the first place unless they are actually paid for it. And before you start berating these "evil capitalists" to have the temerity to demand recompense so that they may earn a living, you might want to look at yourselves in the mirror because no laborer (let alone you) is going to work unless they are compensated too. So just accept the fact we're all financial whores, not out of evil or greed, but because it's necessary for us to live and survive.

Regardless, immediately we see a problem with, not so much Obama's infrastructure plan, but his fiscal policy in that he is going to raise taxes on not only the rich who employ the majority of people, but also corporations. Envy them and hate them all you want, increasing taxes on them will lower the incentive for them to invest, let alone start a new venture in the first place. And with the rapidly integrating global economy, if they really do have a great idea, why would they set up shop here in the first place? Ireland has a 12.5% corporate tax rate. Dubai has 0%. Russia has a flat tax. And "communist" China has a 20% corporate tax rate.
The good ol' US o' A has a 39% corporate tax.

So even though we haven't addressed Obama's specific infrastructure jobs creation plan, it's quite possible other parts of his fiscal policy will impair it or destroy more jobs than it creates, simply because it destroys the incentive to create jobs in the first place; profit.

As for the specific plan itself, it's not an issue of whether it will create jobs as much as it is a question at what cost.

Understand that to finance this infrastructure plan Obama has two choices; taxation or borrowing. And both options are going to cost jobs as well as efficiency.

In taxing people (no matter how "rich" they are) that takes money that would have been invested or spent anyway which would have created jobs as well. So if you tax the "rich jewelry dealer" an extra $50,000 so 2 employees in Obama's Civilian Conservation Corps can pour concrete for a bridge, that's all fine and dandy except for the fact the jewelry dealer now had to lay off his assistant and his admin to compensate for the cut. Congratulations, you created a big fat zero net new jobs.

Borrowing is no better in that the money borrowed by the government to finance the infrastructure jobs creation plan could have been borrowed by a company, an entrepreneur or even an individual to be used to create a new company, expand a factory or just plain spent, all of which would have created jobs too. Congratulations. You not only borrowed money and destroyed as many jobs as you created, but you've managed to increase interest rates as well! Thanks!

But the real cost is this, and is often the forgotten about or never-thought about aspect of economics, and that is efficiency. Specifically, as it relates to production.

If the money was left in the hands of the people, the people could then spend or invest that money as they saw fit and to their best benefit. Allowing people to make their own decisions as to how to expend their resources is the best way to make sure the goods and services produced in the economy are those that most benefit the people and increase standards of living the most. Of course, people make mistakes. The sickening, gluttonous binge of using one's home equity as an ATM machine which has brought upon this financial crisis in the first place is a perfect example where the people will make mistakes. However, for all their flaws, recessions and depressions, free markets, ie- the people have historically been proven to be the best determinants of what to be produced.

Governments have not. And herein lies the flaw in Obama's advisor's plan; taking massive amounts of resources either through taxation or borrowing, takes money out of the hands of individuals and puts it in the hands of government. People now no longer get to decide what to spend their now dwindling resources on, and are instead forced to spend it on roads, infrastructure, and schools they may not need.

Now people may rightfully point out that things like roads, bridges, infrastructure, etc., are hardly foolish investments, and they're right. But again the question is at what cost? Who would be better judges of how to spend this money and who would do more to help the economy out of recession;

A handful of bureaucrats and former Fannie Mae and Freddie Mac advisors now consulting a no-real-world-experience-president-elect determining what the best use of your money is?

Or

300 million Americans who are intricately familiar with their own personal financial situation and the problems/opportunities they face?

This is where the real costs come in that what determines our standards of living is whether we use our resources efficiently to produce the goods and services we NEED. We just promised $700 billion (more like $2 trillion) to bailout those same Harvard ef-ups who ran Wall Street and the government into the ground. Could the people not have used a $700 billion tax cut? Would that not have solved our little economic growth problem? No, we're stupid, we don't know what we're talking about, now shut up and give us the money.

Obama's infrastructure plan is no different (although, I will admit spending the money on bridges and roads is infinitely wiser than bailing out Ivy League deadbeats). We don't know what's best for us. You don't need that money. Give it to us and we'll build shinny new roads and bridges. Just what you wanted. No, not that new icky gross Pontiac Solstice that would ACTUALLY HELP OUT DETROIT WITHOUT A TAXPAYER BAILOUT. No Captain, that's not what you want. You want an addition to the elementary school named after Barack Obama where a newly hired teacher will brainwash...errr....I mean "educate" the children about the evils of capitalism...errr...I mean "global warming." That's what you want.

It is this that is the true cost to this Keynesian nightmare. The loss of productivity and efficiency causing American's standards of living to go down. Not because of a loss of jobs (for I'm optimistically assuming this infrastructure plan will ONLY destroy one job for each one it "creates") but because the stuff we're producing with it is not what the American people optimally want.

And finally, permit me a third point.

I know building bridges, though not optimal, is not a waste of money.

I know roads, albeit not optimal, are not a waste of money.

But notice how education was thrown in there?

Please. Please, just stop with the "we don't spend enough on education."

It's a sickening lie and you're not fooling anyone. By every **measure**, **every stretch** of the imagination we **spend WAY TOO MUCH on education** and the fact education is part of Obama's jobs creation plan shows me just how inefficient this plan will be. Bridges, fine. Roads, fine. But more money for education would be on par with bailing out the losers of Wall Street and sub prime deadbeats.

Alas, appetizing as new roads and bridges are, it was the inclusion of education, above all else, that made me supremely confident the stork will not be bringing any new jobs to Obama with his little infrastructure plan.

Minimalist Art - Art Only a Mother Could Love

It was above 60 degrees today and since it's November and we're in Minnesota that means you have to take a motorcycle ride. So off Natasha and I went on my motorcycle and as I usually do, I took a spin around the Lake of the Isles area where the trust fund babies of Minnesota live (and where **subsequently the trust fund is running ou**t).

However, as we were driving around, we came up on a "sculpture" that was put up this earlier this summer on this pristine piece of real estate in this Lake of the Isles area. I've been meaning to take a picture of this "sculpture" for quite some time, but I keep forgetting to bring a camera. I finally remembered this particular trip and managed to take a picture of this beautiful "sculpture." Remember this is on PRIME REAL ESTATE IN THE ENTIRE STATE OF MINNESOTA.

I've mentioned **minimalistic "art" before**, but the long and short of it is this - it's like a crappy drawing of a 3 year old kid. No matter how bad, the loving mother will still put it up on the fridge because she is proud of her kid. However, sometimes the 3 year old never grows up and never leaves the house. And mom isn't some regular mom, she and the father are filthy stinking rich. And instead of putting up the crappo drawing of the three year old on their fridge INSIDE THE HOUSE, they put their now 38 year old's crappo sculpture in their front yard forcing everybody to see it.

Therefore I decided to do some "art" myself to see if I could get a super rich family on Lake of the Isles to perhaps endorse me (or at least put it in front of their yard).

This I call "The Death of the Burning Mouse." You can see I am a super awesome artistic genius. The reason why you can tell this is because you cannot see the dead mouse in this picture whereas I can.

This is called "Bottle Opener in Milan Summer Nights" It is a very deep and meaningful painting with many layers and emotion. It's one of those paintings you would probably have to pay to see in the Walker Art Museum and end up looking at for 50 minutes to really get to appreciate all the different angles. But again, you are not a super art genius like me, so at most you will only see 3% of all the aspects. But still, it should move your soul and make you aspire to at least try to become a super awesome art genius like me.

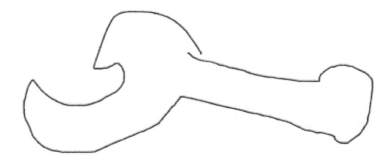

I call this "The Frog of Socialist Caring" Super art geniuses like me can obviously tell he is a frog, but to close-minded evil capitalists I labeled it with a "ribbit" and a fly so you non-artistic rubes could tell what it is. I really didn't want to do this because I don't like doing "commercial art." I mean, it isn't all about money. But every once in a while I have to lower my standards and make something that will sell so I can put food on the table (even though my trust fund does that for me anyway and I live in my parent's basement).

In any case, if anybody in the Lake of the Isles area or Kenwood area or even the lesser Linden Hills area would like to purchase these fine masterpieces and display them in your front yard, let me know. You may also donate to me by clicking on the girl on the top right of the page to feed the starving artist.

Cripes.

How the Female "Romantic Wish List" for Men Corrupts the Functionality of HR

Originally I had in mind doing a post on "The Vanishing 24 Year Old HR Ditz." The reason why was that it has been 7 years now since I've been interviewed by a young female in her twenties, obviously oblivious to my profession, the job I was interviewing for, let alone the industry she worked in. I termed them "HR Ditzes" because they were exactly that. 20 something ditzes asking me inane, pointless questions like

"So, um, like, uh, what's your favorite color and why?" (not joking)

"And like have you ever been in a situation where you disagreed with your boss and how did you resolve it?"

"And so, like what is your biggest weakness?"

"So, like uh you do like Dogs or cats?" (not joking either)

I could never understand how a company could ever attract any talented labor with these dolts doing the initial screening for them and why you never interviewed with the hiring manager directly. Well seven years and not one 20 something HR ditz later I finally got my answer from a friend of mine who unbeknownst to me at the time was an HR manager.

Short answer - "Oh, yeah, sorry about that. We found out that didn't work so they're phasing those generalists out."

Really? You mean having young, idiotic, inexperienced morons who don't know a damn thing about the company or the job being your front line of defense for interviewing because the hiring managers are too damn lazy to do it themselves didn't work out so well? NO! Well, good thing it only took 2 decades to phase them out. Otherwise there might have been some real costs to that!

Regardless, what was infinitely more interesting and important was what I learned about how HR has changed since. Namely "check lists."

Since the elimination of the HR ditz, HR departments are now employing different and automated screening tactics. For example the much-hated "Taleo" or "Brass Ring" application forms where you regurgitate your resume (that you just uploaded) into little fields so a computer can scan for "keywords" that show you're a qualified candidate. Or the use of not only criminal background checks and drugs tests, but now credit checks. Or requiring a cover letter and analyzing the writing quality.

It was here I started to inquire if she ever thought about the unintended consequences of using such tactics?

For example smart, or at least, efficient people know they can apply for 10 times the amount of jobs where it only requires attaching your resume in the time it takes you to fill out a Taleo form. If you require they fill out a Brass Ring application, you may get less efficient or smart applicants. Same thing goes for the cover letter, that alone it 3 more applications, and you just lost an (admittedly) potentially smart applicant. Background checks, all well and fine. But you're going to do a *credit check* on me? You're going to pull my personal finances? Uh, not until I see your credit report first pal.

Her response?

"Well, we have 9% unemployment and we have literally hundreds of applicants each job. We have our pick of the litter and we have to filter and screen them out somehow."

And then I started to see what was happening. Not consciously, but it definitely WAS happening and there was a relation. And I only ask myself why I hadn't seen it before.

In short HR is coming up with a longer and longer check list as there are more and more applicants. This isn't necessarily a bad thing in that how does one filter out a larger and larger applicant pool. But HR is still coming up with a longer and more detailed check list.

(Does this sound familiar yet?)

There are so many applicants and jobs are so highly sought after, HR has their pick of the litter.

(Anybody going to be able to finish my line of thought here?)

I'll give you the one last hint here that might link it together - HR is still dominated by women.

And now you are having the epiphany I had the other night.

The employment check list is eerily similar to the lengthy and long check list women have of men when it comes to courtship. And not only is it similar, it's also made and created by women.

It is here while we were continuing our conversation I started to realize the parallels as well as some of the pitfalls to this;

One the impossibility factor. I didn't believe it when I was younger because frankly I couldn't believe women would have such lengthy and detailed (and some times) mutually exclusive lists. Oh, sure I knew they had STANDARDS, but I did not believe women would refuse to date a guy because he "was too short" or "wore ugly clothes" or "had a bad hair cut" or "didn't have blue eyes" or "made less than $XX,XXX." Of course come to find out in my aged 30's women actually DID have these impossible lists. I now wonder if the lists they create for potential applicants (male or female) are now just as impossible.

"You want a leader who thinks outside the box and will turn your company around, but you're only going to hire yes men who have impossibly perfect resumes, perfect credit scores and are yet docile enough to spend 2 hours filling out a Taleo application form?"

It's no different than,

"I want an alpha male, who's still sensitive and will write poetry who drives a Harley, but won't have sex until we're married, but still rocks in bed, but only once a year, who works out and makes $250,000 per year, but will do chores and housekeeping and is an Orthodox Jewish, Catholic, Muslim Agnostic."

Two was the eerily similar market to men in their teens and twenties versus today's labor market. Back in your teens and twenties women held ALL the power. Men had no clue what the rules were, were told the rules were something completely different than reality and were so desperate they'd do anything and settle for any price. Job seekers today are no different. They're desperate for a job and will do anything (including lie on their resume to make them seem perfect). I couldn't help but notice the unintentional air of arrogance or power in her voice where she said, "we have our pick of the litter." You did in your 20's and you do now today.

Three, the lead up to an inevitable collapse in the market. Understand for anybody to be getting through this impossible HR defense shield you either have to;

1. lie or

2. be so abnormal and so flawless you'd be dysfunctional

It's again why men who lied in their teens and twenties did well and honest schmoes like us kind of flailed along. But even more analogous to the courtship list vs. the HR check list is the beta male or "beta employee." The employee that magically meets the impossible checklist or the magical boyfriend who magically meets the romantic checklist.

Of course, if women were to get that "ideal" boyfriend who would write poetry, who would hyphenate his name and open doors and do whatever she wanted, what did she end up doing anyway?

That's right, dumping his weak beta butt for some motorcycle driving alpha bad boy with a criminal background. But in the employment world it's slightly different. Instead of getting dumped, they get laid off after however many years of loyal service.

However, there is another cost to hiring the obedient, behaving beta employees and this is the true economic cost - it brings about a Black Swan Event. Namely the collapse of the company.

Talk about diversity all you want, if you employ nothing but conformists and yes men, no tolls are going to be sounded and no alarms are going to rung when there are real problems (or opportunities). Because the selection and filtering method really does screen out any genuine "outside of the box" thinkers, you have nothing but highly functional automotons and no real leaders or critical analysts. Couple that with a desperate labor market and your employees are NOT going to rock the boat (for better or worse). This leaves the employer in a horribly risky situation because unless people in executive management are intimately in-tune with every aspect of the company, the company can slowly be piloted towards disaster because nobody dares to speak of the iceberg ahead or problems within their division.

Laugh as you might and say my speaking of Black Swans is all poppycock, may I point out the Black Swan events of GM going belly up? The entire banking industry going belly up? The US retirement system about to go belly up? The US government finances going belly up? Many people tried to sound the alarms for this, but they WEREN'T the well behaved beta employees just trying to hold onto a job. It was the likes of Roubini, Shiller, Schiff and others (and how many of them I wonder would pass the HR created check list let alone had women pining for them in their youth?)

In the end, like courting, the participants in the labor market will become disincentived and leave. You already see this with a collapsing labor force participation rate, people more willing to take and stay on unemployment, higher turnover and shorter average stays on a job, or people just refusing to have kids they can't afford and get by on a lower paying job and not jump the hoops.

The result? Well, as I **highlighted before in the "courtship market" you will have a decrease in marriage or courtship**. Economically the impossible HR check list translates into less employment, CERTAINLY less innovation, but overall less economic growth and lower standards of living. Which once again proves there's only one thing do to.

Enjoy the decline, people. Enjoy that bleeping decline.

She Did NOT Get "Hit By a Truck"

I was accidentally eavesdropping on a cell phone conversation at a cigar lounge I was at recently. It was a young kid (20 something man) talking to either a female friend or his mother (I could not tell which). And far as I could tell he was trying to figure out why a girl who had agreed to go out with him at the last minute the night before canceled. I could not hear what the other person was saying, but the conversation went something like;

Boy - "Well she said she wanted to go out, but when I called her, she didn't pick up. I tried texting, but she didn't respond either."

Person on other line - "Well maybe she was sick"

Boy - "Well yeah, but if she was sick the least should could do would be to text me back saying so."

Person on the other line - "Well there could have been an emergency of some kind. Maybe she's just really busy and hasn't been able to get back to you."

Boy - "How busy can you be to not call somebody for 4 seconds to tell them you're not able to go out?"

The conversation went on, but I needed not eavesdrop anymore because I could already finish the conversation myself. Regardless, it showed me there is a vital and necessary lesson needed to be passed on to the younger Cappy Capites of the male persuasion about the fairer sex, so please take out your note books and pencils and take note.

1. She was not "sick" or "in the emergency room" or "really busy." She just plain didn't want to go out with you.

Understand that women in their 20's and late teens will say yes to avoid the hardship of telling you no. Of course when it comes time to actually show up for the date, then they will bail and just not return any calls that could lead towards a cementing of a time or a place you pick them up. This is why the Rule of 505025 exists (look it up, I won't link to it).

2. How did I know the person on the other line was a girl? Because only women will go to great lengths to rationalize what is empirically and obviously a rejection. They will always try to make you feel better, even though deep down inside they know you just got stood up. Ergo the "well, maybe she got sick." Or " Well, maybe she's just really busy." Or, "Well, maybe she just forgot. *You know, people with their busy schedules and all.*"

Honest to truth when I was a youth in college and had a similar such conversation with my mother she said in ALL SERIOUSNESS (no sarcasm intended) "Well, maybe she got hit by a truck and is in the hospital. *You never know!*"

Actually, you do, because I'm telling you now.

In every case, no matter what the excuse, the rationalization, explanation or theory, in the end the girl just plain didn't want to go out with you.

Now you have a choice. You can waste your time worrying about it, worse still you can somehow think it reflects upon you personally, or you can follow the Ole Captain's simple rule;

"The **Why** Doesn't Matter, All that Matters is What **IS**."

In short, what matters is the reality of the situation - she didn't show up.

You can rack your brain and burn out a 100 terraflop supercomputer trying to figure out the reason and rationalization "why she didn't show up," but in the end all the matters is you wasted your Friday night thinking you had a date. Not to mention calories of energy trying to figure out why she didn't show up.

And to come up with and opine about outlandishly pathetic excuses for her standing you up is foolish and frankly, self-DISrespecting.

Many a man has wasted untold amounts of time, psychological energy and fret/worrying about the "why she didn't show up" when the "why she didn't show up" doesn't matter (and should be self-evident). All that matters is what IS. And that "is" "is that she didn't show up."

The poor guy got stood up and instead of wasting time worrying about it he should instead just simply realize that he got stood up and move on. Perhaps next time being sure to have a back up plan and CERTAINLY NOT put any hope or faith in the fact he "might" have date the next time a girl agrees to go out.

Therefore men (of the younger Cappy Cappite persuasion), save yourself a LOT of stress and learn from the old man's experiences. Realize she didn't not get hit by a truck. She didn't forget to call. Her cell phone was not "not charged." And she was not abducted by aliens. Please have some self-respect, accept the fact she flaked, move on and hold your head higher with a little bit more dignity and simply remember that the next time a girl says "yes" to a date to have a back up plan, if not, fully plan on doing something else that night.

This has a been a public service announcement to the 20 Something Male

Capposphere.

"300 is NOT a Date Movie"

Many years ago the Captain was set up by a listener of his radio show with this listener's cousin. Our first of only two dates was a very innocent and kind one on my part because I was simply that. Innocent and nice. I asked her if I could take her out for sushi during lunch.

Fast forward to the present and while enjoying a cigar over a bonfire with some friends, the conversation turns to appropriate behaviors in dating. A friend of mine says, "Yeah, don't you remember that 300 is NOT a date movie?"

I looked at him quizzically because I remembered hearing that before.

Where did I hear that before?

So I asked, "Where did I hear that before?"

He replied, "Don't you remember? The cousin of the girl that sent you that e-mail listing all the things you did wrong on the date?"

I said, "Yeah, but I recall getting lectured for having an older car. Not taking her to 300. You don't still have the e-mail, do you?"

And for the luck of all my readers, my good friend still DID have the e-mail and forwarded it to me so that I may share it with all of you.

Understand this is a treasure trove of insight into the psychology poor men have to deal with. It is empirical evidence of everything you see in the dating world and the socio-psychological observations made in the mano-sphere such as the Rationlization Hamster, entitlement princesses and delusional expectations of themselves and others. It's been about 4, maybe 5 years since I've read this, but my gosh, re-reading it again only provides vindication, if not great insight and wisdom to any poor schlep still having to deal with this insanity. Please enjoy;

First, I want to tell you I have this thing about dating. I can predict pretty much anything that a guy is going to do. I guessed within 2 hours of when you'd call Terri. Guys are predictable. Not just you. So to have an advantage you need to be different. I think a lot of guys got bad advise from married guys who have no clue what it is like to date in the 30's or from a girl that really doesn't want you to find someone so they can use you as their back up if they can't find anyone else.

This being said Terri has not told me all that much information. I just pick up on a lot more than people usually say. So do not judge her for what she may have said because I am just picking out the things that can help you. Plus, I have been prompting her for details.

I really hate to see people single. When life is so much more enjoyable with the right person. If my thoughts are unfinished or grammar is incorrect you need to bare with me because I am having contractions that are a little distracting. I am sure it is not the real labor as this baby seems to not want to come out:)

-You date like you are 20. Dating in your 30's changes/matures. You can take a 20 year old to Applebee's and it is fine but a 30 year old has had time to eat at nicer restaurants and expects more. I am not saying your choice of a restaurant was cheap just showing an example of what is acceptable. Also, the type of person you date expects different things. A waitress who still lives at home probably is fine with a movie for the first date. A woman that has a career, her own house and is indepedant expects more because they give themselves more and will give you more. I am not just talking money things I am talking taking time to think of good things to do. Taking time to do nice things.
- Phone conversations are a great way to get to know people. You should only call when you have time to talk. And after a few dates call just to talk.
-Group dates are for once you have established you do indeed know you like each other and will continue to date.
-After a first date if you want to ask the girl out again you need to call within 24 hours, best if it within 12 hours the sooner the better in most cases. No likes to wait around and figure out if you like them or not.
-Feedback at the end of the date is good. Like I had fun I'd like to do this again.
-Movie dates are for once you are dating (like a month). You can not get to know someone over a movie. Plus 300 is not a date movie!
-First and second dates should be spent getting to know the person so you

will know if it is a waste of time for a 3rd date. Personal things should be talked about. What personal things do you know about Terri after a date and couple phone conversations? In 30's if marriage is the goal by date 3 deal breakers should be brought up. Like if there is something you are not ever willing to compromise on. Kids, religion etc. Which I think most things you should be willing to compromise on. Since you really can not predict your feelings in 10 years or how you will feel once you are madly in love with this new person.

-Don't imply you have your whole life planned out already. A woman wants to feel like she can be part of the planning if you were to be together. Not just fit into your plan.

-I am not sure how you are on this one or not but here's some advise if case. Sleep is something that can be put aside to get to know a girl. Girls love when a guy is willing to stay up getting to know them (over the phone or in person). This is an investment in your future happiness. It should be taken seriously.

-Always offer to pick the girl up at her house/work. Let her be the one that decides that you should meet at the place instead of drive together.

-Make a lady feel like a lady. I don't know any woman who are over 30 and single that don't want to be treated like lady. Open doors, pick them up, walk them to their doors, etc. Like the guys in the romantic movies. Women over 30 who are single have had a lot of time to think about "how" they want a man to treat them.

-My husband told me about your cheap car. I think it is great but definitely not for dates.

-Practical and cheap are not for dates. They can be brought into a relationship later once you are actually dating but not for dates.

-The date you have lined up for Thursday sounds bad for a couple reason. It's like well I am already going to be there so just meet me there. There is no room for the date to go long if you have a commitment right after dinner. It sounds like you are just fitting her into your schedule not opening your schedule for her. Woman do not want to feel like you are fitting them it. I am going to suggest you rethink the date and plan something else. Make it special. With no time limits. You only get a couple chances before a woman makes up her mind and you need to use those dates to your benefit. Make her feel like she is a priority.

-Dating is work. It does not come naturally to most people. You need to put time and effort into it since a good relationship could last you a life time. And bring you more happiness than everything else on this earth.

When You Abandon Fundamental Value

Retirement programs.

There's a novel concept for you. 60 years ago there was no such thing as a 401k, 403, IRA or SIMPLE plan. People retired by selling the family farm, enough heads of cattle or the family business. Less fortunate people had to rely on their children for retirement and some unfortunate souls, believe it or not, had to work till death.

But retirement programs are funny things and they have funny consequences. Especially when ALL of the retirement programs designate financial securities (read stocks) as the only medium by which you can save for retirement.

Let me repeat that again;

RETIREMENT PROGRAMS ARE FUNNY THINGS AND HAVE FUNNY CONSEQUENCES ESPECIALLY WHEN ALL OF THE RETIREMENT PROGRAMS DESIGNATE FINANCIAL SECURITIES AS THE ONLY MEDIUM BY WHICH YOU CAN SAVE FOR RETIREMENT!

Translated into English, this means with the advent of 401ks, 403bs IRA's, etc., this has channeled all retirement money into the stock market with little regard as to whether or not this would artificially inflate stock prices, thereby causing a bubble.

ie-are the cash flows below;

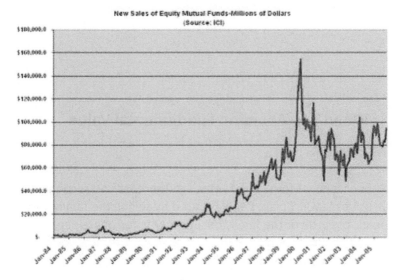

New Sales of Equity Mutual Funds-Millions of Dollars
(Source: ICI)

contributing to a long term bubble?

Of course history has told us that any time you abandon fundamental value as the only reason to invest in something, bubbles always occur.

For example, the famous Holland Tulip Bulb Bubble shows you what happens when you no longer value a tulip bulb for the fundamental value that it will bloom and look pretty, but rather value it based on the idea that you can sell it for more than what you paid for it because the person buying it from you doesn't care what they pay for it, because they know they can turn around and sell it to another person because they don't care what they pay for it because they know they can...etc, etc..

Or Beanie Babies. Paying $600 for something that is nothing more than cloth and beads. Doesn't clean the house. Doesn't pay a dividend. Just sits there. Once again, you have abandoned its fundamental value and paid $600 for (as far as I've been able to figure it) something to feed a middle-aged woman's midlife crisis.

Alas, today's modern stock markets I contest are no different For people no longer invest in stocks for their potential cash flows, profits and dividends, but rather invest in stocks as a vehicle for retirement. And in a very zombie-like fashion I might add.

Every month, every paycheck, without even thinking, there they are, millions of them, zombie Americans doing what their HR overlords and financial advisors told them to do;

HR Director - "You WILL invest in a 401k"

In unison - "We will invest in a 401k"

Government - "You WILL invest in an IRA!"

In unison - "We will invest in an IRA."

With little or no regard as to whether the mutual funds (and underlying stocks) are actually worth the value.

Now couple this dramatic change in investment behavior with several factors;

1. The entire Baby Boomer generation is the first generation en masse to use the financial markets as their mainstay for retirement

2. The Baby Boomers are a plurality of the population

3. And are in their prime income earning years

Is it any shock the average S&P 500 P/E ratio has been consistently trading above its 80 year average of 15?

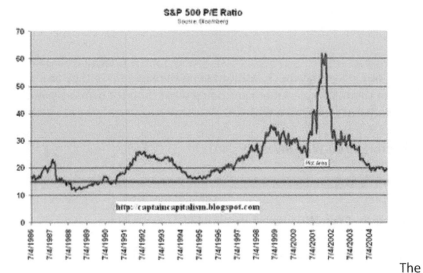

S&P 500 P/E Ratio
Source: Bloomberg

The question is what will happen when the Baby Boomers start to retire? And instead of contributing every month to their 401k's like sheople, *they withdraw*?

Of course, there are arguments that a rise in the average P/E is legitimate and sustainable. One could argue that this is a behavioral change that is permanent. That the Gen Xer's are contributing nicely and will pick up any slack. One could also make the argument that with the advent of the internet and online trading that prices to trade have fallen, allowing millions of Americans to flood the market with billions of dollars that would not have been invested otherwise.

Good arguments, and I agree.

But I wanted to check out to see how much of the past stock market performance was due to the market just being flooded with new money and not necessarily an increase in the profitability of companies.

So the first thing I did was compare the S&P 500 against new mutual funds sales (going back to 1984 which is as far back as ICI has the data), resulting in the chart below.

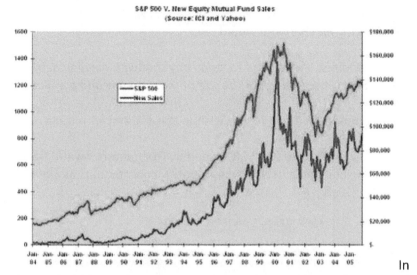

S&P 500 V. New Equity Mutual Fund Sales
(Source: ICI and Yahoo)

In obvious bubbles and crashes you can see the correlation, however, the S&P, as well as monthly contributions to mutual funds are in nominal dollars. Inflation alone would increase the correlation, so I adjusted the figures (and the S&P 500) for inflation (this causes for some unconventional measures, but they are meritous just the same).

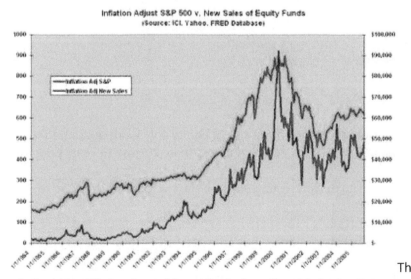

Inflation Adjust S&P 500 v. New Sales of Equity Funds
(Source: ICI Yahoo. FRED Database)

The relationship still stands, and is particularly noticeable in the Dotcom Mania/Bust days. But girls aren't impressed by economists who only adjust for inflation. Economically savvy and drop-dead gorgeous girls that

272

have IQ's of 490 and double as super models can see the obvious shortcomings of this chart and would say,

"Hey, Mr. Economist. If you want to stand any shot with me, you better darn well adjust those figures for the size of the economy and population!"

And we accommodate them, for we wish to stand a shot with them.

So then you have this, the S&P 500 divided by GDP (another weird figure, but interesting enough in itself) versus monthly contributions as a percent of GDP

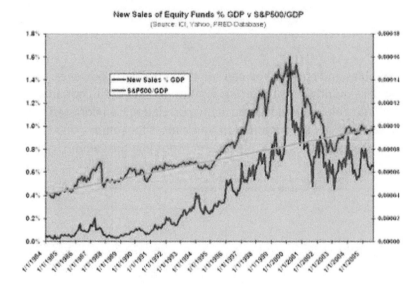

New Sales of Equity Funds % GDP v S&P500/GDP
(Source: ICI, Yahoo, FRED Database)

(notice in Dotcom Mania, new sales of equity only funds accounted for more than 1% of GDP, as opposed to less than .2% just 15 years prior).

This is where it gets interesting because the two data series alone tell us many things;

1. Our broadest stock market index divided by GDP provides an interesting ratio, showing that it has consistently been increasing as denoted by the green line. *ie-We apply more value to stocks, regardless of the amount of wealth our economy is producing.*

2. Monthly new sales of equity only funds are amazing in themselves.

Going from literally less than 1/10th of 1% of our GDP as late as 1992, monthly contributions have skyrocketed to .6% of GDP in all of 13 years! Furthermore, the insanity of Dotcom Mania had convinced people to forefeit money on the order of **1% of GDP** a month into equity only funds for a solid year (**1.6% in one month!**).

3. Of course this could be because people had higher profit expectations of companies, and thus flooded the market with money, driving up prices, but it had nothing to do with the actual increase in our ability to produce wealth (from which profits derive). Even after the crash, we're still on an upward trend contributing a higher percentage of our wealth into the stock market, thereby increasing the value of the stock market, regardless of our wealth producing abilities.

However, there are more pertinent adjustments to be made.

In trying to find the appropriate base by which to adjust for inflation and economic growth, I was predisposed to use GDP as GDP is typically the base you adjust for. But after contemplation what mutual fund flows and indices should really be compared against is corporate profits as corporate profits are what ultimately drive the value of a stock.

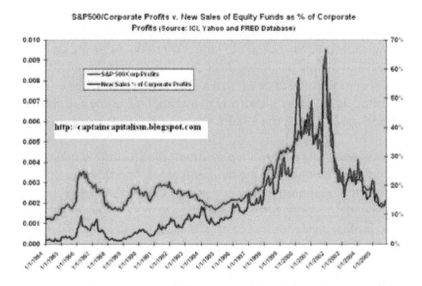

Here, a similar correlation again, but this focuses on the heart of the matter; corporate profits. The only one true thing that should dictate stock prices.

Note the behavior of the S&P 500 relative to corporate profits. The stock market bubbles of 1987 and 1999 are obvious. Also note the highly correlated behavior of the monthly new sales of equity only funds as a percent of corporate earnings.

Ideally this should be a constant ratio, meaning people apply the same amount of market value to corporate earnings, thus, if corporate earnings go up, demand for that stock would go up by a corresponding amount, thus keeping the ratio constant (ie-if corporate profits go up 5%, demand for stocks would go up by 5%). Of course this ratio is not going to be constant because people's expectations of future profitability is changing and people's perception of value changes as well.

This is VERY obvious in the run up to Dotcom Mania. Traditionally sales in new equity funds would amount to no more than a percent or two of corporate profits. However, when people started having irrational expectations of corporate profits, this skyrocketed monthly sales to almost **70% of corporate profits**. Arguably the clearest sign there was a bubble.

Regardless of temporary and irrational fluctuations in people's perception of value and expectations, look at the long term trend. After the stock market crash and people becoming disenchanted with stocks, new sales of equity only funds dropped down to a more "sane" 20%. While a significant drop, it still is significantly higher than the 2 or 3% and shows a general trend upward since the 1980's.

This suggests something a bit more permanent than just the random and chaotic whims and emotions of the market is afoot. And this something is disconnecting the relationship between what we pay in stock price and their corresponding profits, further suggesting to me we have once again abandoned profits, dividends and cash flow as reason to invest in stocks and are purchasing them for ulterior reasons. Given the high correlation between the increase in the S&P500 relative to corporate profits and new sales of mutual funds as a percent of corporate profits (.89) it suggests to me that gains in the market are primarily due to retirement money flooding the market and not so much increases in corporate profits.

All this being said, there is one final adjustment that should be made. Thus far all the charts and correlations have been made with "Monthly New Sales of Equity Only Funds" provided by **ICI**. This tells us nothing of redemptions that were made, ie-people pulling their money OUT of equity only mutual funds. If pure volume of retirement dollars flooding the equities markets is to blame for higher prices and not corporate profit-chasing dollars, then the net flow into equity only funds would be a more appropriate measure. Thus I ran the same figures of "NET New Flows into Equity Only Funds" as a percent of corporate profits versus the S&P 500 divided by corporate profits.

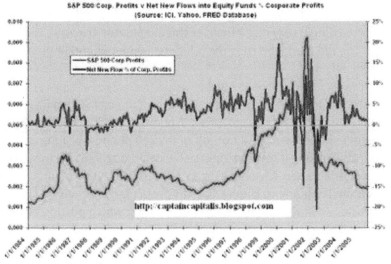

S&P 500 Corp. Profits v Net New Flows into Equity Funds % Corporate Profits
(Source: ICI, Yahoo, FRED Database)

Albeit not as pretty as the previous charts, there is a correlation again, .30. Not as high as the New Sales figures, but a postive one none-the-less. And with with 262 data points, it is probably statistically significant.

However, speculate as we might that all this is being caused by new retirement money entering the market, we cannot know for sure. In Dotcom Mania was it just people's irrational expectations of unrealistic profits that flooded the market with money? Is the rise in money entering the market now due to lower trading costs? Will Gen X continue this investment behavior? Or all of these things in play at once?

Alas, it seems all we've accomplished is proving that when a market is flooded with money, prices tend to go up.

Economists are very good at proving something that we already know.

Jim Beam, Cusano Cigar and a 1940's Motel

I originally was going to take pictures, but then it dawned on me I don't want to ruin it with digital precision and am going to let you imagine it.

I am currently sitting outside in my fold-out chair at my dirt cheap motel in a very small town nestled within the Black Hills of South Dakota. A place none of you will find. It's 78 degrees, about 2130 and the red neon lights just came on casting a very nice hue over the dilapidated trucks in the parking lot. The old man who runs the joint just came out and lit up a cigarette himself.

I am currently puffing on an M1 Cusano Torpedo Cut cigar with a flask of Jim Beam. I have no cell phone reception. Nobody can get in contact with me. I no longer suffer from the jilt or jolt of my cell phone vibrating or ringing, thereby making it my master of a Pavlovian dog-like response to some request or another. My only concerns for tomorrow is to determine which mountain I'm going to climb OR, if it's particularly hot which swimming hole I shall visit OR if it's particularly cool, which portion of the Badlands I shall hike straight through.

Additionally I have not listened to talk radio for about the past 3 weeks and am blissfully unaware of the debt and deficit problems I have tacitly paid attention to when I do decide to visit the Drudge Report. Though I have noticed on my sidebar plug-ins my dollar-short positions against the NOrwegian Kroner and the Canadian dollar are doing quite well - thank you Barry.

I did download some **Tom Leykis** so I could listen to something while I was driving my motorcycle around the Black Hills today, but otherwise right now I hear nothing but crickets and the occasional motorcycle or car driving by on the only paved road in town. I think I will drink myself my flask of Jim Beam and retire watching the history channel or the military channel.

If there is a way to enjoy the decline. This is it. Not trying, not working, and living as cheaply as possible on the minimum amount of labor you forfeited to the labor market/government-taxing machine. In the meantime I authorize all junior, deputy, aspiring, official or otherwise economists to pour themselves a hefty pour of whatever they got and make a long-range toast (wherever you may be in the Capposphere).

Enjoy the decline!

The Arrogance of Divorcees

I have, and will continue to contend until evidence proves me otherwise, that most people in America today who have children have children first and foremost for themselves, and somewhere after matching drapes, fancy SUV's and new shoes, comes the children themselves.

In other words, they never ask the question, "would I be able to provide a good environment for my child? Will I be a good parent for my child?"

No, the question is simply, "Do *I* want children?"

ME ME ME ME ME ME!!!!

Now I have caught mucho guff for heralding the benefits of being single and having no children. I got a vasectomy a long time ago and and it was one of the best decisions I made. But what particularly irks me is when people then accuse me of hating children, because it is the ultimate in hypocrisy.

I have actually THOUGHT about having a child.
I have actually considered the RAMIFICATIONS of having a child.
I have actually asked the tough questions of "WOULD I BE A GOOD FATHER?"

While most of my child-ridden critics have not.

And the fact I decided I should NOT have children because I would be a bad or inadequate father means I (ironically) would actually probably BE a better father than those with baby rabies in that I actually thought about the kid first.

So you can imagine me seeing red when I **saw this article**.

What I can only surmise to be a spoiled American Princess (anybody want to look her up to confirm if I'm right?) who has never given any consideration to anybody but herself, actually writes an article that so completely misses the point, it should raise the ire of any responsible adult and parent. The title alone is so contradictory and exposes her for the failure of a mother she is;

"Maintaining happy, healthy children during a separation and divorce"

Eh, hmmmm....let me see here. Could you maybe maintain "happy and healthy children" by...oh I don't know....

NOT PICKING A FREAKING MORON TO MARRY AND HAVE BLEEPING CHILDREN WITH IN THE FIRST PLACE???!!!!

But it gets better. A couple quotes from the article;

*"Divorce is never easy the first time around, but learning from your mistakes can make the **second divorce** a lot less stressful when making decisions for you and your children"*

Did she just say what i thought she did? Did I hear that right? She is preparing, EXPECTING a second divorce????? Forget he kids coming in around 4th or 5th place in her life. I think the kids are now ranking lower than the house plants.

Another gem;

"help our child have an emotionally safe, happy life as she will now have two families."

Yes, of course, that makes things simple! Two families!

Look, you morons out there, let me explain something to you. My old man has been married three times. You know what pissed me off as a child? Having to figure out how many gifts I had to buy progressively less and less important step-family members for Christmas. Do I send my mom and my new "Step-mom" a mother's day card? What about my step-dad? What about my new uncles I just married into? The budget of a 10 year old child is not limitless.

And of course, yes, TWO families makes it just that much more fun!

Another pearl.

"By communicating with your child frankly, but lovingly, you will be helping your child to accept the new changes in their life that are occurring. This will help them become more adaptable to any future changes in their life."

Oh you think there might be some 'changes' in their lives too? Thanks Ma, you got divorced twice. You've now doubled the kids chances of drug use, alcoholism, oh...and what else...ummm....OH YEAH! DIVORCE! But apparently divorce is a-OK in this woman's book. Perhaps you can celebrate when your children get divorced and try to explain to them why it's not only a good thing, but why they should be preparing for the second divorce that is sure to come.

BUt this takes the case;

"Separation and divorce causes stress on all parties involved--parents and children alike. In this second divorce, I've learned that regardless of how difficult it is and who is to blame, my children come first."

You disgusting, lying hypocrite.

Men Are Intimidated By "X"

Dalrock once again reminded me with his post that in addition to my daily duties of Swinging Bachelorhood I have to occasionally dispense wisdom to you guys. Otherwise lord knows you would all be jumping out of tree and running into bushes. And we wouldn't want that would we?

He invokes **The Word of Grerp**, who should write a book (it could be like the bible! - "*In Grerp's second letter to the Corinthians - "Be not a cumbersome annoyance to your husband, for he hath too much on his plate to deal witheth*") which then prodded me off my lazy butt to address something I've been meaning to for a while. And that is:

"Men are intimidated by X"

"X" being one of three things that I can think of:

1. A woman taller than him
2. A "strong" woman
3. A woman that makes more money than him.

And I am here to put the kibosh on all three.

Not that men are intimidated by these factors and I somehow wish to "hide" this fact in a propagandist move. I am here to put the kibosh on it because all three are false. And nothing puts the kibosh on something better than the truth (just look at socialism, feminism, worthless degrees and the other tenets of leftism).

Here's the skinny in order of the three:

1. I don't know one guy, personally, who has said, "Oh no! Not a a TALLER woman! GASP oh GASP! You mean her legs will be LONGER THAN AVERAGE!? Horrors of horrors. How will I ever survive?"

Now, admittedly I do know of TWO GUYS in the THOUSANDS I have met in my life that did not like their woman being taller than them. This then triggered a banning of those girls wearing high heels.

But frankly, not only are these guys the minority, they are MORONS!

For the most part ladies, men care NOWHERE NEAR as much about the height of a woman as much as women care about the height of a man. Matter of fact, I think almost 40% of the women I've dated have been taller than me because frankly I want to be "that guy."

You know "that guy?" That short SOB who walks into the club with a tall drink of water that you can't get? The guy who everybody is thinking, "how the HELL did HE get HER!?"

Yeah! I'm THAT guy! It's great!

So ladies, if you think men are intimidated by taller women, eh. a REAAALLY small percent are. But otherwise, I'm sorry, if you're taller, you're just going to have to stoop to our level.

2. No, we are not intimidated by strong women. We are attracted to strong women. Women who work for a living, who support themselves. The problem is "strong" is confused in today's **Moxie world** with "loud, arrogant or obnoxious." Most of the girls I have dated who were truly strong simply demonstrated their strength. They didn't wave their finger, give me the hand, bark orders nor tell me every 10 minutes how strong and independent they were.

To put it in contrast in my 20's I would occasionally cross paths with a HOT young lawyer who was working at a firm a friend of mine also worked at. When invited out to various happy hours, I would have a drink or two, socialize and try to get to know this girl. It was like trying to warm up to liquid hydrogen. Every ounce of body language said, "don't you dare talk to me." She never smiled. She never would even say, "hello." The only way I would get any kind of conversation out of this girl was indirectly through group conversation. And ALL she talked about was making junior partner and how hard she worked and how nothing was going to get in her way.

Fast forward 8 years later, and I run into her at the local salsa club. This woman is now WAAAAY into her 30's. Still has that pissed off look on her face, still dressed in clothes that screamed, "I'm a super powerful woman and by god you better do what I say," and wow, is that yet ANOTHER aging 30 something woman without a ring on her finger? I didn't even bother to try to talk to her because I doubt she would have remembered me, but she sat at the bar

all alone

by herself

unapproached

and not one man asked her to dance (and this was a scene where very few men are loth to approach a woman).

However, this was not because she was a "strong woman" and she "intimidated people."

It's quite simply you could tell she wouldn't be enjoyable company.

First, what guy wants to dance with a woman who isn't smiling?

Second, if you get good enough at dancing, you get kind of picky with the women you choose to dance with. I prefer women that follow. Not those that fight and can't grasp the concept of the MANDATORY lead-follow dynamics of dancing.

Third, inevitably, yes, men will want to test the waters to see if there's some dating potential. Sadly "strong" has been corrupted to mean "difficult" and "obstinate."

I'll take a strong woman, not a poser who thinks she's strong.

3. You Captain is largely poor. This is a confluence of factors including (admittedly) his impatient attitude, his inability to tolerate politics and BS, a crappy economy and largely a dying work ethic that is being replaced with enjoying the decline and the evil forces of HR that are always conspiring against us like The League of Doom. So naturally the LAST thing I would want is a woman that makes a lot of money. I mean, that's what EVERY guy is afraid of! A woman with LOT'S of MONEY! I wake up late at

night, soaked in sweat because of the nightmares I have of some woman showering me with $100 bills and buying me nice things. It's horrible, I've had to go talk to a therapist several times to get my mind right. I mean, if you want to scare a man away, if you want him to run for the hills, or if you're just looking for a crafty way to dump him, don't tell him you're secretly married.

No.

Don't tell him you have children.

No.

Tell him you have LOT'S OF MONEY!

That'll send him packing!

Sadly ladies, this is just another example of people in the media, politics and education circles telling you what you want to hear and not the truth.

Thus behooving the question;

What is more important, your short term feelings (in which case you can tell me how evil I am and how you know this ONE girl who isn't like that, etc.), or your long term happiness (in which case you may forward this link to as many people you want)?

I'm indifferent which one you choose, because there's only one truth. I'm merely entertained by how much of a fight people put up against the truth because their feelings are so fragile.

Enjoy the decline!

You Started It, But We'll Finish It

Warning - this is a long one, so pour yourself a martini or a Rupmie.

As I age I get more and more of this thing called "hindsight."

Commensurate with this I also gain confidence when I look back and realize that, yes, though I made many and horrible mistakes in my past, for the most part I played it straight, played by the rules and was a good guy. Even more so when you consider what information I had available to me at that time and what environment I was in and sometimes the outright lies I was told were "truth." Whether my decisions panned out for me or not is irrelevant. I tried my best and sometimes am amazed I even succeeded this much.

Regardless, you combine these two traits, hindsight and confidence, you get authority. The authority to look back at life and start making claims that aren't opinion, they're fact. Facts like HR is a worthless profession that has caused more damage than helped. Facts like just because they're older than you does NOT mean they have more experience or intelligence (matter of fact, they're just more prone to corruption, age does not command respect). Facts like democrats play on the ignorance and feelings of well intentioned people as well as fan the flames of jealously and merely bribe people to vote for them with other people's money. These are facts. Not opinions.

But the fact I'm going to talk to you about to day is a fact about the "war of the sexes."

Oh yes, there is a war. That's a fact that I don't even have to defend. But who started it in its most recent form? Some will claim that is a matter of opinion, but sadly once again hindsight and confidence permit me to authoritatively **state it was women. Hands down, and that's a fact**.

It is here that the "enemy" in this battle of the sexes will now go into knee jerk hyperdrive reaction. Claims of sexism, mysoginy, blah blah blah. We've heard it all before for the past 40 tiresome years. They will ignore my claim it was women who started it (let alone be open minded enough to ask why I've come to this conclusion), in part because they're rank and file enlisted soldiers, brainwashed not to think, but react immediately to protect the hive and the ideology. There are others, let's call them "officers" who know full well what they were doing, but will still feign ignorance and act appalled, because if they didn't, then it would belie their ulterior motives.

But again, I'm not some 18 year old rube who is fresh off the assembly line. I'm not some "nice guy" anymore who was brought up by a single mom in a very asymmetrical manner when it came to the sexes. I'm not that honorable guy why kept on thinking "what's wrong with me" and never developed the courage to say, "what's wrong with society." And I'm certainly not the guy who is going to take it personally when I start pointing out genuinely inconvenient truths and am called a bigot or a racist or a misogynist or pick any term from the communist/feminists playbook.

No, I'm the experienced guy who went through the meat grinder and amazingly has found himself in Bayeux alive, intact and only strengthened because of the experience. And given the hell I had to go through, you damn right I know what's going on. And like hell my experience isn't going to help the boys landing on the beach right now, because nobody, absolutely nobody deserves to go through that hell again.

So let us start out with a very simple question - why is there a battle in the first place?

A simple question, but one that needs answering. What did men do that was so horrible that we deserved the ire, the hatred and the war that was waged against us? The reason I ask this is at least in the beginning, I did nothing to offend or hurt women. As a boy and a young man, I did everything I was told. I was nice, I was kind, I was sweet. I did PRECISELY what they women told me to do. And not only did I not succeed in dating any of the women I pined after, I was actually ridiculed, berated and demeaned. I remember girls acting like they were going to go on a date with me or show up to a dance with me, only to find out it was a joke. I remember getting slapped in the face no less than 4 times before graduating from high school and for reasons that were so innocuous the only one I could remember was flirting with a girl and rummaging through her purse (which obviously earned me a slap across the face). Not once in my entire life have I ever struck a woman.

Now, if it was just one guy, one lousy nerdy guy out of 150 million American men with these experiences the evidence could be considered anecdotal. But it isn't. You ask the majority of men who are essentially NOT of the WWII generation or older and I guarantee you the majority of them (not all) were the exact same way and had the exact same experiences. Started off nice, with the best of intentions, tried their best, maybe even bought a girl flowers and probably have a score of 0-4 when it comes to slugging the other sex, all of which resulted in a big fat zero when it came to courting success.

Of course at the age of 18 or 19, your average man is still too clueless and lost to know what's going on. It's like they landed at Omaha and just got pounded by some German 88's. They're dazed, they're confused, they aren't even cognizant enough to ask "why." They're just taking a beating.

Of course that is the question. "Why?" What on god's green earth did we do to you to deserve this in middle school, let alone the following decade? We came with flowers and innocence and kindness and with the best of intentions and asked you on dates, only to get slaughtered.

I personally cannot answer the question why. I can only guess. And if I had to guess I'd say it was because feminists from the 1960's had so indoctrinated you as children via the schools or even feminist parenting you had a predisposition to view men as the enemy. Never mind the then 13 year old boys of our generation and successive generations never did anything to "oppress you" or "keep you down." Never mind for that matter the men of the WWII generation and Baby Boomers didn't do anything to oppress women either. No, you just were programmed to view men as the enemy, as your oppressors. Dirty disgusting boys that "you should throw rocks at" if I recall the t-shirt logo correctly.

Perhaps it was because of a lack of fathers or father figures given the new penchant women have for divorce. No man in the house to teach you how to treat boys, or perhaps there was a man in the house, but he too is still being shelled by his wife into submission and becomes the complete beta male incapable of providing a decent male role model.

Media? 90210 anybody? Melrose Place? I'm trying to think of other demented shows targeted towards young girls that would warp their formative years in how to treat boys, but I'm grasping at straws as my memory fades. To quote Humphrey Bogart in Casablanca, "Perhaps it was a combination of all three."

Ultimately though, sadly, the reason "why" is moot. It doesn't matter why

Japan bombed Pearl Harbor. It doesn't matter why Islamic-nutjob assholes bombed the WTC. And it doesn't matter why boys received such a hostile reception upon hitting puberty. All that matters is what happened.

Second, along the same lines of "why" is something more fundamental to men and women and courtship in general.

Shouldn't we like each other?

I mean last I checked men and women were kind of designed for each other a little bit. And I ask this one question as it applies to a whole bunch of different levels.

Isn't dating supposed to be fun? Shouldn't we go out and have a good time? No, there has to be drama, chaos, crying, rules, stipulations, rule changes and that's just assuming the poor guy can navigate the mine field and actually land a date. And oh goodie! Look what he gets to look forward to!

Sex anyone? Is it not enjoyable? Why "hold out?" Why attach strings to it? What evil possesses you to use it as a bargaining chip whether you're married or not? And dare I suggest using sex to extract resources is the definition of prostitution? Or is that cutting it too close to the truth?

And the ultimate one that will confuse me till I'm dead, marriage or committed relationships. Aren't you supposed to SUPPORT your husband? I don't mean financially, but emotionally, aren't spouses to support each other? You know, be there for each other. If there is empirical proof that the war was started and continues to be waged by women, this is it. The reason why is it is the EXCEPTION when a wife actually supports and takes care of her husband. He comes home, beleaguered from his work. And she dons some heels and a little outfit and pours him a martini. That's what I'm talking about! Unfortunately, the VAST MAJORITY of marriages the women AT BEST slightly nags him or leaves him alone. Most of the time the women are harassing, berating, lecturing, complaining or just plain fighting against their husband. Why on god's green earth did you get married in the first place??? Better yet, why should men get married at all if instead of supporting them you are constantly fighting against them, if not just simply wearing them down? What's the upshot? And again

WHY???? What did we do to you?

Third is a very shrewd observation on my part. You already know about me getting hit 4 times in high school because the girls at the time liked the power trip. But there were other instances of what was completely unacceptable or idiotic behavior on the part of women/girls, primarily in their teens and 20's. One that is a bit innocent is the "I have a boyfriend in Brazil." This was a popular one when I was in middle school and high school and it was amazing how many girls had real boyfriends in different continents. Another more dangerous, if not psychotic one was suicide threats. I had no less than three women threaten suicide while I was dating them. Temper tantrums were also very popular. I remember trying to drive on 35W (just south of where the bridge collapsed) when my girlfriend at the time just started screaming (she was from California). Another girl from California punched me because I refused to have sex with her. I remember third throwing her phone and pictures and everything around her apartment (the argument of which again I can't remember). And I cannot fully recall the infinite number of head games, mind games and flake outs I suffered in my 20's.

"Pick me up, I'm ready!" 30 minutes later, "Oh, I'm sorry, I have a headache."

"Let's meet at Mancini's!" "Well my morbidly obese friend decided to show up with us, you don't mind do you?"

"Here's my number. Call me!" ....

But isn't it interesting...

very interesting....

(can any of you guess where I'm going with this?)

(I'll give you a couple more guesses)

(it is quite shrewd an observation)

how after the age of 28, 29 30 or so, all that drama goes away?

I haven't had a girl threaten suicide on me since I was in my twenties.

I haven't had a girl throw a temper tantrum on a busy interstate since I was in my twenties.

I haven't had a girl hit me in quite some time.

And you know, there's been a shocking lack of mind games and flake outs since I passed the 30 year old mark.

Could it POSSIBLY be that this was nothing more than FULLY CONSCIOUS self-created drama to get attention? And could it be that they fully well knew what they were doing? And it is NOT that they "grew up" all of the sudden when they hit 30. That they KNEW FULL WELL it was wrong to hit men at the age of 10. They knew FULL WELL throwing temper tantrums were wrong at the age of 10. They knew FULL WELL threatening to commit suicide was wrong at the age of 10. And they knew FULL WELL it was wrong to lie at the age of 10.

They just had no problem using it till the age of 30 because they knew us men/boys were naive enough to think it wasn't on purpose. That there might have been something psychologically wrong with them, or worse, we blamed it on ourselves.

But again, I'm not here to lecture people about such stupid behavior. I'm just asking the question WHY?

What in the Patron Saint's Name of Frick is the purpose in doing that or employing such tactics? It certainly wasn't "well intentioned." It certainly wasn't "in our best interests." It's like using biological warfare against orphans. It was an act of war.

And finally (though there are many examples more) is something that I will intellectually honestly admit I do not believe women do consciously or maliciously, but still has an effect (and this is actually a matter of opinion, so I will grant you that). And that is your voting preferences.

Not so much in a "republican" or "democrat" sort of sense, but rather how you vote or what governs how you vote. You vote with your heart. Admirable. Honorable. But sorry, stupid and naive. Not because of your aims to help out the children or help out the poor, but there are no brain cells in the heart! ie-You only look at the intended consequences of policies and politicians you vote for, but so poorly think through the unintended consequences and ramifications, let alone what ulterior motives politicians and their political donors might have.

Hidden behind the socialist agenda of "helping the children" or "helping the poor" is a huge and financially IMPOSSIBLE price tag. It's not feasible, but nefarious politicians know how to tug at your heart strings and make you vote for them. And since federal and state government finances are not as exciting as The View of People Magazine, you fail to understand how the true costs of making everything free to everyone are simply masked and deferred with debt (if you don't understand that last sentence, then I strongly suggest reading more Cappy Cap and watch less Sex and the City). With the right to vote comes the responsibility of being an informed voter. And just "going with your heart" or "voting for the little guy" without bothering to look up the budget or the finances of the country/state/county simply destroys the nation and your future AND the future of your kids (which is an argument for another time).

But that's not the worst of it (at least as it applies to the battle of the sexes).

The worst consequence of your voting patterns is the replacement of men with government.

And, frankly, it's already done.

You really don't need us.

You have affirmative action, tons of social resources at the state and local levels, welfare, WIC, EBT and a legal system that is pretty slanted towards your side when it comes to divorce and the divvying up of a couple's assets. You have a public school system that is progressively taking a larger and larger role in baby sitting...errr....bringing up...ummm...

"educating" your children and more and more laws passed governing and regulating how children are to be brought up. If you don't have a husband but want children you can adopt, have an IV fertilization, surrogate, etc. etc. Society is on your side because no individual is more celebrated than the single mother or the single woman "living in a man's world." In other words you have voted in a system where the only role men play is that of a tax payer and not that of a father or a husband or a lover, leaving us to ask once again the question, "why, what did we do to deserve financial slavery?"

Now, of course, some of you like that idea. Which only proves my point further because it shows some of you really just wanted men as financial slaves. But there is a consequence to this. There is a cost. And you may be starting to notice this. That there is a price to pay for all the mind games that were played. The dates that you flaked out on. The tantrums, the drama. The dishonesty and lying to men about what you wanted and what you didn't want. The divorce, the alimony the child support. And myself, along with every other guy who made it to Bayeux alive can see it now in beautiful hindsight.

Some of you in your 40's, 30's, even upper 20's are asking "where are all the good men?" Some of you have given birth to BOYS and now you have disadvantaged-skin in the feminist game you may have helped create. Some of you, fresh off divorce and enjoying "**post-marital bliss**" are realizing the men are not knocking at your door like they were in 1981. So continuing with our "battle of the sexes" analogy, perhaps I can describe what is happening and the consequences for waging an uncalled for war on us.

There is a battlefield. On one side are the girls and on the other side are the boys. BOTH of us have been told by society, media and nature or "genetics" to go and find somebody from the opposing team. It is a strong urge, arguably the strongest biological force there is, and thus the attempt to meet ensues. If this was 1940, the battle would look something like this.

Girls liked boys and welcomed them over.

Men were happy to oblige. Not really a battle.

Of course, that's too easy and remember, our WWII grandfathers were of course abusive, misogynistic sexists. So the sexual revolution of the 1960's was absolutely necessary so we could punish future, unassuming, innocent generations of boys for the evils of our WWII generation grandfathers. The Baby Boomers beget Gen X and beget Gen Y so that when teenage boys hit the NEW and IMPROVED battlefield today it looks like this:

It is a veritable battlefield.

One sided, but veritable.

Now, let's ask ourselves a simple question. "How long will the dismembered stickmen boys stay on that battlefield?"

And the answer actually varies depending on the stickman. I got out at 25. I know some men left the battlefield as early as 18. I know men in their 60's who are still wandering around on the battlefield just as dazed and confused when they first landed 42 years ago. Some never get it together and stay on that battlefield till they die in the real world. But I would say on average 15 years.

So by the time a young man hits 30 or so, he starts questioning why he is there taking a pounding. He starts to question why he is even trying to date one of these girls in the first place. He starts to remember his parents getting divorced or a friend's parents getting divorced or ONE OF HIS OWN FRIENDS GETTING DIVORCED. He even starts to question whether he should follow his biological imperative or just get a vasectomy and live the bachelor life forever. And it is at that point he crawls over the hill, stumbles over all roughshod and shot up with holes and joins us in Bayeux.

Sadly here the battlefield analogy ends, because unlike real soldiers thrown onto the Normandy beachhead, we have the option to stop fighting. We have the option to stop participating in the battle. We can give up. Unfortunately I don't believe that is the same for women. Oh, sure, some women can throw in the towel and go on and lead happy lives, but whereas I would think only 5-10% of women can genuinely override their genetic hard-wiring, I would say nearly 60-70% of men can do it. Besides, you've been giving us great practice and incentive to do so since we were 14. So it's not that hard of a jump.

Naturally, when men declare they are leaving the battlefield or women find out they are leaving the battlefield the question of "what??? You're just going to give up?" follows.

And then comes the textbook fear-mongering questions that REALLY are a sign of desperation from the "enemy." I've been so kind to answer them too;

Q - "So don't you want to ever get married and have kids?"

A - No, like my freedom and my money

Q- "Do you want to die ALOOOOOONE in a nursing home?"

A - No, i won't die alone, I presume there will be other people there my same age and as I always have done I will make friends there. Additionally, if I make it to a nursing home, because of the fact men die 10 years before women, I will be a mack daddy and will have multiple women chasing after me. Besides, isn't it pretty arrogant to marry some one, let alone have children for the sole purpose of them providing you entertainment when you age?

Q - "Who's going to take care of you when you get older?"

A - Well, thanks to your voting patterns all health care and social security is free. In short, your children will be taking care of me. Additionally, again, are my children to be slaves to take care of me? Is THAT why I should have children and get married? To have slaves? Thankfully I had a vasectomy while you had 4 children from 3 different guys and you voted democrat all the time. Tell them I say "thanks for being my unwilling and unwitting slave."

and so on and so forth.

The reason for the questions is women (and people in general) can't really understand or believe you're giving up. They can't believe you're abandoning your primary biological motive and just up and going. People, but particularly women, can't fathom what would be better than a life with them and can't imagine a place where you'd be going once you leave the battlefield. But here ladies is where the men are going:

You see, they are leaving the market. And the reason why is that yes, as youth we had these dreams of meeting a beautiful cool, intelligent woman. We had dreams of finding a really neat girl and maybe settling down with her. And yes, the biological drive was very strong. But when our entire youth was not just wasted, but a negative experience, nay a

PUNISHING EXPERIENCE you realize around the age of 30, that is was all just a lie. That or a bill of goods somebody was trying to sell you. At this point most men go through a depression (notice how suicide in men jumps around age 34 and then drops), but most of us look at life and say,

"OK, maybe I'm not going to find that really cool chick I wanted to meet, and maybe I did waste my youth at bars and clubs, and maybe there is no need for me as a role of a husband or a father, but now I'm no longer wasting my time. I'm doing what I want."

And BOOM! They enter Bachelorland.

Bachelorland is a magical place. A place where you get to keep the majority of your money. A place of true freedom where you get to do;

what you want
when you want
how you want
say what you want
hang out with who you want
do what you want
say what you feel

and there's no guff or nagging about it.

Once we pay our taxes to subsidize other people and other people's children, we still have the majority of our money to spend on ourselves. More importantly we have the majority of time to spend on ourselves. And better than that, society has advanced to the point there are LIMITLESS intellectual, physical, video, artistic and other pursuits to pursue and enjoy a happy, fulfilling life. We got our pals, we got our friends, we got a life.

And that (and you need to sit down for this) IS WITHOUT YOU!

No nagging, no crying, no drama, no divorce, no child support, no "my child comes first" BS, no jumping through hoops for sex, to abuse, no slapping, no flaking, no psychotic behavior, no mind games, no half my assets, no nothing.

You're gone, you're outta here, you're irrelevant.

Congratulations! You "won" the battle and men have surrendered! Now leave us alone.

Now who are the winners and who are the losers in this? Well, unfortunately there's more losers than winners.

The losers number many. Notably the women who continue fighting on the battlefield when there's nobody left to fight. Be it because society, media and feminists constantly barrage them with images of Sex and the City or EPL or they can't override nature or they just plain can't believe there are no more men left on the field, they continue to fight essentially no one. Ironically "fighting" against men while trying to attract one Enjoy the cats!

Also in the losing category are the men who had to suffer such BS for most of their youth, and worse, those men who never realize they're being shelled. They wander through life confused and befuddled about something that must not only take an inordinate amount of brain power obsessing about, but something that certainly must lower their life expectancy. They never achieve true happiness because they think it lies through the battlefield instead of getting off the battlefield and living their own life.

But, third, is the biggest and most innocent victims of them all. Admittedly this post has been very broad with the brush. I talk about women and men in general because it's impossible to have a conversation about it if you don't generalize (of course feminists and liberals love to use this technicality as a means to accuse you of sexism, but as I pointed out before, we know their political incentives and I plain don't give an ef anymore). However, there are obviously women who do not fall under this category and are not the malicious or warring types. These are the innocent and most undeserving victims.

The reason why is that the bad girls ruing it for the rest of the good girls. And it doesn't take a lot. It just takes one bad woman to divorce one good guy, and that good guy is off the market for good. I have PHENOMENAL,

WONDERFUL, LOVELY women in my life who would make a great wife for any guy willing to get to know them. They ARE the ones who want to make a man happy. They'll cook, they'll clean, they'll not only dress sexy, but stay sexy because they WANT THEIR MAN TO BE HAPPY. They are the ones who not only claim to be independent, THEY ARE INDEPENDENT working REAL JOBS, producing REAL WEALTH. They want REAL MEN and when they vote, they think. They think not just for themselves, but are actually good, educated and informed stewards of democracy, thinking of society as a whole. The LAST thing they want is what feminists to them they should want. They want to be happy. Matter of fact, feminists HATE them and would call them "female Uncle Toms," but that is because they are jealous that my friends have better lives and are happier than these feminists could ever be.

However, sadly they are all in their 30's and 40's. And by that time the men who are left are either;

1. Confirmed bachelors
2. Divorced men who have no incentive to go back
3. Jerks and #%%holes that they don't want to date.
4. Desperate effeminate men that had too much single mother upbringing or too much brainwashing in the schools and frankly don't turn them on.

Did they do anything to deserve this?

No.

Did they sling a single arrow at the boys on the battlefield?

No.

But they are the ones paying the price for their fellow "feminists" sisters" assault on boys/men.

So ladies, or rather should I say "girls" because it's too late for the ladies, you have a choice.

You're either with us or against us. If you're with us we can ALL enjoy great lives which is what I really think we were programmed to do. We can enjoy each others company. We can go out on dates. We can get married and raise families. We could just jet set around the world getting drunk, eating good food and having great hot monkey greasy sex. We can work, we can play, we can HELP EACH OTHER OUT IN A MUTUAL BENEFICIAL RELATIONSHIP.

However, if you want to be unnatural, if you want to fight your biological drives and subscribe to feminism and make yourselves men. If you want to be childish. If you want drama and chaos and put attention above meaningful relationships. If you want to ruin it for other girls by destroying men through mind games and psychological "drauma." If you want to "dominate" over men or make them pay for some injustice at the age of 14 that they were completely incapable of doing, or if you just want to toy with the hearts and minds of men and boys, go right ahead and declare war. Because in the end, you won't win the battle of the sexes. And it won't be because men will ultimately counterattack and "win this round."

We'll just forfeit the battle

and in doing so win the war.

The Bubble and Burst of Ballroom Dancing

Tonight was an epiphanal night for your Captain, and he wishes to share it with all your fine upstanding junior, deputy, aspiring, official or otherwise economists, and that epiphany is about the realm of ballroom dancing.

I am often faced with a quandary when middle aged women ask if their young, teenage sons should learn ballroom dance. Understand this is a quandary for me because my experience has both pros and cons to it, neither of which (until tonight) has edged out one over the other.

The battle between learning and not-learning basically boils down to two things.

1. When I was literally the best swing dancer in the entire state of Minnesota in the late 90's and early 2000's, it was grand. Swing was hot, I

was hot, and I think I racked up over 200 dates alone in that 3 year time span. Dated the hottest (and most psychotic and dumbest) girl on the scene. Icing to the cake was the Salsa craze that followed. I wasn't necessarily the best dancer, but any "gringo" who wasn't all hands and didn't have a green card as an ulterior motive to dance with the ladies came at a premium. Again, life was grand.

but

2. Inevitably all good things come to an end, and they come to an end in an eerily similar pattern. First there is the craze. Everybody wants to do it, hot people, ugly people, people who climb on rocks. Then the skill level of everybody increases. Some people get better than others and this insults the former "kings and queens" of the dancing world. Cliques form in a very middle school manner, and of course, there may have been some dating going on, not all of which ended successfully. Sure enough due to failed relationships some people leave the scene, one clique won't dance with the others, and it all goes to pot. But worse, hastening the "goes to pot phase" is the entrance of two very different types of men, but PRECISELY identical effects on the dance scene - Green card searchers (latin dancing) and Single Christian Middle Aged Males (swing/ballroom scene).

These men, desperately incentived by ulterior motives, ABUSE ballroom dancing and essentially scare all the women away. Women now can no longer just "go out dancing" and enjoy a good night of it. They are now harassed by illegal aliens looking for a green card or desperate middle aged men looking for a wife. The dancing no longer has merit unto itself. It becomes a tool for desperate men.

This, more than anything else, scares the women away in droves and leaving the dance scene a nerdy-remnant shell of its former greatness.

Thus the cycle is complete, boom to bust, and ballroom dancing returns to where it "normally trades at."

The question then becomes, should the young man ever bother learning to ballroom dance? Does he learn in the hopes he times it right like I did, and with the added benefit of timing two ballroom bubbles and avail himself of (literally) limitless romantic opportunities? Or does he just pursue other pursuits and move on with his life?

I'm happy to tell you I've found the definitive and correct answer;

Do not learn ballroom dancing until you have a girlfriend or wife you dearly love.

The reason I say this is because of the "stable market value" of ballroom dancing.

Understand, though in the past I was a big proponent of ballroom dancing, that is only because I was lucky enough to live through two bubbles. Bar the great 90's swing dance craze and the early 2000's salsa craze, inevitbaly these things come to an end. And if you look back at the past 100 years, maybe, MAYBE 7 of them cumulatively were ballroom dance crazes of any time.

Regardless, that's what they precisely were.

Crazes.

They weren't "normal."

They weren't "the base line" of society.

These were fleeting, ABNORMAL phenomenon in society.

And if you timed them just right, fine, all was well and good (pretty great actually).

But if you got on the bandwagon too late, it was single Christian groups and green-card potlucks.

So you have to determine whether you should learn to ballroom dance based on the other 93 years or 93% of the time when ballroom dancing is "trading" at its normal market value and is not in a craze or "bubble" stage. And it is most decidedly NOT worth it.

The reason I say this is because of my experiences tonight. I went to about the only place in all of southern Montana to do some ballroom dancing. The venue was actually quite large. The band was quite good. And there was no less than 300 people. I walked in thinking I hit gold.

But the a couple observations.

1. NOBODY knew what they hell they were doing. Bar the SCARCE old couple who genuinely knew how to two-step, the remainder of the dancers were just flinging each other around and faking it about as bad as you could. Pockets of "woo-girls" filled the center of the floor as they danced with their beers in hand, and not one man on that floor could have ever been called a "leader" because the women were just turning themselves. I've seen mosh pits more organized than that.

2. Because of #1, even if you KNEW how to ballroom dance it wouldn't matter because no women knew how to follow. And conversely for the Lady Cappy Cappites, it wouldn't matter if you knew how to dance, because none of the men could lead, let alone keep the beat. So again, you could be the best dancer in the state (and I'm not joking when I say, I think I quite literally was), but it won't matter because you ultimately need a partner who knows what they're doing.

3. A reminder that suburbanite princess mentality transcends all rural, suburban and urban borders: There was one time I was at The Times Cafe in Minneapolis. I was in a suit, Vic Volare and the Volare Lounge Orchestra was playing. They had a GREAT floor open and martini's were pouring. It was probably the single best dance floor/joint in the entire Twin Cities and you could not ask for a better floor or band. After getting shot down 4 times in a row, I just decided I would plum ask every single looking lady to dance in the joint. After 30 minutes, I was summarily shot down by every girl in the joint. The floor remained open, until a cackle of woo girls decided to go out on the floor and dance with each other.

Tonight was a repeat. New to the venue I asked a lady sitting next to me at the bar if the band "ever played anything danceable." She said it was her first time there, but her friend from across the bar had been there plenty of times and would know. So we BOTH start beckoning her over and she yells across the bar, "But I don't want to dance with him!' We roll our eyes, continue to beckon and inevitably she comes over. I asked her, "Do they ever play any danceable music? Let alone does anybody here REALLY know how to dance?"

No, not really, she said, and I thanked her for the information.

Of course, fresh in my mind was her presuming I wanted to dance with her. Yes, who else would I want to dance with besides her and her fellow 40 something, aging women friends, with 1980's clothes and noticeable aging physical features? Brushing it off, I could brush it off no more when 10 minutes later I see these same women, acting like veritable 14 year old girls as they start dancing with each other on the dance floor. And I'm not talkign the jump up and down, wiggle butt dance. I'm talking they're trying to swing dance with one another, while there is literally over 100 genuine, tall, good-looking cowboys of their same age.

In short, it was tonight I realized just what a bubble ballroom dancing is when women would just plain prefer to dance with themselves than perfectly capable guys.

So the lesson to learn here gentlemen of the Capposphere is that unless there's a ballroom bubble, there's no point in learning how to ballroom dance. Most women, in a stable market of ballroom dance, will have no interest in dancing with you. Most women will shoot you down. And most women, would actually prefer to dance with each other than a clean cut, good looking guy 10 years their junior who is a stranger. And if you do enter the ballroom world, you can be prepared to join a world of middle aged to elderly single folk looking desperately for some kind of edge or skill that will give them game.

The conclusion is obviously not to learn ballroom, but I will provide one caveat.

Ballroom dance is worth learning if you have a significant other. THe reason why is it is a currency for men. Just like flowers, poetry, buying drinks, paying for dinner, all of that is WASTED on girls you are merely dating or trying to date. All of those, including ballroom dancing should be reserved for a special girl that actually DESERVES those things. Do men REALLY like ballroom dancing? Sure some, but even I tire of it. Did I like writing funny, witty poems to impress the girls in college? No, but I thought it would work, of course it didn't. And how much money did you waste buying soon-to-be-dead flowers, soon-to-be-eaten-chocolates, or soon-to-be-drank drinks?

You will soon realize ballroom dancing is merely one of many forms of what is ultimately categorized as ATTENTION.

And all men, maybe not today, maybe not tomorrow will soon realize you don't use attention to get women (that's where indifference, ignorance and lying about your income come in). You use it to reward the nice sweet ones that treat you nice and don't play games and like you for you.

Therefore, the Captains' new official policy on dancing (as well as poetry, buying dinner, paying for drinks and any other form of attention) is reserved for those special women you are either seriously involved with or married to, or good female friends you really do like and respect.

Wasting these talents or efforts on women as a means to cajole them into dating you, is simply that. Wasting talents and efforts.

I Solved the "Giggle Complex"

Men in the ballroom dance community will know what I'm talking about and will appreciate the great advancement I've just made.

The "Giggle Complex" is when you go to a table of girls at a dance hall, and in order to not seem like you're a stalker or targeting any one girl, you say,

*"Would **any** of you like to dance?"*

Without fail, what reliably ensues is giggling. This is then followed up by the different girls at the table pointing at each other,

"No, you dance with him."

giggglelgiglglegiggle

"No, YOU dance with him!"

giggleglgiggleigiggleggiel

*"Tee hee, I don't know how to dance, **you** should dance with him!"*

giggilgeiglggigglggilgglegiggle

You stand there like an idiot for about a solid minute that seems to last an eternity as they unknowingly mock you in front of many people (I however immediately do an about face once they giggling and pointing and "no you" BS begins, and have seen women continue pointing at each other not realizing I've left). If you have confidence, you actually take it in stride and perhaps even revel in the irony of how these girls are no doubt the ones complaining about where "all the good guys are," while there stands before them the salsa-dancing, motorcycle riding, fighter-pilot, surgeon, alphamale they all dream of having, but loathe the concept of dancing with.

Regardless, this presents a problem to men in the dance community, because while this strategy is still one of the best approaches to notch up some dances, it is draining, not terribly successful and is insulting.

Introduce a little Alphamaleness.

Was at the local dance club in town. Not a lot of dancers here, but there is a dance hall and it gets reasonably packed on the weekend. Fed up with the past 3 weekends of getting shot down and by none-too-pretty ladies I might add, my attitude was not a patient one. I saw a girl that was in shape, went up to her and her group of friends at the table and said,

"Hey, let's dance."

The giggling and pointing was about to start, and she said,

"You should dance with my friend she..."

I cut her off. I said,

"I didn't ask her to dance. I asked you to dance."

The initial giggling immediately stopped.

Their eyes went wide.

No childish finger pointing or mocking ensued.

She got up off of her seat, walked to the dance floor with me and danced. When I got back to the table, I pointed at the next one and said,

"You're next."

Ended up dancing with the whole table.

I officially believe this is the way now to approach all women when you are asking them to dance, especially when they're securely huddled within the "herd." You single the hottest one out, go right up to her, borderline tell her she's dancing with you, and before the cackling can begin you deliver the silver bullet,

"I didn't ask her to dance, I asked you to dance."

Has not failed me yet.

The only other method I've had that has been more successful is to bring a ringer in. This is where you bring a dance partner who is outstanding. You dance so everybody can see how good you are, essentially advertising to the women,

"Yes, I know how to dance. And yes, you too could be the center of attention just like this woman I'm dancing with now."

Whether they know how to dance or not, they won't care. They want to become that woman on the center of the floor and have all the attention of all the men in the joint.

There's Only One Way Out of This Mess

(my apologies in advance for the font. I have no clue why it's doing this)

I very much dislike writing for posterity. It indicates that at the point in time I was writing something, society was so brainwashed, so ignorant, and so stupid, that I had to resort to writing down something to provide a historical record that, "yes, I know what the hell I'm talking about." And "yes, you people were so galactically ignorant back then, that now, with hindsight, what I predicted has come true, and you must feel awfully stupid for not listening to me." I of course am not talking about you fellow Cappy Cappite readers, matter of fact this post will probably bore you because it is something you, I, and everybody with an ounce of brain know. But I'm going to spell it out anyway, not just to have a historical record permitting me an "I told you so" in the future, but to perhaps crystalize our thoughts about economics, politics, etc., or perhaps to precisely and succinctly make our case.

Right now, whether you are on the left or the right or in the spineless "inbetween," we can all agree that the economy sucks, the future of the US is crippled, and nobody is happy with the direction the country is headed. The solutions deployed thus far are largely Keynesian in nature where we take money and resources from one group of people OR we borrow it from the future and give it to other groups of people in the hope of "jump starting" the economy. This strategy is the "status quo" because Keynesian economics is drilled day in and day out into young economists' brains from high school into college and into their careers.

So when it's blindingly apparent that the Keynesian stimulus has failed, because Keynesianism is so entrenched you get the idiotic, "We just didn't do ENOUGH of it. We need MORE stimulus. We need MORE taxes. We need MORE government intervention." And then the layman on the streets says, "The government needs to do something."
However, let me suggest an alternative strategy. One not based on "sloshing money around the economy" in the hopes it all of the sudden "jump starts" and we have a booming 1940's America once again.

Production-based economics.

You see, if you permit me to just wipe clean your brain of what you think you know about economics and politics, and start from the ground up, I believe I can provide you a much clearer and (MUCH) simpler model in how economics works.

You must understand, first and foremost, what an economy consists of. An economy consists of one simple thing – production. Specifically the production of goods and services. It's a boring term "goods and services," but if I said:
"Martinis, Ferraris, clothes, video games, Ipod's, cell phones,etc, etc," much more exotic stuff, you can see where people are incented by production.

We want STUFF. That's all economics or any economy in the history of the world has been about. STUFF.
If you don't believe me, perhaps an example that will prove it AND teach you a very important lesson about money.
If I have a wad of $100 bills and I release it at a crowded state fair, what do you suppose will happen?

A riot will happen, that's what. People will scramble and knock each other out of the way to get that money.

But what value does the money have? What can you do with a $100 bill?

Functionally nothing. A $100 bill is a piece of paper with ink on it. It has no more value than a scrap of paper or garbage on the ground. But people instinctive, viscerally, and most likely, violently will scramble for it. Not necessarily even thinking about why they are punching the teeth out of grandma to get another $100 bill, but because their brain unconsciously knows full well it can buy STUFF with that $100 bill.

In short, the success of an economy is not based on how much money it prints, but rather how much STUFF it produces. Money is merely a tool by which to convert your time into a medium or tool that you can purchase STUFF with.

Related to STUFF and production is another aspect people don't think about and that is innovation.
Innovation is the creation of new, better and more-kick-ass STUFF.

Vaccines, faster planes, better computers, or whole new inventions we haven't even thought of yet. Innovation is arguably even more important than an economy's mere volume capacity to produce stuff, because it allows an economy to produce better stuff with less time and resources. Take for example automobiles. Before hand you travelled by horse or on foot. Transport of goods and services relied on beasts of burden or canals and boats. But with the combustion engine we could now haul TONS more STUFF, further distances and at a fraction of the cost. The benefit was more STUFF delivered to more people AT A CHEAPER PRICE. The innovation of the combustion engine benefited not just its inventor and the "evil corporation" that made it, but made prices lower for everybody thereby increasing standards of living for all people (ie-why do you hate Wal-Mart so much when it's done the exact same thing today?)

It is these two things – the ability to produce stuff and the ability to create NEW stuff – that determines how successful, rich and prosperous an economy and a people are.

Now, assuming you believe what I laid out above (and if you don't, then I can't convince you because you're psychotic, insane or just intellectually dishonest and there's no reason trying to convince you), ask yourself how today's current government policies help promotion the production of stuff and the innovation of new stuff?

The answer is, it doesn't.

Matter of fact it punishes people who produce stuff or dare to create or innovate new stuff.

The current government policy is not to promote economic growth, but is instead based on spreading out what stuff we make now more "fairly" or "equitably." It also foolishly assumes spreading out the "stuff" will somehow magically result in an economic boom.

The problem is look at who the policies reward and "punish."

Right now we do not champion the producers or innovators of society. We champion the losers. All of our efforts and focus is on people who are unemployed, underemployed, old, aging, decrepit, oppressed, disadvantaged, blah blah blah. And so we tax people who produce stuff and transfer it to those who don't produce stuff.

I am not commenting on the morality of whether those NOT producing stuff deserve it or are oppressed or somehow deserve the transference of stuff. I am merely pointing out the fact that we are transferring stuff from producers to non-producers. And whether there is a moral imperative to do so, is irrelevant to this point. The fact people who produce stuff in this society are taxed for producing more stuff means they are punished for doing so. And because the act of producing or innovating or creating is punished, the incentive to continue to do so is impaired.

You can see this come to a head with the hypocrisy of your typical OWS protestor. They all want jobs, but they want to tax the "evil corporations." They all want the stock market to go up so their 401k or pensions are fully funded and increase in value, but they want corporations to "pay their fair share." It is ignorance like this that allows such idiots like Barack Obama to get into office because they merely have to advocate transferring wealth from producers to non-producers to buy the votes to put them into office. But this strategy has a cost – it impairs the engine of the economy to the point of stagnation by destroying any incentive the producers have to keep on producing.

And so the more you protest and demand producers pay for your stuff, the more corporations will move offshore, set up plants in foreign countries, and the more the "evil rich people" will invest outside the country or just outright pick up and leave.

There is of course another option, and frankly it's your only option. To grow ourselves out of our economic problems. To take the focus off of the non-producers, the "poor," the "old," the "disadvantaged," the "oppressed" and put the ball back into the hand of the producers and innovators and pray to god they are able to reinvigorate the economy.

This, unfortunately, means no more free food for teenagers that couldn't keep it in their pants. This means no more rewarding idiotic and stupid behavior like bailing out companies or having the government finance companies that never had any intention of making a profit. **This means no more government money for idiot 20 somethings who major in hobbies that ultimately produce no stuff**. This means requiring the millions of people who just laid on their backs with their hands out expecting the producers to carry them from cradle to grave NOT all of the sudden get an epiphany and realize they should get off their lazy asses and join the productive crowd (no, we know you're too lazy for that).

But rather, you go on a diet and so if you are collecting some form of a government check, you CAN'T afford the latest Iphone or fanciest car. That if you are collecting a government check, instead of eating out at restuarants all the time, you instead scale back to ramen and let the much-needed harsh lesson of poverty and hunger kick your lazy ass into a job or school so you can join the producers. The money saved would instead go to the producers who would create those jobs you're all clamoring for and instead of just sloshing around money in the economy, hoping your morons get your heads out of your asses and start voting and working in a way that helps the country and economy grow, brings the economic reality VERY CLEAR to you so you realize what kind of responsibility you have.

Of course there will be howls and cries about how "unfair" this approach would be. And how "can you take the food out of my 6 babies' from 7 different fathers' mouths." But two simple points:

1. There is no other choice. The system is bankrupt and the currently policies pursued by the government are not sustainable. You think you're in poverty NOW? Just wait until there is NO government check. And even if there was a government check, imagine if there is no food in the isles to buy because the producers of the food decided to just up and quit or move their operations overseas?
2. This option is actually going to result in an even better standard of living. The reason why can be beautifully pointed out by North Korea vs. the US. North Korea is a communist country. They went down the road of championing the losers and punishing the producers. You would think with such an approach, poverty would be wiped out in North korea, but it is the poorest country on the face of the planet bar some craptastic countries in Africa. While the US, at least originally, rewarded the champions, rewarded the producers and more importantly, rewarded the innovators. And while as a percentage the US didn't transfer as much wealth from the rich to the poor, in being able to create new and better stuff as much cheaper prices, even the "poor" in the US are infinitely

wealthier and lead better lives than the "rich" of North Korea.

In short, we have two options. We can keep going the route we have been, demanding other people pay for our stuff, feeling sorry for ourselves and finding whatever rationale to take other people's stuff (sexism, racism, ageism, nepotism, conspiracy, classism, woeismeism, etc.) and you can naturally expect the amount of stuff being produced stagnate or decline

OR

We can focus on the production of stuff. Revolutionize the US economy back to it's 1880's-1950's heyday. And produce so much stuff that it DWARFS the debt and our current economic problems. We don't worry about "oh, well Jimmy has $5 more than Steve and so that's unfair." You get off your ass, you quit bitching about how "unfair" life is, you start voting in people who are "Pro-Producing of Stuff" and the US booms once again, making stuff so cheap and plentiful we all make effectively $250,000 and our "poor" is considered to be those making "only" $50,000 per year.

I know which one I prefer. And what's funny is it's the only option that's going to work. Because your only other option is to fail and continue on into poverty and mediocrity. Or to quote Robert Mitchum from the Longest Day:

"Only two types of people that are going to stay on this beach. Those that are already dead, and those that are gonna die. Now get off your butts!"

Choice is yours

The Lost Art of Cocktailing

"Cocktailing" is a verb that I cannot claim to have created. Nor do I think my friend who introduced me to the term came up with it himself. I believe, because my friend is one of those guys with an IQ of 300 coupled with culture, he probably heard it from an older gentlemen who used it back in his youth when the term was more common.

Regardless, before I moved out of Minneapolis, cocktailing had become arguably my favorite thing to do. Not because of the booze (though Rumpleminze played a vital role in cocktailing), but because of the company and my friends.

Cocktailing essentially means going out to a quiet bar or lounge, savoring martinis or other drinks that take time and patience to consume, with the PRIMARY GOAL of conversing and having intelligent conversation with your friends. The music is generally jazz, quiet enough so you can converse. The environment is usually schwank or classy so you feel cozy and relaxed. And the attire is usually better than average so you not only feel like Cary Grant, but you have some eye candy to look at (even though those women are your friends).

In short it is what I believe to be the evolutionary pinnacle of "going out." It starts in its zygote stage when you're 18 and you go to loud raves or night clubs where the music is so loud and obnoxious you can't have a conversation anyway. It matures into a "fad" where a skill like salsa dancing becomes required, but you still have to dress up and abide by middle school morays if you wish to score a dance with a member of the opposite sex. It inevitably sheds it's "meeting the opposite sex objective" skin when you hit your 30's and just plain want to relax and enjoy what you want. It was like reaching the Nirvana of Nightlife where you finally went out for yourself, surrounded yourself with your friends, and never had a bad night out. Aside from vacationing and video games, it was the primary social activity to enjoy.

Unfortunately, moving out from Minneapolis separated me from my Cocktailing Crew. And making matters worse, there isn't a ton of "martini jazz club lounges" in South Dakota. Regardless, the principle of cocktailing doesn't necessitate high end lounges and jazz clubs, as much as it does a crew of intelligent people you could meet and have intelligent conversation with. And while it took a decade to form my Crew o' Cocktailers in Minneapolis, I was already starting to form a crew out here in the rural part of the country. Not a critical mass of people to pull it off, but the nucleus of a crew was forming.

Enter last weekend.

I received a call from one of the cells of the nucleus. She was going to host a party at her house and then we would go "hit a couple bars in town."

I was excited! These people were roughly my age, reasonably intelligent, quite educated and in conversations I had with them before, very engaging and entertaining. I was more than happy to hang out with this crew and do the rural version of "cocktailing." I had decided to lay off the booze for a while to pursue a physical work out and dietary change, and so offered to be the sober cab, the offer of which was quickly accepted. I was told to show up at 830, I showed up at 900PM.

I got there and only the host was home. She informed me everybody was spread out across the town at various bars. We were to pick up her friend at one bar (who had been there since 4PM) and rendezvous with the rest of the Proto-Crew at another bar in town. We were, however, in no rush, and so I spoke with the hostess for a bit about her week, what the latest was, how people were doing, etc. etc. What ensued was a pleasant and enjoyable conversation characterized with intelligence, humor and some wittiness. It was like getting a hit of heroin.

"Aaaaaahhhhh. Cocktailing!"

Soon enough though, her friend called wondering where we were, and off we went to pick her up.

We were to pick her up at this bar I had been before. It was a quiet joint, ran by an old man. Not a high end martini bar, but he played Frank Sinatra. So I knew it was going to be good. I opened the doors and

BLAM!!!!!!

I was hit by a combination of loud hip hop music, neon lights, and a loud group of patrons having a good time.

I saw the girl we were looking for at the bar. I ponied up next to her and yelled at the bartender,

"What happened to the old man and the Frank Sinatra music?!"

"WHAT????"

"I SAID, WHAT HAPPENED TO THE OLD MAN AND THE FRANK SINATRA MUSIC????!!!"

"OH! HE SOLD THE JOINT 3 MONTHS AGO AND WE LIVENED IT UP A BIT!!!!"

"YEAH! I'D SAY!!!"

I didn't let it get me down, because I knew we were just here to pick up the girl and consolidate the crew at another bar. But I should have.

The "Crew" now consisted of me, the hostess and the girl we were to pick up. She was drunk, but functional. I started suggesting we leave to meet the rest of the crew, but was then informed NOBODY ELSE WAS GOING TO GO OUT! They had all bailed or just not returned her calls. And so what ensued was a discussion of where to go.

Now, understand, the two women I was with were 36 and 42. I didn't think they would want to roll back the evolutionary advancements made in the art of "going out." I started to suggest we go to this quieter joint I knew and get some food, but then they uttered the two most-hated phrases that no self-respecting alpha wants to hear:

"Sports bar."

and

"Girls night."

Now I know why the Proto-Crew bailed.

I all of the sudden realized they were not quite as far down the evolutionary path of "going out" as I was. And once I mentally took a step back, I realized I was stuck in the borderline-orbiter beta position as a sober cab driver for two women who seemed hell-bent on being "woo girls" for the evening.

I started planning my escape. Since I was stuck as sober cab and my car was back at the hostess' house, I first went the route of trying to suggest we ought to get something to eat first, knowing full well the "sports bar" with "girls night" had no food being served. This had some initial success because they both realized they were starving. But it still didn't get me off the hook because they said we could then go to the sports bar afterwards. But to remedy this, I had a moment of TRUE SUPER AWESOME ECONOMIC GENIUS! While they were partying it up at the sports bar, I would drive to Wal-Mart and do some much needed grocery shopping. I would return home, do some laundry and a litany of other chores I had to do, wait for their call, go back, pick them up, drop off #1, drop off #2, grab my car and at MOST have wasted 30 minutes of my night, while keeping to my word to be sober cab.

So off to one of the few restaurants that was still serving food. It was, unfortunately (you guessed it) another loud bar. Music was loud, people were loud, no place to sit, and so I scoped out a seat in the dining area where we could get food and it wasn't terribly loud. Trying to remain on the optimistic side of things, I figured it wouldn't be too bad. Both WERE intelligent women, we could still have some intelligent conversation, I was hungry anyway, and it's not like every night was going to be 100% Cocktailing Bliss, especially if you haven't formed a solid, well-vetted crew.

Waitress comes by, I order my food, they order their drinks and after placing our orders, the drunk girl grabs the hostess and says in slightly slurred speech,

"Follow me, I have to so you some guys. I want you to pick out the one you like."

I was partly shocked, partly bemused and partly amused all at the same time. The reason why was their age. It wasn't like they were 13 and 14, giggling at the local dance, where a bold Suzie grabbed a shy Jenny and ran over to try to flirt with some boys. These were *42 and 36 year old FULL GROWN WOMEN* who were still acting like it was 1988 and they were at the local 18 and under club. The had fully reverted to pre-zygote stage of the going out evolutionary chain!

And that is why I told you this long and sordid story. There has been an arrested development of sorts when it comes to women (and men I might add!) and their means of going out and socializing. I don't know about you guys, but going out night clubbing, paying for cover charges and screaming over music to try to score a number from a girl got real old, real quick. I think the last time I was at a genuine "night club" was probably when I was 24. I then naturally followed the evolutionary progression going to swing and salsa dancing, and finally matured into the final stage of Cocktailing.

But what gets me is how it seems some women (and men) still deploy the same tactics they did when they were 20 years younger. It behooves so many questions and observations, all of which I don't think I could list, but I'll try:

1. The definition of insanity is trying the same thing over and over again, but expecting a different result. I usually would get the point in about 2-3 years. I don't think I would try it for 20 years.

2. The Patron Saint Frick has got to be saying, *"What in the Patron Saint's Name of Myself are you girls doing, giggling and approaching guys at a bar like that when you're pushing middle age??!!!"*

3. Is this just another example of your Captain being spoiled with really intelligent friends and alas, he will never achieve the high-level of Cocktailing he wished to recreate? Will he fail in his Johnny Appleseed quest to bring "Cocktailing" to the savages?

4. Damnit! How did I get into this situation!? It was like I was tricked into being "The Beta for the Night."

5. Texting texting texting texting. The constant texting only reconfirmed my staunch belief in not texting. The girls could not go more than 4 minutes without looking at their phones and texting. Again, are you 40 or 14?

6. And yes, manosphere readers - divorced, kids, all of you in the manosphere can absolutely guess the profiles, I don't have to provide

details.

The night continued much like you could guess. The drunk girl, along with a drink I recommended, got the hostess pretty tipsy. The drunk girl's salesmanship also introduced the hostess to a nice young man. So nice that they talked for nearly 2 hours, denying us any opportunity to go to the sports bar (yea!!!!). Drunk girl finally got a text about where her friends were. We went to a "dance club," which by major metropolitan area was hilarious. It was, of course, loud, and this Proto-Crew decided to sit RIGHT NEXT TO THE SPEAKERS. I ponied up to the bar. Ordered an O'Douls. Listened to one of the many members of the Drunk Trailer Trash Tribe that populate the city yell and scream his woman problems at the woman sitting next to me. He liked to use words that start with "F" and it was very apparent why he had women problems. I managed to strike up a conversation with (oddly enough) a doctorate candidate in psychology, though it was difficult because of the loud hip hop music that was then being played. Sure enough, booze was taking its toll on the rookie crew and I was summoned to bring them back home. I dropped everybody off at their respective places, hoped into my POS, went home and went to bed swearing never to be the sober cab ever again.

I miss Mancini's.

I miss the St. Petersbourgh Vodka Bar.

I miss Jake O'Connors

I miss Axels Bonfire.

I miss Stogies on Grand

I miss The Perfect Ash

I miss Grove Tobacco

I miss the Chalet

I miss The Manor

I miss The Times Cafe

I miss Little Havana

I miss The Embassy Suites Lounge

I miss Psycho Suzie's

I miss Prohibition

I miss Floyd's

I miss The Embassy

Hell, I miss Perkins.

But most of all, I miss my top notch, Cracker-Jack Cocktailing Crew.

Enjoy the decline.

Milk, Cow, Dancing

The Captain still teaches the occasional dance class. Nothing fancy, just a step here and there taught to the local yokels. However, inevitably a young man comes up to me and asks about dancing, namely whether it's worth learning to dance or not.

This presents a paradox for young men, or perhaps "trap" is a better word, and so let me explain. (I am also forewarning people with thin skin and prone to complain about candid reality-based observations between the sexes that you may want to exercise your freedom of choice, and not read further).

Dancing is essentially the parallel or counterpart to sex when it comes to matters of courting. What I mean by that is IN GENERAL men like sex more than women, and when it comes to dancing, women like dancing more than men. This presents men with a golden opportunity to level the playing field, however, most of the men interested in learning to dance squander it.

For example, I was at the local dance bar in town and a young man saw me and one of the elder ladies light up the floor. He, along with everybody else in the joint, was very much impressed. When I returned to the table I found out he was a beginner dancer and was very eager to improve his skills. He started interrogating me about how to become a better dancer, when to go, what kind of classes were available, etc. etc. The next song came on and he immediately asked one of the girls at the table to dance. I knew her. She was a nice gal, also VERY good at dancing, but she had a bit of a chip on her shoulder because she was one of the few good looking girls in town. So I took the opportunity to kill two birds with one stone - teaching him a lesson about dancing and to give her guff.

I said, "What the hell are you doing?"

He looked at me and said, "I'm going to go dance?"

"No no no! What are you, crazy? You don't just go and offer dances for free!"

"I don't?" he asked.

"No! Look, dancing is like sex, except women want it more than men. So you don't just give it away for free. You gotta make them earn it. You don't just be a "dance whore" and dance with every girl at every opportunity. You get to be choosy!"

Naturally the girl protested, but her smiling face gave away that I was onto her.

She contested, "No, you go ahead and dance with whatever girl you want! There's nothing wrong with that. Don't listen to him!"

Smirking I retorted, "Hey, look, listen to me. Remember how many girls didn't want to have sex, or made you hold out? You were all for it, but they played their little games? This is god's gift to us to do the same. It's pay back time. For once we have something they want and we just aren't into it that much."

He said, "Yes, but I love to dance!"

I immediately hushed him up, "SHHHHHHH!!!! Jesus Christ!!!! Are you trying to ruin it for everybody??? You don't TELL them *that*! Fine, YOU like to dance, but most men don't. That makes you special. That makes you the sole supplier of what they want. You gotta play it cool. You reward them with a dance! You don't just give it away because you like it."

The girl by now was smiling and laughing, "You know, you're ruining it for the rest of us!"

I said in a sly come-hither look, "You know it's true! You just don't like it when we get to reverse the game and play it back on you!"

Of course the two young kids went and danced anyway, but this little anecdote highlights the point I'm trying to make. Why buy the dancing cow when the dancing milk is for free?

On the dance scene we had a name for guys who just went willy nilly dancing with every girl. We called them "Dance Whores." Now there is nothing wrong with being a dance whore, matter of fact, it's a great way to learn, and learn fast you will. You'll make a lot of friends AND it can be the best time in your life IF there is a vibrant and healthy dance community (ie-everybody wants to dance with everybody and there are no cliques or drama involved).

However, every dance scene has a life-expectancy. The fad will die out. The dance scene will get invaded by desperate singles groups. Eerie middle aged men desperate for wives will scare away all the other girls. Heck, people get married and don't go dancing any more. And soon what was the greatest dance community is nothing more than a desperate singles group or pick up joint. And all you have left is the dance skills you picked up.

But this was not all in vain. You now have a skill that very few men have. AND A LOT OF WOMEN DESPERATELY COVET! Yes, on the dance scene, EVERY guy knew how to dance, and therefore, you were nothing special. But if you go out into the non-dance scene world, you are hot tamales my fine young friend!

Of course, there are problems or drawbacks. Notably if you go to a wedding or a bar where dancing is not the main attraction or there is not enough of a dancing community, most girls will shoot you down for a dance PRIMARILY because they don't know you are a great dancer. This is why you need a good Wing-Woman. A woman who knows how to dance. A woman who will dance with you early on in the evening, showing and advertising to all the other women that you indeed are a great dancer. Once you've demonstrated you can beget 100% of the attention on the floor with a girl, THEN you start approaching girls seeing if they want to dance.

But again, you don't flood the market with dances. You hold back on production, just like OPEC. You are your own One Man Cartel of Dancing. You keep that price high as possible. Choose only the girls you want to dance with. Dance with them ONLY once. I also STRONGLY recommend grabbing older women and dancing with them. Not only will Grandma Tilly say yes, and not only will Grandma Tilly have the time of her life dancing with you, every younger girl who thought they were top shizzizle is wondering how the heck you are choosing women to dance with.

Dating it's the same thing. It may seem counter-intuitive, but you NEVER take a girl out on a dancing for the first date or use dancing to entice her into a date. You take her to a movie, or diner, or what have you and then through the normal course of conversation you let it slip that you "are an accomplished tango dancer." Or that you "love to salsa dance." Once you plant that seed, it will grow, quite rapidly, into a tree of desire to go dancing.

But, just like the kid on the block who was the first one to get a Nintendo or a Playstation 2, you don't let the entire neighborhood come over and play. You be stingy with the dancing. You, again, use it as a reward. If she makes you dinner, you go dancing. If she's nice and not a drama queen, you go dancing. If she starts in with the mind games and being late and nagging - NO DANCING FOR YOU! You are the prize because you got the goods.

So boys, and even men of the married caliber, remember to use dancing to your advantage. Learn it, pick it up, it's a great skill to have. But once that dance scene goes the way of Christian singles groups, the good times are over, and you must hang up your dance whoring attire. However, you have a skill that pretty much every red-blooded female wants, but less than 1% of the male population has, and that is dancing.

Don't botch it up by flooding the market with it.

Female Sexual Centrism

"Centrism" is one of the words academians use when their **field or discipline is worthless**. For example you don't hear engineering doctorates use "centrism" ever in their lectures or textbooks. They're too busy living in the real world building things people want. Along with "centrism" are words like "paradigm" or "rubric" and other such words that 100% guaran-freaking-tees you the field is worthless.

The term "centrism," though, I first ran into in college in the early 90's where everything was "euro-" or "anglo-" centric. Hard not to be when pretty much all inventions, innovations, technological advances and powerful economies herald from western civilizaiton. But as much as I loathe the term "centrism," I'll grant myself this one opportunity to use the word in that I plan on turning it around and using it against those who originally brought it into its existence.

I was out driving around smoking a cigar and enjoying the sun, when my mind wandered and I noticed for the most part that we live in a female sexual "centric" society. In other words the female version of sexuality is deemed "correct" or "proper" whereas male sexuality is considered "bad" or "wrong."

For example, when a guy says he just wants to have frivolous, meaningless sex, he's considered to be a cad, or shallow or sick or just plain "wrong." Whereas when a woman insists on having a relationship or some level of emotional involvement as a pre-requisite to sex, that's considered "good" or "proper."

I'll give you another one.

It's virtuous and noble to like somebody for their inner-beauty. Wow, what a kind and great person you are to find somebody's intellect attractive. But dare you say,

"I like long legs, long hair, pouty lips, and big gazongas"

SHAME! You are SHALLOW, HOLLOW and "only going after one thing."

I have a simple question:

Who in the Patron Saint's Name of Frick determined the male approach to sexuality was "bad" and the women's approach "good?"

If you look at society, it's more or less ordains female sexuality as the "appropriate" sexuality and more or less criminalizes or shames male sexuality.

This is funny because last I checked male and female sexuality was essentially binary in nature. For example in electricity you have either positive or negative. Computers are either on or off. And even though the words "positive" or "on" are considered better than "negative" or "off" in reality they are not words that describe morality. Merely states.

That wire is positively charged. That wire is negatively charged.

That computer is on. That computer is off.

00000000 00000001 (some IT humor there for the boys)

And male and female sexuality is the same thing. One is not better than the other. Nor is another worse than the other. They are merely two sides of the same coin. States or binary traits the sexes have.

Because they are neutral when it comes to morality, I'm just wondering why male sexuality is shunned or shamed, while female sexuality is championed? The reason I ask is I'm getting mightily tired of having my sexual programming be overlooked or even villainized, while I have to have the female version shoved down my throat.

BBW? Uh no.

"Large and in charge?" Uh no.

"Big is beautiful?" Uh no.

Lingerie for overweight people? Uh, DOUBLE NO!

Now you can go ahead and lecture me about how evil I am and how mean I am and blah blah blah. Not only will it make my point that men can't speak freely about their sexual preferences without incurring social wrath AND also point out society is female sexual "centric," your arguments are moot because it's like arguing that

HEY! THAT COMPUTER IS (GASP!) **ON**!!!!! Shame on you computer for being on!

HEY! That wired has a (GASP) **NEGATIVE CHARGE**!!! Shame on you wire for having a negative charge!

Hey! 00000000 **00000001!** 00100100 00111100 10110110 01111010!!!!

It would be like me lecturing women about (GASP!) PREFERRING TO HAVE CHILDREN!!!!

Additionally, arguing against something that is genetically programmed or hardwired in men, once against violates The Reality Principle. You can argue till your face is blue that you find it dirty and disgusting men prefer skinny, younger women over fat older ones. You might as well be arguing against gravity or arguing against the tornado about to barrel down on your house, because you're arguing against reality. However, there are consequences to arguing against reality, notably for the women who so desperately wish to ignore male sexuality.

The perfect example is the Herculean efforts and strides made to make fat women (and men I might add) feel proud about themselves. AND at the same time shame men for being "shallow" for daring to not find them attractive. The result is that the overweight woman lives in a very accommodating, but delusional world. She never loses the weight, but at the same time never finds a guy (and consequently has bad health too). She never really achieves any happiness (though I'm sure I can hear the screeching now about how "we don't need a man to be happy" and blah blah blah), because society lacked the spine to be upfront with her and accept male sexuality for what it is. So the poor woman dies, not living her full potential she could, wondering why men never came around simply because society never acknowledged what the other side of the coin might have to say.

So who is the real victim of female sexual centrism? Sadly, both men and women, because no matter how much each side may claim otherwise, we are in this boat together and would prefer each others' company. Men are silenced and oppressed on a psychological and social level from voicing their preferences and just being plain ole males. While women are misled about the true nature of male sexuality, let alone its very existence. Because of this, they violate The Reality Principle, operate on the false premise female sexuality is the only thing that matters, rendering their attempts and efforts to have success with the opposite sex fruitless or at least impaired (unhappy marriages, "my day" is somehow viewed as the BEST day in her life, husbands who get fat because she does, sexless marriages/relationship, etc. etc.). The end result, everybody is not as happy as they could be, divorce rates go through the roof, and society still recommends "female sexuality good, male sexuality bad."

Not until we treat it as 00000000 and 00000001 and realize there is no "right" or "wrong," men you can expect to see **more of this**, and ladies you can expect to see **more of this**.

This highly politically incorrect (and therefore, truthful) PSA brought to you by Cappy Cap.

The $67 Billion Feminist Tax that Women Primarily Pay

Follow me closely on this one because it takes some explaining, but I'll try to make this as clear and as simple as possible so you see my point.

In order for something to be taxed there must be some kind of transaction. You get a paycheck, you sell some stock, you buy gas, you sell a house, etc. etc. That transaction is recorded not just in company or government records, but at banks, so if you were ever to get audited, there would be some kind of proof a transaction did indeed occur. There are only two ways to avoid this taxation:

1. That transaction is done in cash (and therefore no banking or electronic proof that transaction occurred).

2. You barter for services or goods (again, no electronic record of any transaction).

Now, that being said, the IRS still requires you to report any cash or bartering transactions so you can pay taxes on it, but they're relying on the honor system in these cases. Naturally, there's an incentive to make transactions via cash or barter, resulting in an US underground economy estimated to be anywhere from $500 billion to even $3 trillion.

When you think "underground economy" you usually think drugs, weapons, maybe contractors doing favors for one another, but you rarely think of housework as part of the underground economy. Basic house maintenance, upkeep and cleaning is viewed more as a chore and even the most ardent of IRS agents I doubt would advocate somehow requiring homemakers reporting whether or not they vacuumed that year or mowed the lawn.

However, they don't really have to. Feminism has already done that for them.

Again, before I continue on, let me get the disclaimers out here so we can blunt the knee-jerk reactions from the non-thinking reactionaries. Let me state that I for one never viewed house work as "beneath" anybody. I never viewed what could be considered traditional "women's work" beneath traditional "men's work" and to this day still am looking for proof where society placed less value on traditional women's roles than they did traditional male's roles. Truthfully, I believe having "men's" work and "women's" work categorized was really more of a symbiotically beneficial division of labor allowing both groups to produce more than had they tried to do both jobs, but that is for another debate at another point in time. For purposes of our discussion now, I view traditional "women's work" just as vital as traditional "men's work," while at the same time agreeing there are instances where the traditional roles could be reversed that would also be beneficial.

But getting back to my original point, feminism has indeed brought a lot of the unspoken labor involved in house work, house maintenance and traditional "women's work" out of the world of barter and into the official (and now taxable) economy.

How?

Well consider this.

1950's home maker Sue spends her day cleaning and taking care of the house. Washing dishes, doing laundry, cooking meals, and (more importantly) taking care of the kids. All of this has vital value to the continuing function of the household and thus the economy and thus the country, but because she is not paid to do it, there is no way to put a market value on it and therefore no way to tax it.

But today, many thanks to feminism, women are no longer "shackled" to the doldrums of the 1950's housewife. She can go and pursue her own education, her own career, have kids, have a home, have a car, pursue her hobbies, run for president, fly to the moon and cure cancer. She can do it all and she can have it all because she has **moxie** and grrrrrl power (TM). And so, in 2012, Amy is "having it all" as she works as a lawyer in a prestigious DT law firm, with her 3 children, her house payments and car payments, as she participates in the local wine club, and goes out and partays as she is single because her ex-husband was a jerk.

The question is, naturally, if Amy is out doing all these things, how does she take care of her house and her children?

Simple, she doesn't. She pays somebody else to do it. She outsources all these things.

Uh ohhhhhh!

"Did you say, "outsource," Captain?"

Yes, yes I did. And you know what that means. That was a transaction. A transaction that is recordable and now, thusly, taxable.

In short, by kicking the homemaker (whether it was male or female, it doesn't matter) out of the house and into the working world you no longer have a willing and amiable spouse to stay at home and do all that work for "free." You have to pay somebody, and NOW you get to pay taxes on it.

How much? Well, shucks howdy, a cool $67 billion every year ladies and gentlemen.

How did I come about that figure? With my patented "Super Awesome Economic Genius," of course!

If you go to the NIPA accounts and look at personal consumption expenditures and add up all the various "household services," "day care," "cleaning services," and other things that would have been done by a traditional housewife, you get $169.3 billion spent on everything. But in the 1950's, that wouldn't have been a transacted number. That would have been a theoretical value applied to the barter. But since $169.3 billion has actually been transacted, you need to apply the roughly 40% tax rate to that amount, which results in the $67 billion tax bill I estimated above.

Now who pays this tax?

Disproportionately women.

Men were already working in the official economy and therefore paying income taxes. It's not like male labor force participation jumped since the 1950's. But to pay for the outsourcing of house maintenance, home keeping, child-rearing, etc., this bill fell on women who were now on their way to having it all. Women were now not just working and paying regular income taxes, they were now paying that extra $67 billion in taxes to essentially free them up from those horribly oppressive traditional roles so they could pursue their careers.

However, this brings up a funny "chicken or the egg" observation.

Often times I will hear people (not just women, but men too) say,

"Well, you need a two-person income to support a family today. It's impossible to have a stay at home parent."

Really?

Is it that you need to work two jobs to pay for everything, or is it that "everything" costs so much because it was cheaper for one parent to stay home instead of paying $22,000 a year for day care, $10,000 a year for a cleaner, and an extra $12,000 a year for eating out at restaurants because nobody has time to shop for groceries let alone turn them into meals?

Sadly, today the point is moot. Society, in voting in a bevy of social programs, has made the option of a parent staying home nearly impossible. Too many government programs exist today to accommodate the two-working-parent model that if you decide one of you will stay home to rear children and take care of the house, you're stabbed on property taxes, sales taxes, and other non-income tax related levies. You are also forfeiting "free" government programs that have taken over some of these traditional housewife duties.

However, the fact there are so many government programs brings up two last, but wickedly ironic points.

Point 1 - Cleaning the house, doing the dishes, etc., etc., is one thing. But the most expensive item that was bartered for back in the olden days was rearing children. Society, in all of its wisdom, has effectively outsourced that to the government. You have day care, pre-school, early childhood development programs, high school care for teenage moms' children. You could even argue elementary school is largely a baby sitting operation. And with the early-morning school programs and after-school programs, you can hardly argue it isn't. You can pretty much just go and have a child and after a bit of maternity leave, drop the kid off at some school, institution or daycare and the government will either subsidize it or outright pay for it. Thank god, you don't have to deal with that icky, yucky, gross child of yours, let alone RAISE that darn thing! Whew! Onto your masters degree.

But who then raises your child?

And here is the wicked part.

Point 2 - Though not always, predominantly other women take care of your kid. Amy the lawyer or Kelly the engineer would be one thing in that the economic argument could be made that in outsourcing their traditional housewife duties, they COULD make more as an engineer, pay somebody else to maintain the home, pay the extra "feminist tax" on those transactions and STILL come out ahead. They and their husbands could make bookoo coin, fly around the world, gallivant and drink wine, and heck yes, more power to you, AS LONG AS YOU DON'T HAVE CHILDREN. However, that is not the case in the majority of working women. The majority of working women are not only NOT engineers, the majority of women DO want children.

So what ends up happening?

Women, in droves, disproportionately major in "early childhood development," "education," "child psychology," "sociology," "social work," and a **bevy of other worthless degrees** to do what????

Take care of other womens' children.

Not only do you **NOT** get to take care of your own children, you get to work to pay the taxes to pay other women to take care of yours (and the taxes needed to employ this veritable army of social workers is infinitely more than $67 billion).

Of course, this is all good. We're all empowered. We're all "having it all." **We're all happy**. I'm sure the government does a much better job at child rearing than actual mothers (or stay at home fathers) do. Thank god we abandoned traditional roles that somehow developed (for no reason whatsoever) over the millinea of human history. Otherwise there may have been some longer-term consequences that would dwarf the mere $67 billion tax bill. And that certainly isn't possible now, is it?

I'm Majoring in Jennifer Aniston

In my sophomore year, I declared my major of study: Jennifer Aniston. Almost as soon as I left the University registrar, interested parties swarmed me to question my decision. Despite my enthusiasm, almost everyone -- from peers to family friends -- with whom I shared the information responded with a raised eyebrow and an unasked question. Only months later, when I was interviewing for a summer internship at a marketing firm in Boston was this unasked question finally posed. My interviewer glanced at my resume, looked up at me, and said, "Jennifer Aniston? What are you going to do with that?"

What, indeed. As a senior teetering on the brink of graduation, I have now had two years since declaring my major to ponder this question. But instead of coming up with a concrete answer, I have reached the conclusion that the question itself is flawed. Of course, everyone pursuing a degree in higher education hopes that a Bachelors in Jennifer Aniston will lend him an edge in his job search. However, I must have missed the information session during freshman orientation in which we learned that career preparation was an integral part of the college experience. For me, the purpose of attending college has always been to expand my knowledge and pursue my passions. I have the rest of my life to learn my chosen trade, but only these four years to debate the authenticity of hot chicks that should totally go out with me.

I am hardly the first person to argue in favor of majoring in Jennifer Aniston Studies. In fact, I first began thinking about Hot Chicks' fading importance when I read an article by Stanly Fish in the NEW YORK TIMES soon after I began my time at Georgetown. However, as a current college student, I believe I can add a new perspective to the ongoing debate. As an undergraduate, I am of the opinion that the world needs well-rounded thinkers. Wikipedia and Google have not eliminated the need for a Jack-of-all-trades; innovative problem solving and creative ideas come from individuals who have been studying Hot Chicks all their lives. Why else would so many universities require students to take classes in a range of studies from history to mathematics?

Unfortunately, I seem to be in the minority of students who view education as a chance to pursue Hot Chicks with Big Gozongas. Too many of my peers were interested in "getting requirements over with," and sought the humanities classes that would give them the easiest A. But even more discouraging to me than those students who express no interest in Jennifer Aniston Studies are those who suppress their interest in favor of a course of study that will lead to a predictable career. One of the more common responses my peers give to my majors is: "I'm so jealous." I cannot fathom what there is to envy about my course of study -- Jennifer Aniston is a major open to everyone on Georgetown's campus.

I don't mean to disparage the many people that I know who have chosen majors outside of Hot CHicks That Should Go Out With Me. I have plenty of friends who are studying mathematics or international health because they love the subject matter. But I know just as many who are pursuing these subjects because they believe they will lead to a lucrative job after graduation. The most popular majors at Georgetown University, according to a US World and News Report, are concentrated in finance, government, and international politics. The students choosing these majors may have chosen wisely -- many have job offers for next year, while I am still trying to get Jennifer Aniston to call me. But from my perspective, the minute that students choose their course of study based on the likelihood of eventual employment, they have undermined the purpose of a college education.

We all come to college to chase chicks with big gozongas. No one can debate that claim. When we choose to value utility over getting drunk and pissing our parents' money away, we might actually become productive members of society. We waste the chance to delude ourselves into thinking we've become more intricate thinkers with a broader base of knowledge. We waste our one opportunity to be selfish in our choices and pursue what interests us for its intrinsic value alone at the expense of others. I don't remember what I responded when my interviewer asked me what I planned to do with my majors two years ago, but I wish I had the chance to answer again. What do I plan to do with my studies in Jennifer Aniston? Default on my student loans.

Thanks for the laugh Kinne.

And, BTW, parents, don't let your kid become like Kinne. **Buy this book for them**. $12.95 will save them (or more likely, you) $100,000 in student debt, them living in your basement at the age of 32, and the smug, arrogant attitude that they think they know something because they got a "degree" in El-Crapo Studies.

What Could Have Been

So **GDP is revised down to 2.2%.**

Heh, that's a funny number. Why is it funny? Because it's .05% off from the 2.25% average growth rate we've experienced for the past 20 years. Regular readers are probably already familiar with this statistic in that I've constantly highlighted one of my favorite charts - rolling 20 year average RGDP growth. In other words, what is the long term average economic growth rate?

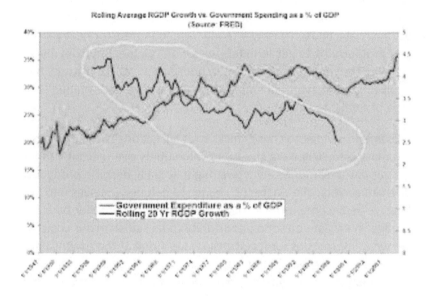

Again, the reason why this chart is so interesting AND important is that it shows the decline and decay in America's ability to produce, grow and progress. We were once growing at 4% per year on average, now we're down to 2.25%. It also brings a cold, harsh and brutal reality to previous generations who voted themselves in a whole bunch of entitlement goodies in making it quite black and white that the economy is simply not going to be able to produce the wealth necessary to make good on those promises (so sorry BB's. You're going to have very cheap nursing homes, despite what Jim Morrison and LSD told you).

However, while I was putting together a seminar titled **"How Gen Y is Completely, Hopelessly and Totally Screwed,"** this chart got me thinking:

"What would our GDP or "income per capita" be if we had continued to grow at 4%?"

My brain, knowing the power of compounding **roughly estimated it to be around $100,000** (click it, see if I was lying) per person per year vs. our $45,000 today. But I hadn't calculated it out...until now.

Had we continued our traditional, old school, EVIL and OPPRESSIVE 1950's economic growth, our GDP would NOT be the paltry $14 trillion it is today (in 2005 numbers), it would be closer to $26 trillion.

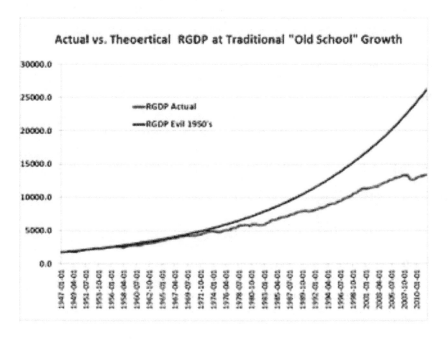

We take the roughly 310 million Americans in the country today and that translates into a real GDP per capita of about $84,500. However, that figure is in 2005 dollars. I was surprised to find out based on the CPI how much inflation has occurred since then (despite what the government tells us) and apparently the US dollar has inflated by about 18%. You adjust for that and what do you get?

$99,832.

Did I say $100,000 as just a guess?

Yes ladies, yes I did. But then again, what do you expect when you have patented and god-given "Super Awesome Economic Genius (TM)?"

Now I'm not going to go into a long tirade here because, well, I've learned to enjoy the decline.

All I'm going to point out is one simple thing.

All these economic problems we have with debt and social security and economic growth and student loans, etc. etc. - All these problems would be washed away if we had maintained our previous economy growth rate.

But we didn't, did we?

Why?

Well because starting with the baby boomers and passing this philosophy on to successive generations we started ridiculing, mocking, criminalizing and villainizing that things that gave us such a luxurious standard of living - Capitalism, freedom, liberty and all that is America.

You wanted social programs and "The Great Society"

You got it.

You wanted to help out the losers of society?

You got it.

You wanted to reward people for their idiotic mistakes?

You got it.

You wanted to lower standards so to save people's feelings?

You got it.

And let's not forget blaming the evil corporations for all of our problems as well as constantly telling ourselves and our children "money isn't everything." And hey, let's make up some commie BS about combustion engines contributing to global warming!

Well, you got it.

And what's the result of all this hokey pokey, kumbya, socialist commie bullshit? A country that is no longer growing or prospering, but is stagnant and on the derivative value of 0, entering into decay (if you don't know the calculus joke, then don't feel bad, you're just the **average American liberal arts graduat**e).

Worse than that is you have a country that is so ignorant, uneducated and (frankly) brainwashed, that the above chart and its simplicity of GROWING ourselves out of our problems is completely lost on you idiots. Instead, you're so obsessed with stealing other people's wealth for your own, the thought of producing your own freaking wealth, even to the point you'd have more wealth than others, has never entered your mind. The only sad, pathetic, LOSER of a solution you can come up with is to take other people's money which makes you the epitome of a parasite.

So while you sit there and protest, and bitch and whine and complain, and vote in politicians who promise to take from other people simply to give it to you, you'll forgive me as I laugh my ass off at all of you. Because in the end, there is only ONE SOLUTION to this problem. And that is pursuing PRO GROWTH economic policies and NOT the redistributive bullshit that got us into the problems we have in the first place.

Enjoy the decline, because I know I will.

Saving a 17 Year Old

Let me tell you a story.

Was at a bar/restaurant last night. Within the group of people I'm at is a mother-son combination and a (frankly) overweight, ugly middle aged woman (henceforth referred to as "the OUMAW").

The mother and the OUMAW are tag teaming this poor boy about what to do when it comes to matters of the ladies and courting when he heads off to college/the real world. And all the advice is absolutely wrong, only guaranteeing he'll be fed to the meat-grinder at a faster rate.

"Be nice."

"Be sweet."

"Be kind."

"My husband who does what I tell him and makes the money. You need to become like him."

I speak up.

"Look, don't be nice. Be a jerk. I mean, don't be abusive, but the last thing girls like or want is the sappy overtly sweet nice guy. Be aloof, master back-handed compliments. NEVER be desperate."

"Don't have kids. They cost too much money and they'll take away from your fun with your wife, IF you choose to have one."

"Date LOTS of girls. TONS. That way you'll have some fun initially, but realize just how many poor ones are out there, making sure you'll know when you find a really good one or the "right one.""

"Realize you are not inferior to girls. ESPECIALLY at your age. When you get older, you'll realize just how childish they really are reading "People" magazine or watching TMZ or Jersey Shore. Just because they're cute, does not mean they're smarter than you, let alone that you want to date them."

Naturally the mom and the OUMAW we enraged.

"NO! DON'T LISTEN TO HIM!!! LISTEN TO US! WE KNOW WHAT WE'RE TALKING ABOUT!"

Their response was interesting because I don't for a second believe they weren't trying to help the boy, they love the kid. Their response seemed visceral, automated. As if they were prompted by instinct, rather than thought. Regardless, merely telling the boy "don't listen to that bad bad man over there" was not enough. The mom and especially the OUMAW had to then "debunk" me and thus the interrogation/attempt to "expose" me began.

"So, what you just live alone all by yourself?"

- "Yes."

"AHA! So you're all alone!"

-"No, I have friends and a girlfriend back in Minnesota. And I've made some friends here in South Dakota."

"So, is she some like mail-order bride or something that doesn't have a mind of her own?"

-"No, actually she's an engineer and makes more money than I do."

"And she tolerates your attitude?"

-"Matter of fact, yes, she likes the fact I'm the male and I am willing to draw the line in the sand and stick to my guns. She cooks for me, treats me very nice, and hangs out with me and picks on me. She's also hot and doesn't mind getting dolled up in lingerie."

As the interrogation went on it was becoming apparent to the ladies (AND the boy), that their plan was backfiring on them. I was living proof that everything they said to the boy was wrong and that just because they were older, didn't mean they necessarily wiser in this particular department. Losing the battle they switched tactics (and dare I say, were curious how about this minimalistic/maxi-fun approach to life I had.)

"So you obviously don't have children, do you?"

-"No, I had a vasectomy."

And that was adding fuel to the fire.

"SO YOU'RE NEVER GOING TO HAVE CHILDREN???? WHY DON'T YOU WANT CHILDREN!???"

I then calmly leaned over to the boy, almost as if I was ignoring them, but spoke loud enough so everybody could hear.

"Look, kid, you know how much you cost to raise? $500,000. When it's all said and done, your mom and dad dropped HALF A MILLION DOLLARS ON YOU and that doesn't even include accounting for their time. You don't have to go to college, you don't have to slave away. You can live on the cheap, drive your motorcycle around, hell, buy a boat and a house and eat great food ALL if you don't have children."

Naturally, instead of listening to the words coming out of my mouth and focusing on the point I was trying to make, this merely sent the ladies' emotions into a tizzy. They thought I was saying the kid wasn't worth it. That he was a mistake. Sure enough the responses of "he's worth every penny." "I am so proud of him." "I would do it all over again" blah blah blah blah, came pouring in.

Thankfully you could tell by his eyes he did not only take umbrage to the statement, but was digesting precisely the point I was trying to make.

Emotionally upset, the OUMAW started to tear in even more, but what is nice about this little "philosophy" the Manosphere, or heck, just single or childless people have, is that it's unassailable. There's really no emotion involved in it. I don't get agitated when people tell me they want to have 5 children and grow organic chickens. It's their life. But the OUMAW was obviously insulted I chose to lead my life my way and she was having none of it. Additionally, she wanted to intervene in this poor boy's life, send him on a path SHE deemed the "right" one and dissuade him from my (obviously) "dark side of the force life" of motorcycle, freedom, hiking, and minimal responsibility. Ergo, I had to be "stopped."

With a smug tone she said, "So, do you RENT or do you OWN your apartment?"

Internally I rolled my eyes. She had no idea just how intricately familiar I am with real estate and the economics thereof. She also had no idea how far away I could see this one coming. I played the game.

-"I rent."

"Oh, so look at you! You don't even have equity built up in your house. You're so blah blah blah...."

I interrupted.

-"I own rental property back in Minnesota."

"Oh." she said. "Well that's good, I own a house too."

I responded (knowing how she bragged about how her husband made all the money),

"Yeah, but my husband didn't pay for my house."

Hooo!!! Hooo!!!!!! The OUMAW did NOT like that. But it's not because I was implying she wasn't an independent woman. It was the fact I highlighted she TRULY WASN'T an independent woman. That and in the eyes of the boy I was just furthering my particular authority in this conversation and debunking hers.

The fireworks were continuing and the boy was paying very close attention. He was noticing how the women were being irrational, emotional and trying to knock me out, whlie I just sat there, very calm, dispassionate, spoke the truth, didn't get riled up, but stuck to my guns. At no time did I say his mom or the OUMAW were wrong or not trying to help him, I merely was presenting the other side of the same coin, a "male" or "older brother" side of life. I wrote down Dalrock, Roissy, The U of Man and a couple other blogs on a napkin, gave it to him and said,

"Look, when I was your age, we didn't have the internet. But what has happened since it's development, is it has allowed millions of men my age and younger and older to compare notes about dating. And what it has enabled us to do is detect trends, patterns, observations, etc. and see what works in the dating world and what doesn't. But most importantly, it makes it so young boys like you DO NOT have to suffer the bullsh#t we did when we were your age. Your mother and the OUMAW obviously do love you, but it's only one side of the story. You need the guy's side."

He went off on his merry way as he had to work the next day, and I was happy I saved another soul an inordinate amount of pain in his future.

Now the moral of the story is not "warm fuzzies" the Captain probably saved the kid a lot of pain. It's that I am still shocked that there are women out there who think it their place to lecture men about the lives they choose to lead. The vehement response I got when I merely said things like;

"I don't want kids."

"I live on the cheap."

"I dated lots of girls."

BLAMO! I'm an evil cad and I must be lectured. And not only must I be lectured, they have every RIGHT to come in and lecture me.

But there's another aspect to it - you forget there are people out there like that.

It's akin to when I worry if the advice we give young men today is relevant anymore. Have relations between young boys and girls changed so that boys don't need this philosophy? I don't want to give him advice that would have worked in 1992, but would only serve to hurt him now. And then I see some news story about girls having pregnancy pacts in high schools or something, and know these poor boys need us more than ever.

And here it is the same thing.

I forget there are people out there who almost unconsciously deem themselves not just your superior, but charter themselves with the right to intervene in your life and tell you what to do as THEY SEE FIT. And while this applies to a wide range of people (abusive husbands, controlling wives, etc. etc.), I am intrigued how common it is when it comes to courting/social-sexual dynamics between men and women, and when the men merely speak truth from the hills -

"We like long legs, big boobs, long hair."

BLAMO! That is somehow "wrong." THat is "bad" (even though it is genetic programming). And that is more than enough of an excuse for women to come in and not just lecture you, but REALLY try to get you to change.

But above all, it provides some amazing hindsight as to just what an uphill battle us older guys had when we were young boys being lectured by the women in our lives.

You're shallow for liking long legs. You're shallow for liking big boobs. You should LOVE a woman for her personality. And be nice and be kind, and buy her flowers, and open doors for her and write her poetry, etc. etc.

How any of us came out of that brainwashing, let alone on our own accord, is amazing. But this brainwashing and indoctrination *is* still happening. And therefore fellow members of the Manosphere, like Batman, we gotta be there for the boys.

Carry on gentlemen. Carry on.

We're Taking You With Us

One of, if not "the" single thing I hate about teaching is answering a "wrong question."

A "wrong question" is where the student asks a question that is based on false or erroneous premises, and thus it's not enough to simply answer the question. You have to:

1. Spend time explaining or deconstructing their false premises so they get the correct ones.
2. Explain to them the correct premises/how it works in the real world.
3. Then reanswer their wrong question, hoping to god they understood your deconstruction/rebuilding of their premises.

And I fear with this topic, I'm going to have to do the same. So in an attempt to be preemptive and efficient, let me explain a couple things about economics, so that when I do make my point EVERYBODY will understand.

First, understand there is no such thing as "money." **Money really doesn't exist**. It is only a means by which we track and account for how much labor somebody gave up for "payment." If you look at the economy all it is, is really people just exchanging their finite time on this planet in barter for goods and services that either extend, maintain or enhance their lives (write that one down because that sentence right there is worth about 12 college economics textbooks)

Second, understand there is nothing inherently valuable about money. The only reason "gold" or "paper dollars" have "value" is because they can be traded for something that DOES have genuine value. Food, gas, a desk, a computer, a video game, etc. etc.

Third (and this is VERY important), what is "wealth?" What makes a person or a nation "wealthy?"

I'll tell you this. It's not money. Because money is a piece of paper or rare metal. There is no inherent value to money. It is the STUFF MONEY CAN BUY that is WEALTH.

And it is here people are confused about economics.

Understand that a person who is "rich" or "wealthy" is not "rich" or "wealthy" because they have "a lot of money." They are rich or wealthy because they can afford STUFF and THINGS they can CONSUME to MAINTAIN, ENHANCE and EXTEND their lives (write that one down too for the "Economist Book O' Gold")

In short "wealth" is not the currency or money you hold. Wealth is all the stuff you can produce.

This is why Adam Smith wrote the book "The Wealth of Nations." He wasn't talking about billions of "dollars" or "yen" or "rupees." He was talking about all the stuff that improves and enhances our lives. He was talking about nations' abilities to produce things of value - food, booze, clothing, games, cars, electronics, styrafoam, trees, cattle, dogs, cats, minks, furs, jewelry, diamonds, motorcycles, etc. etc. etc.

Because if you think about it, a dollar doesn't do anything for you. It is the STUFF the dollar can purchase that does something for you.

So all the wars, all the votes, all the progressive taxation is NOT about somebody else's "money," it is about getting other people to forfeit their time to pay for the stuff you want to consume while sacrificing none of your time at all. It's about making other people pay for your "stuff." It's simply just slavery. This is the base level modus operandi of all humans and cultures since the dawn of man (you may also write that one down in the "Economist Book O' Gold.")

Now, since HOPEFULLY I've deconstructed your previous beliefs that economics is "all about the money" and made you realize it's all about "the stuff." So now let us talk about grocery stores.

I know a lot of you on the left think you're entitled to "basic" things. Food, clothing, and shelter. I've seen some people even proclaim they're "entitled" to health care, education, and even cell phones.

But let's get back to reality for one second.

Who provides "food, clothing, shelter, health care, education, and cell phones?"

If you are a liberal (and I'm not mocking you here) you believe in a philosophy or political ideology of the **"Great Liberal Economic Oort Cloud."** The reason you believe in this is because (and admit it please) you have been too lazy to bother with studying economics, how economies work, let alone - thinking it through. Therefore, you just throw up your hands into the air and think the government/business/industrial complex "figures it out" for you. There's this "highly complex" economic-political-social-governmental-god-like entity that is WAY too complicated for you to understand that just farts out jobs and only truly intelligent people like Barack Hussein Obama can understand.

But in reality, just like money, there is no government.

You TRULY fail to realize that the "government" is nothing more than you and me because we are all in this boat together, and we simply voted our neighbors, colleagues and friends into office. "We" are "the government." Therefore the solution to our current day economic problems....nay....EVERY SINGLE ONE OF OUR PROBLEMS resides within THE PEOPLE. The "government" cannot do anything just like "the corporations" cannot do anything because both are merely composed and controlled by us - the people.

So who provides the "food, clothing, shelter, health care, education, cell phones" and general "stuff" humans wage war over?

We do.

Not the government.

Technically not the "corporations."

It all boils down to people, because there is no other "entity" or "creature" on the planet to provide these things

By this time, I hope we're all still on the same page. We have thus far covered that it isn't money that matters, it's the actually goods or services MONEY CAN BUY that matters. STUFF matters. AND EQUALLY IMPORTANT we have dispelled the delusion that "government" or "corporations" are entities to themselves able to create "magically" jobs, employment, wealth and income. There are "technically" no such things as "governments" or "corporations" as they are nothing more than amalgamations of people.

People - you and me - your brother and your sister - your neighbor and your enemy - are ULTIMATELY responsible for this nation, for this country and for our economic success and future.

So since it is on the people, let's talk about two distinctly different types of people in our modern day America.

I like to be simple so I categorize the many groups of Americans into two simple categories:

Producers

and

Parasites.

Since there is no **GLEOC** and the success of this nation and all others depends on the individuals, you either carry your weight and support yourself or you don't.

"Parasite" is not meant to be a pejorative or mocking term. It is meant to be an ACCURATE term.

Take emotion, political bias, or whatever you want to use to excuse your erroneous thinking out of it, the definition of a parasite is some thing that lives off of others. And there's a ton in these here United States.

Anybody who collects a government check (bar social security, though, some will argue) is a parasite.

I don't mean that to be insulting, I don't mean that to be derogatory - it's simply the truth. If you collect a government check you are NOT supporting yourself and therefore living off the slave labor of others and are a BONAFIED PARASITE. You DO live off of others. If "others" didn't exist, you WOULD NOT exist, end of story, no discussion, take your bleeding liberal heart emotional-therefore-irrelevant arguments elsewhere.

However, that does not so much irk me as I am willing to accept as much as the next man that people get down on their luck.

What irks me is when 50% of the population collects a government check AND HAS THE AUDACITY TO DEMAND MORE, AND CRIMINALIZE THE HOST OF WHICH IT'S PARASITING OFF OF.

There is no end to the "rich doesn't pay their fair share" or the opposite side of the coin - woeismeism.
So a short message to all of you who think "the rich should pay more" to compensate you for;

YOU majoring in a stupid degree and taking on $100,000 in debt to pay for it
YOU breeding children you couldn't afford and never bothered to think about
YOU being too lazy to put down the booze/drugs to find reliable employment
YOU for choosing a cushy government job and daring to demand people who actually produce something of wealth to pay for your bloated government salary and pension
YOU for just be a pathetic, lazy, moronic parasite who expects other people to pay for you

"YOU" cannot live without "US."

WE produce the STUFF. WE are the people who actually produce the goods and services that have value and people want and need. YOU need US more than WE need YOU!

We're the ones that produce the groceries to keep your "WIC Accepted Here" BS grocery isle full of the food you need.

We're the ones that go to school for 10 years to become the doctors to provide you "free health care" when you decide to get knocked up for the 5th time before your 25th birthday.

We are the ones who engineer the buses and cars you ride to enjoy the roads WE designed with OUR MONEY you used for bus fare.

We are the only reason you live and exist today. Without us, you would not exist.

That's not an opinion.

It's not a "wish."

That's not political bias.

It's a fact you have been shielded from by liberal politicians and an ignorant voting population that votes to take our money to pay for your parasitic (again, not insulting - just true) lives.

You're not "independent." You're not "cool." And you're certainly not "oppressed" or "tyrannized" over. You're just parasites enslaving other people who actually produce STUFF and things of value.

Now, you can get all pissed off at all those rich people, and never spend a calorie of energy looking at how much they pay in taxes to pay for your parasitic existence, but here's another shocking bit of fact-

Hate us as much as you want, we're taking you with us.

You can vote to tax us to death. You can vote to make it illegal to be successful. You can villainize "profit" and "wealth" all you want. However, in the end, you WILL realize that we are your life line.

We are the ones producing the food, the clothing, the shelter and the STUFF you NEED TO LIVE.

We are the ones that are producing the doctors, the surgeons the nurses and the RA's to take care of you. The food that goes in your mouths and the 4 illegitimate childrens' mouths you have. We are the ones producing EVERYTHING you need to live. And you produce NOTHING in return (maybe more illegitimate children, who the hell knows).

But you DARE want to piss us off, or tax us to the point it is no longer in our best interest to play host to your parasitic lives? OR you DARE to attack us because you are envious, bigoted, and hate filled?

Go ahead.

Because if we go down, we're taking you with us.

And what's funny, is we don't have to try because we're the ones producing all the stuff.

So I dare suggest for those of you who think you're "oppressed" or "disadvantaged" as you snort coke, knock up girl #14, get knocked up by guy #15, **major in philosophy or some other obvious galactically stupid decision**, to take your complaints and the consequences of your stupid decisions, shove them, and have a strong belt of STFU and be THANKFUL we're paying the taxes to shield you from the full costs, consequences and catastrophes of your inconceivable stupidity.

The Smith and Wesson Retirement Plan

I love truth. It's such a wonderful thing. It makes you sane, helps you make better, more effective decisions and it irks all the right people. But what I really love about truth is how some people seem to have a huge problem with it. How they'll desperately try to ignore it, rationalize it away, or just plain deny it as if they had a choice.

"The sky is blue."

"No it's not."

"Communism and socialism has failed."

"No it hasn't."

"Children need fathers."

"No they don't - sexist!"

I take great entertainment value in watching people lie to themselves as day after day, night after night, the real world delivers anything from minor cuts to crushing blows to their fragile "reality" and how they desperately scramble to find some some kind of explanation, ANY explanation or rationalization why they're still right, and the real world is wrong.

Now we could go on for hours about the many and varied people who choose to ignore reality and mock them mercilessly:

-Liberal arts majors who voted for Obama, joined the OWS movement and still can't understand why they don't have jobs.

-All the aging women who KNEW they could "have it all," with mocking boys in their youth to boot, who sing in chorus "Where have all the good men gone."

-The union members of now bankrupt cities and municipalities who won't be getting everythign they were promised in terms of pension, because, well, the money just plain ain't there.

But today I'm going to talk to you about something that affects all of us, is very important, and only the smart people will realize what I say is deadly serious and very much real, while the delusionals of the world caught up in American Idol or how thin Michelle Obama's arms are, will be aghast at what I have to say and will no doubt pull from the inventory of "ist" names to call me.

The Smith and Wesson Retirement Plan.

"What is the Smith and Wesson Retirement Plan" you ask?

Well, it's a very simple plan.

Instead of socking away $400 a month into your IRA or 401k, spending hours of your life managing it, spending thousands of dollars on various managerial and advisory fees, only to have the government either outright confiscate it or inflate it away you instead spend the small nominal fee of...

33 cents.

Why 33 cents?

Because 33 cents is the price of a single 45 caliber bullet. And with that bullet you can permanently retire yourself.

Now a lot of people will be shocked with such a statement. How dare I suggest euthanasia (which, when I was younger thought was "youth in Asia" and had NO idea what people were all up in arms about) as a viable retirement plan. But, if you're so open minded (as I know many of you liberals claim to be) perhaps you can read on and realize that The Smith and Wesson Retirement Plan is probably a much better plan than your 401k.

First, consider the fact that the VAST majority of people are just plain not saving up enough for retirement. In the consulting I do, I have a never-ending line of 58 year old people coming up to me and saying,

"I'm 58 and just finished paying off my 4th child's doctorate in French Literature. I have a house that's underwater, and I'd like to start planning for retirement. I'd like to retire at 62. What should I invest in?"

I tell them the politically correct thing (you'll have to work till you're 80), and then they go to Edward Jones or Charles Schwab to see if they can find somebody to lie to them (remember what I told you about how distasteful truth was to some people?)

And forget old people, young people don't stand much of a chance either. With no employment prospects, $50,000 in student debts, and an unemployment rate of 8%, even if they wanted to save for retirement they can't. They need all of their money NOW to simply make ends meet. And (to add further mockery to this stupid retirement system we have) even if they did have the money, what? They're going to invest in an overpriced stock market with a P/E of 24 because TRILLIONS of dollars of baby boomer money has flooded the market, making it a bad deal to begin with?

Regardless of the reasons why, most people will PLAIN NOT HAVE

ENOUGH MONEY TO PAY FOR RETIREMENT and THEY NEVER WILL. So why bother saving up in the first place?

Second, don't think Big Daddy government is going to come and bail you out. I don't know if you've noticed this whole Greece thing going on, but no matter what previous generations of Greeks promised themselves in terms of retirement or medical benefits, if the money ain't there (guess what!)

IT AIN'T THERE! (curse you evil truth!!!!)

Did you see any of the articles about how the hospitals are running short on vital drugs? Funny how that works given the government "decreed" they were "entitled" to all that free health care. Let me let you in on another little tidbit of "uncomfortable truth." If there's no money in it for the private sector to create those drugs (say like you regulate or tax pharmaceuticals to death), then it don't matter what who promised who what - there ain't no drugs and you're going to die no matter what you were promised.

Third, let's put a very positive spin on this (and I am not exaggerating or being facetious). Realize the majority of your expenses you incur (or more likely, the taxpayer incurs) in terms of your living and health care expenses come in the last 6 months of your life. The premise of The Smith and Wesson Retirement Plan is that you would us the 45 caliber bullet to off yourself before then, saving society hundreds of thousands of dollars NOT TO MENTION saving you the 6 most miserable months of your life. Now macroeconomic benefits aside (like no government debt, booming economic growth, improved health care through innovation, and yes, dare I say it, longer life expectancies, but don't let this concept confuse you), there is a huge advantage to this - the fact you don't have to save up for retirement in the first place if you're willing to work as long as you can and participate in The Smith and Wesson Retirement Plan when the time comes. That money can instead be spent on the years of your life WHEN YOU CAN ENJOY IT!

I remember, VERY CLEARLY, trying to save money into a IRA when I was making $23,000, commuting 120 miles every day for work and living downtown. Now I'm cheap, but my life had NO FRILLS.

Once I realized that having lifelong employment in America like a 1960's Japanese Keiretsu was laughably impossible, I forgave myself of the responsibility to "do the right thing" and invest in a 401k. For the first time in my life I "let go," went out, got drunk, tried sushi, stay at hotels (as opposed to sleeping in my car at a wayside) went on trips and enjoyed life. The other option was to continue to live in poverty, have no fun, and have what meager savings I had stored up in a 401k confiscated in "*2020 National Wealth Redistribution Financial Solvency Patriotism Act.*"

The single best thing about The Smith and Wesson Retirement Plan is you get to enjoy the ONE life you're given on this planet and don't have to worry about spending the resources to extend your life when you can't enjoy it.

Fourth, you will not be a burden on society. I know hippies who never studied economics love to sit there and yell from their Depends,

"I contributed to the system and I deserve my government benefits!!!"

epically failing to realize they voted in things like "The Great Society" and other programs that blew away the money they "socked away" for retirement, and now literally demand future generations to become their slaves.

You don't have to become such ignorant hypocrites. You can live your life, contribute as long as you can, and the second you realize you might become a parasite upon society, take yourself out. I know that sounds harsh (because we've all been told to ignore the 600 Pound Reality Gorilla in the room), but it IS altruistic. Certainly more altruistic in demanding and voting that OTHER people pay for the charities you wanted them too over your live and then voting to have other people take care of you.

Finally (and here's that damn truth and reality getting in the way of things again), you really don't have a choice. Bar some spectacular economic growth and a true revolution of the economy, the money and resources plain isn't going to be there to make good on all the promises pot smoking commies back in the 50's, 60's and 70's made to themselves, future generations, all humans in the world, not to mention, pay back the debts we've currently accrued. This once again revisits our buddies in Greece who are "entitled" to "Zymorgopentothol (tm)," but the fine men and women were taxed so much to death at Zymorgopentothol, Inc, they decided no longer to supply Greece with that life-saving drug. You will have to make the choice to continue living in a desperate, painful state, or ending it mercifully (and cost-effectively) yourself. I do not wish to be so pessimistic, cynical or macabre, but I'm not. I'm really not. That's going to be the REALITY for a lot of people. And if you don't believe me, or think I'm just engaging in sensationalism how about for once YOU do the leg work and look up the finances of social security, medicare, medicaid, the federal government and general economic statistics of the US? YOU run projections, make calculations and theorize and predict where the economy will go. YOU prove me wrong and tell me where the magical money is going to come from to pay for everything everyone promised themselves.

Because again, I thoroughly enjoy and anticipate the crazy rationalizations, excuses and explanations delusional people come up with so they can keep believing in Lala-Land. And until I execute my own Smith and Wesson Retirement Plan, one of the main forms of entertainment I'll have (in addition to hiking mountains, smoking cigars, playing video games, riding motorcycles and working as little as I can) is watching you fans of socialism, communism and "free" health care blow trillions of your own dollars on private retirement programs that will not only be confiscated later, but never compare to my 33 cent program.

And you wouldn't want to deprive me of that entertainment, would you?

The 2nd Most Arrogant Assumption You MUST Make

I have said it before, and I'll say it again, when you keep failing at a particular task the only person to blame is you. You tried, you failed, and therefore the blame is solely on you. You need to go back, train more, try harder and keep failing until you succeed.

This rule or "law" or whatever you want to call it, is simply commonsense. You are the independent variable. You are the one that needs to improve. You are the sole entity to blame if there is failure

...except in life there are two rare instances where you will NOT be to blame.

One of those instances is for the young and now full-grown adult men who in their youth failed time and time again when it came to interacting with the opposite sex on social, romantic or sexual grounds. You tried, you failed. It's your fault.

You tried, you failed again. It's your fault.

You trained, tried harder, failed harder. It's your fault.

You changed tactics, experimented, tried really hard, and failed really bad. It's your fault.

You went all out, trying crazy new tactics, rehashing old ones, put yourself in your best physical shape, invested thousands of man-hours, burned millions of calories and failed even more spectacularly than Lehman Brothers. It's your fault.

And after anywhere from 10-25 years of failure (depending on how independent minded you were), you inevitably started daring to ask a VERY arrogant question:

"What if there's nothing wrong with me, but something wrong with everybody else?"

Understand why this is a very arrogant question. For something to be wrong with EVERYBODY ELSE, and NOT wrong with the SOLE INDIVIDUAL implies:

1. You are somehow brilliant or very special.
2. You are also so brilliant you are smarter or better than everybody else
3. Something has universally infected other people, while sparing you, putting you into "black helicopter" conspiracy theory territory.

At first you fight this thought that let this possibility enter your mind. And you go back to banging your head against the drawing board to try another thousand slight permutations or variant of approaches to attract some lass. But in the end, by the sheer volume of approaches, experiences, experiments, self-inflection and years of human life spent trying to "succeed" at this challenge, your mind is tortured into forcibly accepting the only remaining explanation:

"No, there's nothing wrong with me. There IS INDEED something wrong with everybody else on a societal level. Don't know what it is, but by god, it's not me!"

Some people call it taking the red pill. (I, however, think to go through the torture yourself and have the courage to make this assumption WITHOUT the benefit of The Manosphere to lay it all out for you, deserves some other title - but that is an aside, NOR is it meant to belittle people who did take the red pill). Whatever we decide to call it, once we entertain this arrogant assumption, it is amazing how everything falls into place and makes sense. NOT because it conveniently benefits us or merely excuses and rationalizes our failures in the past. But because IT DOES EXPLAIN EVERYTHING.

It's akin to fighting on the ground, having no idea where whose lines are, getting shelled left and right, being driven insane by chaos, and then magically being transported to a command center where you have crystal clear satellite imagery with friendlies being tagged with beacons and enemies being tagged by heat signatures, AND proving your hunches were indeed correct all along.

It just took you the arrogance to make such an assumption to get this bird's eye view and save your sanity.

Now, focus all we want on The Manosphere, that is not the topic I'm talking about today. For there is going to come the time many of you, if not all of us, are going to have to man-up again and once again question,

"Is it me, or is there something wrong with everybody else?"

but in a different sphere.

And I'll give you a hint - this has nothing to do with the sexes. Women will have to ask this question too because we're all going to have the honor of being in the same machine-gun strafed boat here.

Anybody get it yet?

Bueller? Bueller?

Alright, I'll tell you.

We're ALL going to have to gin up the courage to ask this question when it comes to our relationship with employers:

"Is it me, or is there something wrong with the employers in the US?"

Again, the two issues parallel each other very closely.

If you have a hard time being reliably employed, you have failed. There MUST be something wrong with you.

You try working for multiple employers, try multiple tactics, you'll still fail. Therefore there MUST BE something wrong with YOU.

You try really hard, volunteer to work more, take on different projects, suggest new ideas and innovations. You still fail (hell, you'll get punished for thinking of new ideas). Therefore there MUST be something wrong with you.

And dare you start to suggest or theorize there's something structurally, fundamentally, or universally wrong with employers, corporate America and our current system of employment/labor market, then you are just (fill in the blank)

....not a team player
....a disgruntled employee
....a slow learner
....somebody who just doesn't "get it"
....a bad employee
....somebody who's just lazy

Never mind you are willing to work hard.

Never mind you did all the right things, got the right degree, got the right certification.

Never mind you came up with ideas that would have saved the company money, or crushed the competition, or heck, **saved the entire US economy.**

No, there's most DEFINITELY something wrong with YOU, and those crafty HR "generalists" with their scripted "pure-extract of inane" interview questions will be able to smoke you out without you knowing it (even though they themselves have gone through three divorces, 47 failed relationships, host 3 cats as pets, and are the world's worst judges of character).

And, much like you were veritably forced to have the arrogant epiphany about courting when you were 25, you will have to come to the same arrogant conclusion about the realities of the labor market and employer-employee relationships in America. And just like me and a handful of people that have gone before you, you will realize once you make this assumption, you'll see employment and employers for what they are and hereafter be able to make better decisions.

Of course, humility and modesty may intimidate you from making such an arrogant assumption. However, permit me to make several observations about corporate America that may convince you that there is indeed something fundamentally dysfunctional about modern day employers and that, no, you're not a bad employee, and no, you're not insane.

First, let's look at HR. I could write a book about HR, but we'll instead focus on the fact that HR is dominated by women which cannot be overlooked and draws many parallels between The Manosphere "world" and the "working world." Much like dating, women are predisposed to believe that they are the prize and you are lucky if you get the honor to date her. You have to do all the leg work, you have to beg and plead, and if you prove yourself worthy, you will be rewarded with a date. Applying for a job is the exact same.

HR operates from this exact same premise - that the job is the prize to be won and that you should be honored to even be considered for the position. Matter of fact you should thank her for pelting you with inane questions that have nothing to do with the job or the industry. What they fail to realize, in both instances, is it is a two way street. Not only do applicants need jobs, but companies need labor. Yes, they can take some arrogant liberties with an Obama-induced 8+% unemployment rate, but now that I've taken the "employment red pill" I sit in awe when an HR interviewer asks me with naked arrogance

"So why do you want to work here?"

as if it's a given I want to work there.

When I reply in a deadly serious tone

"Money."

the look on their face or the silence at the other end of the phone is hilarious. But it still proves my point. They PRESUME you are the one at a disadvantage and are the one bargaining from a position of weakness. When in reality, you are merely the other and equally important side of the coin.

Regardless, the point is not whether unemployment breeds arrogance on the part of employers, it's the fact we have to endure something as stupid as the "HR screening interview" in the first place. None of the questions have any predictive value as to the future performance of an employee. The "best" answers are lies and the furthest thing from the truth. The person conducting the interview is typically clueless about your profession and anything involving math. It does nothing to find and detect the best candidate. And, no, you're not insane for thinking the same. So don't fret it when "HR" doesn't call back. They were never going to in the first place.

Another aspect of HR is that it's "wishlist" for qualities and traits in a candidate for a job is equally impossible as the typical Ameircan woman's "wishlist" for qualities in a man for courtship. **I've spoken of it before,** but when they're asking for 5 years experience in a software that has only been on the market for 3, you might as well be asking for a bad boy alpha motorcycle riding preacher, who's an animal in the sack, but only after you're married, who's also rich, but never married, and no children, but wants to take care of your 3 children from 4 other guys.

Again, you're not insane when you look at the list of requirements, do some quick math, and realize in the 6 billion people in the world, 1/8th of a person would qualify.

Second, abandon HR and look at the management in general of companies today. Corporate America is no longer headed up by hardened, WWII vets who are ready to propel corporate America to new levels of greatness. It's headed up by hippie Baby Boomers, followed by the ranks of Gen X middle management. The psychology that comes with this is nothing as simple or logical as achieving greatness, or revolutionizing industries, or simply going out, kicking ass and taking names. It's been replaced by people who are more concerned about **maintaining the status quo so they can keep their jobs**. To run the firm or their division as their own personal fiefdom. And so when a logical, young whipper snapper like you comes in with new ideas, innovations and creations, understand the reason you're getting fired is NOT because your ideas are "wrong" or "stupid," but because they've exposed just how inefficiently the company or division has been managed and your ideas are likely to result in the layoff of the unnecessary fat - ie - your boss and 40% of upper management.

Third, never discount that fact that unlike you and me, the majority of Americans are HORRENDOUS managers of their own personal finances. They racked up debts going to college. They racked up credit card debts in their 20's. They had kids they can't afford. Ergo, they literally cannot afford the luxury you have to speak out and say,

"Hey, that's a horrible idea! If we introduce that product, then our product will kill 30,000 infants and shave 100,000 kittens!"

No, they have to shut up, not rock the boat, because they need food on the table and little Jimmy needs braces.

Because of the financial mismanagement of the majority of Americans, understand corporate America has the luxury of employing millions of yes-men and yes-women.

Oh, you may be right.

And yes, you may save the company in the end.

But you are rocking the boat with your bachelor and bachlorette ways. And if an employer has the choice between hiring somebody who asks difficult and reality based questions, or somebody who is a slave to their debt, and therefore will never question management, they're going to go with the psychologically defeated automoton every time.

And finally, let's not forget that American employers are spineless. They stand for nothing. They fear everything. And instead of adhering to some code of morals or ethics, they instead cower and fear the slightest bit of criticism in fear they may lose .0003% market share. This allows people like lawyers, sue-happy employees, sexual harassment filers, protestors, nepotists, crusaders and the like to essentially make it impossible for a corporation to hire anybody with a brain or slightly opinionated personality. They hire robots, automotons, preferably the heavily indebted type, as they are the ones with the least risk.

Of course, they're the ones with the least amount of creativity and leadership and innovation, but hey, at least we're not getting sued.

In short, the strategy of American employers is no longer that of achieving excellence or dominance in their field. It's no longer going out, doing your best, kicking ass, taking names and crushing the competition. It's one of self preservation and retaining what little fiefdom they have. If you ask any major (or minor) US company what their "growth strategy" is, it's not to create new and amazing products that will obsolete the competition. It's an amazingly lame, "grow the company outside the US while we bribe congress with our lobbyists to introduce legislation that will give us an edge against our competitors."

Now, you combine all these veritable psychoses that are governing US employers and ask yourself one simple question - can a normal person, with logical thought and the desire to work hard and succeed ever possibly stand a chance to survive in an environment like that? You have a dying domestic labor market where everything is outsourced not just to save money on labor costs, but to lower lawsuit/sexual harassment risk. You have people being promoted not based on their intelligence, ideas, innovations or observations, but by the fact they're enslaved to the company because they indebted themselves to the point they literally had to sell their soul and financially whore themselves out which makes them "obedient" (the most sought after trait in America). You have the primary gatekeepers to employment staffed by the world's ditziest, dumbest people asking questions that have nothing to do with employment, effectively turning away any true leaders, thinkers, innovators, in exchange for somebody who can provide the best rehearsed answer to "have you ever had a difficult situation with an employee? how did you solve it and why?" And the entire thing is being managed by lazy, incompetent aging brats who are so talentless they cannot create their own job security, but instead they must stifle any potential usurpers by maintaining the status quo.

If you consider that, you can't POSSIBLY think there's something "wrong" with you or that somehow you're a bad employee, which only proves my previous case.

Understand, and understand well, that there is nothing wrong with you. You did your best, you did the right thing, you made the right choices, and that's all you can do. If your career is not heading the way you would have liked by now, understand it's not your fault. Even if your boss or former boss lectures you about how you didn't do this minor thing right, or criticizes you on some nebulous grounds of you not having the right "attitude" or not being a "team player," assuming you did the right thing and tried your best, chances are it's more of a criticism of themselves and their inability to lead or make decisions, than it is a legitimate criticism of you.

Yes, this is an arrogant assumption. And yes, it takes a lot of bravado to make such assumptions. But all one has to do is look at the current economic state of the US and realize that is the empirical evidence that you are right. Because if the US economy was booming and US corporate domestic sales were booming, then, yes, you would PROBABLY be in the

wrong - the leaders of the various institutions of the US are probably
doing something right by the fact the economy is doing well. But since
the economy is craptastically stagnant, and the government bankrupt, for
employers and various leaders to have the gall to blame their inadequate
and incompetent leadership on their employees is laughable. For them to
tell you during review time, "well, you really only earned an "average"
rating despite your 60 hour work weeks" is hypocritical.

Thankfully, you have the choice as to whether or not to believe them. If
you choose to, realize this is doing nothing more than believing a lie. It
won't help you in your long term future success, if anything it will hurt you
because you are basing your decisions of a falsehood. However, if you
choose not to, and realize they're nothing but a bunch of ass-kissing,
brown-nosing, debt-enslaved suits, you will be able to make better
decisions about who you want to work for, what kind of work you are
WILLING to tolerate, and (as I've found out) you TELLING them what you
are and are not going to do. It's counter-intuitive, but just ask any girl
which guy gets more success:

The compliant yes man who asks her "whatever you want to do dear."

Or the motorcycle bad boy who dares to tell the girl one word , "no."

The "Minimalism" Threat

So I was talking to our IT guy today and we were talking about stuff.
"Stuff" as in "stuff in the house" and how much he'd like to get rid of it.
Of course he can't because the Mrs. won't let him get rid of the stuff, even
though this stuff has never been used in the past 10 years. This sent our
conversation on a trajectory in terms of how nice it would be to get rid of
most of our stuff in order to live another lifestyle. The IT Guy said he
would love nothing more than to jettison all of his stuff, grab a backpack,
his laptop, sell his house and live in Mexico. I spoke of my desire to pretty
much do the same. I'm kicking around a way to camp in the National
Grasslands during the warmer 6 months of the year, commute to work,
save on rent, and then get a 6 month lease during the winter months.
Again, I'd have to get rid of all my stuff.

But opine as we might about how nice it would be to get rid of all our stuff and lead a Spartan existence, there are consequences men and women don't think about to such minimalism. Consequences so huge, underestimated, unseen and (dare I say) on our front-door step I believe they need highlighting.

First, understand the only reason stuff exists - women.

Women want stuff. Men hate stuff. This is no better highlighted by comparing a bachelor pad to a bachelorette pad. A (true) bachelor pad is sparse. It's functional. Nothing matches. Nothing goes with anything else. All items were a potpourri of hand me downs, Goodwill purchases and charitable donations. The couch is for sitting on, not looking at. The table is for eating on, not looking at. The bed is for sleeping on, not looking at. And if you're a really good bachelor you will eat, sleep and sit on your couch, making the bed and table obsolete. Sure there may be the occasional nice thing (primarily your TV or LCD projection and computer), but for the most part a true bachelor spends no more than $2,000 on non-electronic stuff.

Women on the other hand have to "nest" (a term a psychologist friend of mine was trying to explain). This means no consideration is given to functionality or price, only aesthetics which ultimately supplant functionality and price.

Is the couch for sitting on?

Good god, no! It goes with the drapes.

Are the drapes to keep the sun out?

Good god no! They go with the hutch.

Is the hutch for storing things?

Good god no! They go well with the dining room table.

Is the dining room table for eating on?

Good god no! It goes well with the couch.

Women will also buy crap and trinkets simply because they want "crap and trinkets." Said trinkets and crap have no other function but to ornament the place with cute little things she likes to look at and stimulate the part in her brain that is only stimulated by spending money.

Could that money have gone to pay down the mortgage?

Yes.

Could that money have gone to pay for gas?

Yes.

Could that money have been donated to a small third world country, thereby lifting it and all of its people out of poverty forever?

Yes.

But it's more important to have the "crystal unicorn set" sitting on top of the TV because it goes well with the armour (sp?) and she got it for "50% off!" Malaria infected third world children be damned, she has the whole collection!

Admittedly, I'm being a bit sarcastic, but not by much. In all truth and reality the VAST majority of the "stuff" that is found in the average American home (and I'm saying 90%) is ONLY there because the woman wants it AND it really serves no functional purpose. Because of this, that means by default 90% of the consumer spending in this economy is driven by women. Spending that would not exist if it were purely up to men.

And now you see some consequences on the horizon, don't you?

If it were up to men, consumption spending would tank. We wouldn't be wasting our precious time (in the form of money) on doilies or Beanie Babies or "nice, matching furniture" or general crap that isn't needed. There would be an entertainment system, some dishes, some used furniture and that's about it. But don't think it would stop there. Our

Spartan spending habits would have ramifications WELL beyond that of trinkets and doilies in the house. Notably, the house itself.

Not only would demand for non-durable consumer items tank, the housing market itself would tank. Men need nowhere near the size of a house as women do. This in part because we don't have as much stuff that needs storage, we (frankly) don't want children AND we view the house as merely a place to sleep and retire to from work. ie-our lives are outside the home, while women's spending habits (no matter what they keep contending) proves the majority of their lives are still inside the home. The suburbs I doubt would even exist if it were up to men. We'd have the city center, apartment buildings and condos, and then for our rural brothers small towns with wood cabins in the forest. Vast swathes of 10,000 sqft McMansions used to impress the Suburban Princess Suzie McQue's of the world would not exist.

Regardless of which markets would be affected by male minimalism, the point is that consumer spending would be a mere fraction of what it is today. And since consumer spending accounts for 2/3rd of our economy, you could expect (at least in the short term) a drastically contracting economy should men all of the sudden follow the religion of Minimalism.

Now if you think that prospect is bad, we haven't even gotten to the other side of the economic coin. Because for as important as consumption is, production is even more so. The reason why is it doesn't matter if you want to "consume" a Ferrari or "consume" some sushi. If nobody produces the Ferrari or the sushi, you ain't getting anything anyway (just ask anybody in the former Soviet bloc about empty grocery store shelves despite the socialist guarantees of their governments). And so when it comes to the economic consequences of men en-mass pursuing "minimalism" we must also consider production.

However, understand when I say "we must also consider production" I do not mean men will say,

"Finally, she stopped nagging me about buying all her trinkets and crap! Now I can finally get to work."

and start to focus their energies and efforts into producing more and increasing standards of living for the family.

Quite the opposite actually.

They will look at the lower financial demands of their family and will RE-EVALUATE whether or not it's worth all the production for the compensation they receive. They will RE-EVALUATE whether it's worth slaving away 60 hours a week, 20 hours of which is uncompensated overtime, and another 10 hours that are stuck in traffic. They will RE-EVALUATE whether it's worth 30 years of tolerating insufferable insanity of corrupt bosses, incompetent co-workers and lazy underlings. They will RE-EVALUATE through the prism of minimalism whether the percent of their finite lives they are forfeiting is worth the monetary compensation they receive OR if it's just better to forfeit labor for leisure and suffer/enjoy a lower standard of living. And it is here the true threat of "minimalism" lays for the rest of society.

Understand, in general, men still produce the majority of the stuff. This is not up for debate now, but I guarantee you that if you look at labor statistics you will find the majority of men produce the majority of stuff in this economy that "matters." What do I mean by "that matters?" ie- stuff that has value. Stuff people want.

For example the disproportionately women-dominated field of "day care" does not produce anything people really want. Other women are taking care of other women's children while those women go work (primarily) another government job that is (guess what) taking care of other women's children (though typically in the juvie criminal system by this time) so they can make the money to afford day care for their children AND the increased taxes to pay for other women who work in social work programs. Or take for example, the non-profit sector. By the fact non-profits have to go and beg and plead to get their funding OR have the government force people to pay for it via taxation is proof that nobody really wants it and therefore it is not "stuff that matters." The non-profit industry is again predominantly staffed by females. But whatever the industry, the point is there is a strong correlation between faux economic production or "make work/rent seeking" economic production that really only exists for political reasons and the percent of those industries staffed by females.

Now, are there women who are engineers and doctors who make the stuff we want like electronics and surgery and gasoline?

Certainly, of course.

Is that the majority of women?

No.

The majority of stuff that people want is still produced, created and innovated by men, period (though again, up for a debate at a later time).

So, logically then, since it is men who are producing the majority of the stuff we want, we should make them happy, right? Compensate them, reward them. Cheer them on and encourage them. Support them be it emotionally as a wife or in terms of policy when it comes to law. And certainly not stand in their way of creating, producing and innovating, right?

Right?

RIGHT?

I mean, they are producing all the stuff. They are the engine of economic growth, RIGHT?

Heh heh. Where do I begin?

I guess I could start with the **"family"** in that this is, or at least, WAS a primary motivator in a young man's desire to work hard, succeed and produce. Originally the man would do all the production and the wife would take care of the house and little kinder. He'd come home to a loving wife, obedient children and was rewarded with a family. Of course things have changed.

Now the division of labor between worker and home-care-take was too logical, too efficient and obviously oppressive. Now nobody stays home to take care of the kids, the kids grow up maladjusted, causing more psychological strife for the man at home. A home that he presumably would retreat to, to decompress, relax and be reinvigorated for the next day of work. Now he has a wife that is equally stressed out, the home is in disarray, the kids are misbehaving, they really won't leave until they're 26, and did I mention most men didn't want kids to begin with? If anything, the chaos that has been left in the wake of outsourcing parenting to the government has turned a man's castle into just another office where he works a second job.

Now you would think this would disincentive him to work hard, but ironically, it makes him work harder. He gets to not only pay for the children and subsidize his part-time-working "social worker" wife, he gets to pay more in taxes to support an ever growing parasitic class collecting a government check. **He is the Atlas in Atlas Shrugged, but he cannot shrug. He is chained to his family.** Employers love him because he's their bitch. He cannot afford to be independent minded, he cannot talk back, he cannot speak his mind. He is their little slave at least until his youngest graduates from high school, and given the dependency of young "adults" today, until that kid graduates from college. He is the slave of America.

So far it doesn't sound like a family is a great disincentive for a man to produce. It almost sounds like it FORCES him to produce MORE. And it does. But what people don't see is his childless, unmarried male friends taking note. What people don't see is his sons watching their dad suffer. What they don't see is that for every enslaved **Beta-Atlas** there are 3-4 men who are deciding not to have families. And deciding NOT to have a family is arguably the single biggest thing a man can do to minimize his responsibilities AND CONSEQUENTLY cut his life long production needs by at least 67%. That does not bode well for the economy.

Closely related to family is the only natural course or outcome of getting married - **divorce**!

When you know half your assets are going to go bye bye and there's a 50/50 chance you're going to get divorced, then what do you think happens to a man's desire to work hard and produce? Again, it sucks to be the Beta-Atlas sucker stuck in a marriage whose wife is on the precipice of divorcing him. But for every one of those poor unfortunate souls, there's a score of younger men who haven't taken the plunge, remember their old man getting divorced and are taking very studious notes. They are opting instead to just stay single. And as every guy will tell you, without a wife or a girlfriend, you can get by EASILY on 40% less social expenditures than if you had one. Guess what, that translates into less production.

So good for them. Single, no wife, no kids. You're in the clear, right? I mean, society is going to support you now, right? Young, go getting corporate man, or young budding entrepreneur? Backbone of our society. Right?

Oh, you foolish male you.

See, you are male. Therefore you must pay because you are privileged. So now you get to suffer **affirmative action** and constantly be hounded about the **pay gap.** Less qualified women are passed over you, standards are lowered for them, and let's not forget the devastating effect an attention-seeking-drama-queen can have by launching a frivolous sexual harassment complaint!

The effect on male production? Well most men, when they're young, have a desire to belong to something better and bigger. To belong to a team. To find a good institution, pledge their loyalty, give it their best, achieve great things and take pride in their accomplishments. But when the rules are point blank unfair and the institution is corrupted by petty office politics AND their careers can be extinguished instantly by chaotic whims of a petty drama queen, not so much. Their loyalty fades, their allegiance dwindles and I'm no HR expert, but I believe high employee turnover is bad for a company's bottom line. So instead of being the loyal corporate man for 35 years, you're lucky if you're on one gig for more than three. Again, the result? The production of the average man today is only going to be a fraction of what his unharassed, undiscriminated against 1940's counterpart was.

It can't get worse? Right? I mean, we don't discourage men from production beyond that, right?

Well let's look at **progressive taxation**, no small part in which was brought to you by disproportionately socialist-and-democrat-voting women who want more of your money to take care of their...er...I mean "the" chilllllllldreeeeeennnnn. Again, I'm no economist (oh, wait, I am), but it seems to me the more I work the higher percentage of my money you're going to take away from me is going to provide a disincentive to work. The enslaved married Beta Atlas can't shrug, but I and millions of other unmarried, childless men can. Again, congratulations, production reduced.

Well, at least what I worked for I get to keep, right? I mean it's not like the government would **CONFISCATE** my assets or anything? They'll tax my income, but not my wealth, right?

In 2008 the democrats were kicking around a way to nationalize (read - confiscate) people's 401ks and 403b's. It has already happened in Bolivia, Ecuador and Argentina. Now, MOST men I admit are unaware of this. However, more and more men *are* becoming more and more educated about economics. And as they read more and more about economics and study this here country's fine federal finances they can put two and two together and see that there is an increasing chance the government WILL inevitably start taxing our wealth and confiscating our assets. Now, I know you girls are too busy reading People magazine or watching Kate Perry's drama with Russel Brand, voting democrat because you care for the children, and studying for your masters in communications, but for us men who DO look up the federal budget occasionally, we're starting to see it's more and more likely whatever we produce today will be confiscated in the future. And not just that, but the MORE we produce today then progressively more of it will be confiscated in the future. End result? Less production.

But let's say we men wanted to be charitable. We still wanted to work knowing full well our effective tax rate would be 60% at state, federal and local AND there would be a 75% at least 50% of our wealth would be confiscated in the future. Because by god, it's for the chilllllllldrreeeeeeennnnn.

Just one problem.

We can't work even if we wanted to.

I'm not talking about the overburdensome employment laws foisted on employers many thanks to disproportionately-female-voted-in socialists and democrats.

I'm not talking about the incredibly inept and corrupt HR industry which I do not believe to be dominated by males, that has completely impaired the labor market.

No, those are hurdles we get to suffer anyways.

I'm talking about the **regulations** that (once again) disproportionately-voted-in-by-females socialists and democrats have enacted making male-dominated industries either impossible to work in or have just driven them overseas. You know like energy, oil, construction, fields and industries where we produce all the stuff you need, but like to regulate and punish for the sake of the chilllllldreeeeeennnn or "mother Earth."

I don't know if it's your grand economic scheme to get everybody to work as barristas at Star Bucks or we all work as school teachers or something, but I do know all those regulations make it quite difficult for us men to produce. So congratulations, even LESS economic production.

And finally the cumulative effect of this veritable war waged on men - it's **toll on our loyalty**. I'm not talking loyalty to an employer. I'm talking loyalty to the country. I used to want to join the military and even to this day kick it around. But then I ask "who would I be protecting?" You see, all of the above really grinds mens' gears. We don't take kindly to being accused of automatic sexism, we don't like being enslaved to a government that does nothing more than take our money to bribe parasites into voting for more government, we don't like paying the taxes so you can play "pre-school teacher" and claim your 9 months a year job makes you an "independent adult," we don't take kindly to divorce (even though most of us haven't been), we don't take kindly to you ruining the industries we are predominantly employed in, we don't take kindly to the childish mind-games girls played on us during our teens and twenties, we don't take kindly to watching naive, spoiled, brats destroy the world's formerly greatest country and thusly steal our birthright and we get down right pissed when you start complaining that we're not "manning up" and choose to "sit on our asses all day playing X Box." Because when it comes to us men "investing" in this country be it buying property, starting a business, marrying, starting a family, whatever...

why should we?

Seriously, I want somebody to answer that question.

Why the hell would we work more than we have to than to support our meager little selves? Why would we invest in anything that can be taken from us (either assets by government confiscation or family via divorce). And why would we try to EXCEL when the majority of our production will merely be taken from us and given to not just ungrateful parasites but people who hate us and demand more? There's no incentive or upshot to it. Congratulations, you've effectively stalled you engine of economic growth and production.

But wait, there's one final aspect you haven't thought of, and it's particularly precious.

Men are infinitely better at being minimalists than women.

I don't believe this was always the case. Say the pioneer or the Great Depression days. Men and women had to watch every penny, and there was no such thing as "nesting" or getting "matching curtains." But after roughly 90 years of uninterrupted economic growth (not to mention HEAVILY subsidized consumer spending financed by our Chinese, Arab and Gen Y Generation Forced Mortgaged Future Volunteers), the women alive today have never really had to suffer, scrape or scrimp by. They EXPECT a luxurious house or apartment they can't afford. They **EXPECT clothes they don't need**. They EXPECT every little aspect of their material goods lives to be perfect. They CANNOT (or very few can) scale down to a **small studio apartment from a house**, sell all their stuff, and downsize their car. They cannot get rid of the daily Starbucks. They cannot fathom utter poverty and what they'd have to do to survive it.

Men on the other hand (of the non-OWS, pansy commie type) can. Part of the reason I'm kicking around the camping 6 months a year is to see if I can do it. And though I don't know for sure, part of the reason my IT Guy wants to go to Mexico with just a backpack is to see if he could also do it.

Men forecast and run "worst case scenarios" in their heads in anticipation it might just happen and we're prepared for it. Poverty is ALWAYS licking our feet, driving us to stay one step ahead of it. However, whereas in the past poverty would be beaten by working hard and making more money, when that route is merely punished or impossible, the only alternative is minimalism.

This situation where making more money is impossible hits every almost every guy during college, forcing them to become experts in minimalism. They can't get a job, but have the tuition-cost demands of college. They MUST resort to minimalism. I graduated with no debt only making $16,000/ year in college. Factor out tuition costs and factor in inflation, that's still around $16,000 today. But that's if I had a lot of stuff. If I got rid of my stuff and did the tent thing or the roommate, I could probably get by on $11,000/yr, roughly the standard of living of South Africa or Colombia. I'd like to see a modern day western woman do the same.

Sadly, most can't. But this is where it gets particularly precious.

With economic growth stagnating and the population growing, our standards of living are decreasing. Additionally, nobody is loaning us money anymore so we can maintain our "I'm a Barbie Girl, In a Barbie World" lifestyle. The can cannot be kicked down the road any more because it's been kicked off the cliff. Sure, we can move money around and rely on Europe's economy being "slightly more sucky than ours" to delay the economic realities from hitting our domestic shores, but ultimately there is no more money left to maintain unsustainable lifestyles. This puts the ball back in the court of men. Men who have the know-how, the ability, the creation and the innovation to produce the economic production necessary to solve all these problems. Men who can make this country dominant as it once was. Men who literally could make our standard of living jump from the $43,000/capita it is today to $70,000/capita I believe in just 10 years. Men who could make our debt and financial problems go away.

Just one problem - the aforementioned problems and disincentives are making these men go the route of minimalism instead of production. And we men can do that because we CAN survive on $11,000 a year. We won't have a nervous breakdown. We have no problem hocking our stuff and living out of a van. But the social worker who is accustomed to making $80,000 a year and $20,000 in fringe benefits on our dime who loses not just her job, but her pension because her California city filed for bankruptcy, she'll break down in tears.

So, whether you like it or not, the threat of minimalism is very real and it is very present. So present in fact that the people of America (primarily women, but men too) have to ask themselves a question - are you going to cut it with the "socialist, woe is me crap," give us producers the ball and let us run with it, or are you going to **demand even more from men** (and the productive women of this society), in which case we can pursue our minimalism and by default, force place it on you?

The Costs of Playerhood

Roosh in his book "**Day Bang**" explains arguably the key ingredient to being a player. It isn't confidence. It isn't working out or looks. And it isn't money.

It's failure.

It's knowing that you are going to get shot down the majority of the time and to simply keep at it until you inevitably succeed. Oh sure, there are some things you can do to "tighten up" your game (environment selection, practice, situational awareness, working out, clothing, etc), but even Roosh admits players at the top of their game will have a maximum close rate of around 40%.

Now, the reason I bring this up is because (hubris and arrogance aside) I was a player. And when I was a player, my friends would always ask, "how did I do it?" I'm not particularly tall, I'm kind of skinny, when I was at the "top" of my game I least physically fit, and for the majority of my 20's I was making less than $30,000 per year. But sure enough pretty much every hot girl that walked into the dance scene was mine. If there was a social event, I would be "that short skinny guy" who brought the "Russian ballet dancer" to the party (true story). If I wanted to and had enough forewarning, I could pretty much guarantee myself a pretty girl for a date. The irony is of course, that's what people saw from the outside. The finished product. The tall drink of water on my arm. What they didn't see was the behind the scenes action of how sausage was made and thus thought it was all puppies, chocolates and unicorns. They didn't realize there are genuine and severe costs to being a player, costs so great it makes you quit.

First, understand the time commitment involved. Again I reference Day Bang (though I'm sure Roosh mentions this in all of his books), where Roosh, right up front addresses the amount of time you will have to commit in order to succeed. He does not beat around the bush, likening being a player to a sport. You NEED to practice, regularly, everyday, 3 hours a day to get good at it. And he's right.

Now, did I go out and treat it like a sport? No, but I did get to the point of being able to remove any emotion from getting shot down. And I did get to the point to not take any personal offense or umbrage when a girl shot me down. It requires you give up a little bit of humanity and treat it like a genuine, real and passionless game. You almost have to get to the level of ignoring the fact the girls are fellow humans and look at them more like hurdles or benchmarks to overcome. I never achieved 40%, maybe at best 30%. But for all the tall drinks of water I brought into a club or a party, there were at least 7 or 8 that shot me down.

Regardless, the point is not how you need to become dispassionate about it (though that helps), it's to point out some math. To get shot down 7-8 times just to get one date means you got to spend at least 2 hours failing before you get that 15 minutes of success. And that's a low estimate. The average guy is more likely to spend at least 10 hours getting one date, the majority of that time will be spent being shot down. Consequently, unless you can remove your soul a little bit from this process, it will start to affect your personality, ego and self-esteem. Both of these (the time commitment and the constant assailing of your ego) are costs that often go unnoticed in the sausage-making process that is known as "playerhood."

Second, say you do succeed. Again, to the outside observer, all they see is you punching above your weight with that tall drink of water on your arm. "See" being the key verb here. They don't TALK to the tall drink of water. They don't LISTEN to the tall drink of water. All they see is her physical beauty, 95% of the time is her best and only asset.

Until a woman has a child, gets divorced, has to support herself or goes through some other life-trial or tribulation that builds character, you can expect an inverse relationship between the looks of a woman and her personality. The old adage - intelligence, sanity and beauty, pick two - applies here. Out of the 200+ women I have dated (not lying) there was a DIRECT and STRONG correlation between their beauty and their insanity or lack of intelligence.

The drop dead gorgeous blond that took all the oxygen out of the air at a hangar dance I went to?

2 DUI's, 1 year of "cosmetology school" and kicked out of her parents' home, on again off again collector of welfare.

The Russian ballet dancer?

Former mail order bride of an American sergeant who abused her while they had sex to the point she was hospitalized and was thusly thereafter afraid of sex.

The hot latina that I was going to impress with tickets to the opera? (I was young and stupid)

Wasn't ready until the doors to the opera were closed and we had to wait till intermission (I did not wait till intermission).

The professional trainer?

Talked 3 hours straight. I LITERALLY got TWO SENTENCES IN. What did she talk about? Her ex-boyfriend THE ENTIRE TIME.

The hot ex-girlfriend of a Minnesota Viking whose parents were also billionaires with direct family ties to the Kuomintang party of Taiwan?

Threatened suicide when I didn't buy her a soda at a gas station in St. Louis Park.

Now, I could go on (and on, and on, and on), but you get the point. You just see some guy driving a Ferrari down the street and envy him. YOu don't see the drama and psychological BS the poor guy has to pay maintaining such a high-maintenance vehicle.

Third, speaking of costs, you still have to spend money. This can be controlled or limited to a certain extent, but if you want to be a player you at minimum have to GO OUT. That includes (on the very cheap end) gas to a coffee shop and at minimum $5 for coffee. On the average end, $10 in gas, $20 in drinks for yourself, maybe even $5 in covers. AND YOU HAVEN'T EVEN GONE OUT YET. This is just to get into the game and start wooing potential candidates for a future date. The dates themselves (if you follow Leykis 101) should not cost more than $40, but heck, that's what you drop on them. That again doesn't consider ancillary expenses, let alone your time. You prorate your time at $20 an hour, with $20 in gas and $20 on actual expenditures on your date, you're looking at total costs of at least $100 each date. Figure a low-end player gets 4 girls a month, 48 girls a year, that's $4,800 a year ON VERY CHEAP DATES, the real figure is certainly higher.

Now you throw all these together and what do you have?

An already impoverished 20 something blowing AT LEAST $5,000 a year on dates, not to mention committing an amount of his finite time that is equivalent to a part time job ONLY to get shot down the majority of the time and SHOULD HE SUCCEED, it is a 95% guarantee the dates will be pure psychological torture.

Now, you do that for 10 years and (not to be crass) I don't care how long the legs are, how nice the boobs are, or how great the sex is (usually pretty bad), there IS going to be a burn out rate. I personally don't know how the likes of Roosh, Roissy, etc. do it. In the end other aspects of life start to appeal to you.

A quiet night on your own listening to Johnny Coltrane, playing video games, hell, even reading a book is better. You discover working on motorcycles proves more enjoyable than dating Bambi the Drama Queen. You discover studying a foreign language proves more intellectually rewarding than suffering another outting with Monique the Sociology

Major-Turned Realtor. You discover hanging out with your buds having a cigar will provide better life-long memories than suffering another ignorant-laced conversation about politics with Lilly the "I'm a Progressive Feminist" Liberal.

The point is, playerism and playerhood is all great and wonderful. But there's nothing wrong with you if you decide to give it up and opt for more of a MGTOW type lifestyle. The reason being is it's your life, not theirs. You don't have to spend your precious few moments on this planet suffering the drama and psychoses of tall drinks of floosy.

Why You Philosophically Must Ride Fast and Take Chances

This is a long, but very important one. So first pour yourself a drink.

Second **READ THIS** because it will provide the context to what I'm about to write.

Did you **read it**?

DID YOU?

Ok, let's begin:

By most conventional standards and measures I am a failure.

I don't make a lot of money, just enough to get by.

Despite a spectacular track record of predicting economies and assessing risk, I have spectacularly failed in a financial/economic career.

As much success as I've had with the ladies, I've had Tsar Bomba levels of failures.

And understand, this is all while facing an economic environment that is not only very poor, very hostile to capitalist American males, it's likely to be unviable and get much worse.

But how am I so happy?

Very simple lieutenants, agents in the field, and junior, deputy, aspiring, official and otherwise economists.

Context. Plain and simple context.

You see, I took more risks and have suffered more highs and lows, successes and failures by the age of 25 than most men will by the time they die. It was and still is exhausting. It is akin to hiking out mountainous terrain instead of merely driving on the road that bypasses the mountains to reach the same destination.

But, when me and my driving counterpart reach the same destination, I have context.

I know the lay of the land better, I've got plenty more vantage points and victories by summiting all the mountain peaks, and just as I know failure when I was in the deepest valleys. I know what's in those mountains while my counterpart who merely drove around them is still wondering.

And over time knowledge will serve you better than wondering as you age.

A small example is 401ks or retirement plans.

It's a fool's game.

Oh, I know that, and you know that. But how did we get to this epiphany? We had to journey through a trek of economics, research, philosophy and data crunching. We also had to dare to have independent thought.

But try explaining that to somebody who didn't hike through the mountains and took the easy route their HR department told them to with their 401k investment options. To them you're a "kook" a "whack." Just some sensationalist trying to stir up drama. Heck, try being in financial advising and telling people, "um, hey, better have a plan B incase the government nationalizes your 403b."

Another example is moving around and job hopping. I am a job hopper. Why?

Am I disloyal?

Am I a bad employee?

No, I just can't tolerate politics, lying, indecision, inefficiency, bureaucracy and mediocrity (which, actually in today's America makes me a very bad employee, so um, yes, I am a bad employee).

Is there a consequence? Certainly - lack of steady income and the stigma associated with job hoppers. But that reputation or stance is the official one that comes from taking the road. Let me throw a different spin on it or a different perspective from the mountains.

Loyal employees are suckers.

How many people do you know that slave away, loyally and then get laid off because of ineptitude on the part of management or the economy tanks? Additionally, how fun is it being the yes man and suffering day in and day out reconciling what you know to be wrong with what you're told to do. Also, how much suffering and abuse must you sustain because you bought a house you couldn't afford, married a profligate spending spouse and bred children you can barely support? And good thing you're moving up in income tax brackets to pay those progressively higher taxes! Right, the loyal corporate stooge is the way to go.

But what's funny is this observation can only be made from a mountain top as you watch the lemmings slave away with no self-respect, just barely scraping by. They don't see it. They think there's going to be that gold watch at the end of that road. They think their company is going to be around forever. They don't see the road construction around the bend and the bridge out another 3 miles further that you do perched atop your peak.

But arguably the most important thing I've learned or gleaned from taking the trail-never-travelled is what's really important - other people. And here is where I have to make a confession.

I told all of you I was in South Dakota working in collections. That was not true. I was working at yet another wonderful community bank in Wyoming. I was already on my way to get a 2 year degree in computer networking, but then out of the blue a recruiter called me and wanted to know if I was interested in working a job in Wyoming.

No state income taxes.
It would put me closer to the west and I would finally be able to explore all the national parks to my my heart's content.
I would recapitalize my bank accounts, pay down the mortgage more, purchase some fixed assets.
The pay was decent.

So off I went knowing full well this was going to be another crappy community bank with the same crappy prospects. But you'll all be proud of me.

I shut up.
Did what i was told.
Made no waves.
Made no decisions.

I made the job work for me.

I was excited about moving out west and living my childhood dreams. But, again, this was taking a chance. Doing something different. It was climbing another mountain and not taking the road. There were going to be lessons.

While I was able to hike more miles and discover more fossils in one single year than I did the past 7 I paid an egregious price. Not in terms of work (I already climbed previous mountains to know what was in store with another podunk bank), but in terms of society and socializing.

Wyoming is hands down the dumbest state in the world.

Are there smart people?

Yes, certainly.

Are there interesting people?

Yes, certainly.

But those people are married right quick, have children and do not socialize and if the do, it is usually before 10PM.

Additionally, another interesting aspect of living in Wyoming is that you take the mountains and parks for granted. Ironically NOBODY hikes or does any kind of physical activity in Wyoming. There was no limit to the number of people who had LIVED ONLY 2 HOURS AWAY FROM THE BLACK HILLS BUT NEVER WENT THERE. 4 HOURS AWAY FROM BADLANDS NATIONAL PARK AND NEVER BEEN THERE. They were so convenient, nobody thought to avail themselves of the opportunity.

The result?

The majority of single or socially active people are fat, drunk, uneducated, unintelligent and uninteresting. The only social activity they engage in is drinking and breeding illegitimate children. For once I agree with the coast liberals.

Unaware of this sociological trait of the state, what ended up happening was an interesting transformation. During the first few months I excited and happy, I tore up after mountains, rode my motorcycle wherever I could, shot guns, hunted fossils. BUt at night I'd come home and there were no friends to **go cocktailing** with. There were some places that had dancing, but the men are incredibly possessive of not just their wives or girlfriends, but their ex's. Plutonic activities involving the opposite sex (ballroom dancing, motorcycle riding, etc.) were impossible. There was nobody to go dancing with. I tried to finding hikers and hiking clubs, but there was nobody to go hiking with. And in the end you could be in a town of 50,000 people, but all alone. Not because you are unsociable, but because it would be more enjoyable to be by yourself getting your intellectual fix over internet discussion boards with genuinely intelligent people than hanging with the locals at the local dive bar listening to how they can't make their payments on their used pick up truck because they knocked up another girl.

Soon I started drinking. Even more than I normally do. And with winter set in, there was really nothing else to do. Oh I joined a gym and jiujitsu, ran and worked out twice a day, I got right ripped, heck, I wrote **"Worthless"** in two weeks. But that still isn't enough time to kill the entire day. The booze would inevitably flow at the end of the night because my friends out east in a later time zone had fallen asleep. It was the only thing to stimulate my brain and also knock me out to dreamland. This was the valley that taught me my lesson. BUt this was the valley that provided me the most important context of my life - that the number one thing, the most important thing you have in your life is other people. They mean more to me that my hatred for Minnesota liberalism and socialism.

I had already decided there was no way my friends or my girlfriend would move out to Wyoming. I wouldn't do that to them. And it was very apparent I wouldn't befriend anybody in this state to make it worth staying. So I crunched some numbers and realized if I made it another 3 months I'd be able to keep my signing bonus and build up enough cash to last about 2 years. It's not a lot of cash, but with super low living expenses and no children, you'd be amazed how long you can last in the field on little money.

Four days ago, at 8:01 AM on my one year anniversary, I gave my boss my two weeks notice. The hike was over, I reached my destination and with the KNOWLEDGE that people are the most important thing in your life. My road-driving counterparts finished their drive, but without that important lesson which is why I'm happier, though a "failure."

The story gets better, as icing to the cake was the bank was worried about me hacking the system or firebombing the place (I thought I was being professional giving a 2 weeks notice, and such a fear would be unfounded). But then again, with the hypersensitive nature of modern day American employers, a man's word is not worth the risk. They said they would pay me 2 weeks anyway and I could just wrap it up (I wasn't doing any work anyway).

And so to celebrate the end of this journey, I decided to do a victory lap. The great western motorcycle ride I'm on right now. While I'm out west and getting paid, I figured i might as well drive down to Phoenix and visit my friends, and head back a different route through the Rocky Mountains.

The story will end in about 2 weeks. I will return to Wyoming this week. My boxes have already been packed, ready to move (i've even estimated the amount of time it will take to load up the truck - 20 minutes). A convoy of friends will come out here to retrieve my gear and my vehicles, and I will drive my motorcycle back to the Twin Cities, straight to "my bar" in "my town" to a homewelcoming party. A year and 2 weeks of pure hell, and of course your Captain racks up another "failure," but I will return with the context and KNOWLEDGE of what's most important in life - my friends and loved ones. And, not that I didn't appreciate them before or somehow took them for granted, but I will appreciate them on a whole new level, be much more thankful for them and enjoy their company at least twice as much as when before I left. Because of that context, I will be happier than my "more successful" road-travelling, obedient counterpart as he vainly tries to go for that gold watch, gets divorced, and wonders why the government is nationalizing his 401k account when he "did all the right things."

Enjoy the decline!

Onward Christian Rationalization Hamster

The St. Leykis Clause is in effect for this post

Because of my unique background (secular, but very familiar with and informed about religion - specifically, Christianity), I can hypocritically sit on the sidelines and mock and ridicule what I see happening inside the church. Specifically, I savor watching the realities of the modern day "real world," human nature, socialism, and a progressively-debased society run full-force into the old religious beliefs, tenets and principals of various established religions. But for the best show, the one where I like breaking out my lawn chair and lighting up a cigar, is to watch when feminism and Christianity collide. Not when secular feminists criticize the church and lobby for abortion rights, etc., but rather when Christian women adopt feminist ideals, doctrine and philosophy. It results in a spectacular train wreck as they try to reconcile two (more or less) mutually exclusive ideologies and the ensuing explosion ensnares scores, if not hundreds, of innocent Christian male-bystanders.

Oh, I laugh, but a piece of me cries as I see the clueless men of the church flail about with no idea what's going. Even incredibly intelligent ones who are very aware and observant of the political forces of feminism and are definitely alpha males, also suffer. Not because they are somehow duped, but because their faith blinds them to the bird's-eye-view observations secularism affords me. **Dalrock, U of Man, Last Christian Standing, Elusive Wapiti**, observations are correct, but through the lens of Christianity. So if those of you from the Christian side of the Manosphere will permit me, allow me to make some of my secular observations (which I do NOT mean in a condescending way, just wanted to share).

First, though you may disagree, for the sake of argument assume the majority of religious people do not deep down inside believe in their religion for one second. Most go to church, synagogue, mosque, whatever, not because they actually believe the doctrine, but because that's what they were told to do as kids. It is a rare person (like say, Dennis Prager) who really believes in his religion, and even those who would presumably be the most ardent believers (the clergy) use religion more often than not as a means of employment first, ego satisfaction next, and then somewhere in 4th or 5th place is "god."

Second, also assume the premise that what prompts most people to join and stay in a religion are social or at least "ulterior" motives that have nothing to do with the religion. The religion serves merely as a vehicle or an excuse to congregate and socialize.

Now, you make those two assumptions and religion takes on a whole different dynamic. It is a medium or a catalyst to achieve other, non-religious based things.

What do I mean by "other non-religious based things?"

Well any kind of ulterior motive.

To meet a spouse, to have friends, to have belonging, to provide your mind an explanation (you deep down inside don't believe anyway) as to what happens after you die so you don't have to worry.

The religion is like Play Doh or clay. It can ultimately be morphed into serving whatever purpose its "believers" desire. But beyond that, religion also carries "authority" which provides the legitimacy that people need to confirm that what they're doing is virtuous, true, noble and correct. And it is these two traits that makes religion the most perfect, most powerful, most disastrous weapon a rationalization hamster just plain can't resist.

Understand what a Rationalization Hamster is. It is up for interpretation, but I think we can all agree that a rationalization hamster is a vehicle which allows a person to deny reality. But it's more than that. A person just can't "deny reality," they need a rationalization so that their weak minds will fall for it. The rationalization or logic the hamster generates doesn't have to be sound, reality-based or have any level of intellectual honesty, but if you can reach out and attach some kind of approval or ordainment by an "independent third party," all the more power to the rationalization hamster.

Tell me how religion, specifically, Christianity, does not fit that bill perfectly. It has all the traits and characteristics that could feed an army of rationalization hamsters.

Fateism - The inane and cowardly "the lord will provide" or "the lord has a plan" is only uttered when the utterer has made one or many galactically stupid decisions. You don't hear the electrical engineer who waited till he was married to have kids say, "well, the lord will provide." You hear the single mom of 5 children from 3 fathers who's attending cosmetology school at the local degree mill on our dime say, "the lord will provide." The appeal or the attraction of "fateism" is that you get to jettison any responsibility for your actions.

Slept around, knocked up a chick, got an STD, dropped out of college, collecting welfare?

Oh no, that's not your fault. "The lord has a plan."

Consequently, when you run into these fateists they have no problem claiming responsibility for their good decisions. Oh no, the lord had nothing to do with you getting your MD, that was all you. But the one night fling you had that brought your unwanted child into this world, yep, that was JC all the way.

An Amorphous, Intangible Doctrine - Clear rules are bad for rationalization hamsters. They're too black and white. And while you may think the bible is clear on a lot of things, those very clear things account for about 5% of the total pages in the bible. The remaining 95% is stories, parables, poems and a bunch of other amorphous, touchy feely stuff that can be interpreted however anybody wants it to be. This gives the rationalization hamster another gift "from the heavens." (yuk yuk yuk).

A rule book where the rules can be changed and interpreted however the rationalization hamster wants.

It's like **Calvin-ball** dating Christian girls. YOu never know where you stand, what you're supposed to do, what they want, and what the goal is. If you try something, it's ruled illegal. But if some other guy tries the same thing, that's all good because in Romans Chapter 89 verse 312 subsection A the lord said,

"Kiss not the upstanding young Christian man in your church. Nay. Make out with the criminal, bad boy with 2 illegitimate kids who wanteth to get downeth your pants, so that you may help the poor, impoverished man by showing him God. For it is he who needeth you, sayeth the lord."

A Christian man just cannot win playing Calvinball against a Christian woman.

Moral Superiority -Another aspect of religion that makes rationalization hamsters salivate is the moral superiority religion provides. This aspect of religion yields many benefits. First, it provides that "third independent party" needed to "ordain" or "approve" all the actions of the rationalization hamster. And as long as the rationalization hamster bases her decisions in the scripture, no matter how horribly misinterpreted and construed for her own benefit, she is doing the right thing. Additionally, because it is a religion, it is an "authoritative" third party, not some journalist or professor. It is GOD who is ordaining your decisions. How can you go wrong with the ONE TRUE GOD on your side?

Second, because of this divine authority, all other arguments are moot. Logic doesn't apply. Statistics or facts don't apply. The other person's feelings don't apply. This is GOD, need she remind you. This leads to, third, inferiority.

This a Christian male is not going to run into as much as it will be secular males. Date a Christian rationalization hamster and you are immediately demoted to "heathen" status, obviously inferior to the rationalization hamster. And even then, on second thought, I take that back. Christian men no doubt do suffer from this inferiority trait, namely by what I guess could be considered "christian shaming language." How many of you have heard "Well I guess you're just not a good Christian." Or "I guess Jesus isn't in your heart!" In short, if a rationalization hamster embeds itself enough in religion, any men (secular or christian) who dare criticize, argue or disagree with you can be written off as inferior.

Jesus, Rockstar Alpha - You ever date that girl that wouldn't shut up about her ex that rocked her world, treated her like crap, but how she pined for him anyway. Yeah, well JC puts that Alpha Bad Boy to shame. JC is the ULTIMATE alpha. Take the multiple male suitors in Harlequin romance novels, the World's Most Interesting Man, George Clooney, those Vampire/Wolf guys from all those vampire books/movies, put them in a blender, take pure extract of Alpha maleness out of them, and then refine it further in secret government labs and you still would have Mortimer Snerd compared to JC.

JC is "perfect." He is always there. Always forgiving. All powerful. All loving. And guess what, a figment of her imagination just like all the vampire movies and Harlequine romance novels.

You are real. You are mortal. You are human. You stand no chance against a dream or a figment of imagination. If there is any turbulence in your relationship, you will immediately be compared to JC just like other girls will compare you to the rockstar alpha in their past. And good luck winning that battle pal.

Additionally, JC brings in yet another tool the rationalization hamster can "lord" over you (yuk yuk yuk). "He" is more important than you. What always irked me about weddings is about 85% of the time it's the same damn sermon:

"Through Jesus you two will succeed."

or

"YOu are getting married to serve Jesus."

or

"Your wedding and your family will help glorify Jesus."

I call a secular "BS" and have said crassly to the few christian girls I've dated "I'm not having a threesome with Jesus," but for the Christian male this really puts you in a bad position. You can NEVER be #1. It's like marrying a single mom - you are default-ranked #2. You marry a christian single mother, you are default-ranked #3. Regardless, it provides another chess piece the Christian rationalization hamster can invoke to manipulate the relationship.

Get Out of Jail Free - Akin to "fateism," I wanted to separate this because it's an aspect of Christianity I very much dislike - ALL IS FORGIVEN. This means you could have been, or could be the most evil, maniacal, disgusting person, and it's alright, it's all OK, all is forgiven.

Now I am agnostic and I'm a pretty gruff and callous guy, but the number one thing that hurts me, haunts me and I even have nightmares to this day are the handful of people I did wrong to. If you are a real human being with a real soul, you will realize not only were you wrong, but there's NOTHING you can do to undo the harm and hurt you caused other people. Even if they forgive you, you can't forgive yourself because of the pain you caused them. It doesn't go away. It isn't washed away, it still happened. In short, what I'm trying to say is I don't understand how people can do something wrong and horrible and because some book or guy in robes says,

"Don't worry, Jesus forgives you."

how they can then just skip along your happy way without the slightest cringe of guilt or shame. And not only that, how they can delude themselves into thinking it never happened.

The perfect example is the "born again Christian" or worse, the "born again virgin."

Are you kidding me? What, your past doesn't matter? Not to mention all the consequences of your mistakes and who you hurt along the way (innocent illegitimate children, impoverished people, tortured souls, victims of your crimes, etc. etc.)

But again, this is a rationalization hamster on religious steroids. Anything is possible, including your ability to pretty much blank out your past, forgive yourself and then believe your a much better person than you really are.

Again, I don't envy my Christian brothers.

Now, you take in all these traits, all these variables and aspects of religion and tell me how in the eyes of a rationalization hamster it is nothing more than an irresistible tool box or a steroid buffet to use, abuse and unleash for its own selfish purposes. Also tell me how a Christian male is supposed to find a genuine Christian woman in a church full of poser rationalization hamsters. Also tell me how a Christian male, who is genuinely interested in finding a good church, finds one, and not some watered down, acoustic guitar playing hippie church where your pets can be baptized (St. Mark's Episcopal Church in Minneapolis, if you're interested) and Jesus is hidden somewhere in the basement all to pull in more people purely for marketing purposes?

This isn't to say all women are using and abusing Christianity for their own ulterior motives. This isn't to say all members of our churches, synagogues, mosques and temples are nothing but posers and crusaders looking for a date or some business contacts. And I'm certainly not asking anybody to abandon their faith. All I'm asking is the men (and women) of The Manosphere take another red pill.

We already took one when it came to the dating/social dynamics of courting women. We should also be taking one for employee/employer dynamics. But in order to understand what is happening in our places of worship all religious men and women (regardless of religion) should be taking a third red pill to prevent what is nothing more than a political ideology from corrupting, infiltrating and destroying our religious institutions.

Stay Frosty

I was once again sitting at "the" bar in town. Minding my own P's and Q's, enjoying a top shelf cocktail on the cheap because in this small town everything costs about half what they do in the city. Mike, a 100% USDA certified cowboy, was in the house and we discussed ex-wife #3 of his portfolio of wives he accumulated in the past. Mike is an interesting fellow.

Time went on and a couple of the other locals came into the bar. The locals were also joined by an out of state concrete crew enroute to the Bakken oil field. Booze was flowing, somebody put some "happy" country music on the juke box, this is about as festive as it gets at this bar.

There were of course girls in this bar, but the thing with small towns is you already know who they are, not to mention (if you're a local), you've already dated them all by now, sometimes twice since the 6th grade, and they're either all married, spoken for or ruined by booze, drugs and too many children.

Enter in a hot little number, decked on in some serious sexy business attire, that walks through the door.

The old timers finding refuge at the bar from their wives raise an eyebrow and send confirming smirks to one another. The younger locals are not so clandestine nor couth and gawk. My peripheral vision picks up somebody walking in the door, I naturally turn, confirm it's a hot girl and turn my attention back to my drink. The concrete workers immediately invite her to join them.

The night goes on and female friend of mine shows up. We throw a couple bucks into the juke box and dance to some country swing and Frank Sinatra. The dance floor isn't terribly big, but it's more than enough to accommodate the only two people who know how to dance in the county. After a couple dances my buddy has to get back home and I figure I better call it a night as well and "mosey" (which is an official word here) up to the bar to pay my tab. But before the bar tender can even get to me, the hot little, business suit wearing babe jumps into the barstool next to me.

"Hi!" she says.

A little surprised I say, "Hello."

"So, um, you know how to dance, huh?" she asked.

I said, "Yeah, used to teach back in the Twin Cities."

And it is here I must interrupt the conversation. By this time I already figured I knew why she was talking to me. She saw me dance, she's from the city, probably here on business, is dreading what this podunk town has to offer and wanted to see if I would dance with her sometime too. I figured she would continue her line of inquiry about dancing, but then she surprised me and shifted topics.

"So, do you live here?" she asked.

Not particularly phased I said, "Yep."

"What brought you out here?"

"No state income taxes, the economy doesn't suck as much as Minnesota's and you can actually find a job without having to have a triple doctorate and 40 different certifications and kiss some HR dolt's ass." I said.

"So what do you do?"

"I'm in collections."

By this time it was starting to feel like an interview and the conversation was no longer what I'd consider "natural." Natural in the sense that it was clear what her intentions were.

Oh sure, have I had random female strangers come up and inquire about my dancing?

Yes of course.

But this was different. We were no longer talking about dancing and now she was asking questions about me. Girls don't interrogate me about me, they interrogate me about dancing because they're interested in inevitably becoming the center of attention on a dance floor. I just happen to be their ticket to that destination. But now a girl wanted to get to know "me." Asking personal questions about "me," what I do, what I like, etc. etc. Ironically, you'd think that would be nice. "Awwww!!! She really likes you and wants to get to know you!" I had a different take. I was suspicious.

The conversation continued down its new path, her inquiring about all that is Cappy. But then I noticed two things. One, her body language changed. She was now leaning in closer to me, her body completely turned into mine and her face looked like she was hinging on every word I said (and I wasn't saying terribly impressive words). This stood out because we had only been talking about 5 minutes, way too soon for a girl to become acclimated to the idea of getting physically involved with you. Two, Mike and some of the old timers at the bar were smiling and smirking. But not in the "Oh, look who's gonna get lucky tonight" kind of look, but they were almost laughing at me.

Now I knew something was up.

She continued her interrogation, but on account I already have a girlfriend and I was tired, I decided to cut it short, but in a polite manner. I said, "I'd love to stick around and chat, but I really do have to get to bed. If you're in town for a while this is the place to be on Wednesday nights. Me and the handful of other ballroom dancers in town frequent it on Wednesdays. Maybe see you then."

And with that I left.

Couple days later I'm at "the" bar again and sure enough Mike was there (not even sure he ever left). We started chit chatting and through the course of conversation I brought up the hot little business babe that walked in a couple nights ago. I said,

"Hey, you know that girl that was talking to me at the bar the other night?"

Mike started laughing. He said,

"Ooooo, yeah. I remember her. What about her?"

"Eh, there was something off about her. Girls just don't come up and start talking to guys at bars. It was like she was interrogating me or something."

Mike started shaking his head, he said,

"Oh, I shouldn't tell you."

I said, "Tell me what?"

"No, you'll kill me if I do."

I said, "Jesus Christ Mike, just f@cking tell me what it was."

"Well," he said, "her and those mason workers were wondering if you were gay and they put her up to seeing if she could get you to proposition her."

I said, "GAY??? What the hell made them think I was gay? My dancing?"

"No," Mike said, "it was the way you were dressed."

"How the hell was I dressed that made me gay?"

He said, "You had those ironed olive slacks on with that black shirt. They thought you were gay."

I went on to continue to defend myself and point out that just because I had ironed slacks on with a nice black shirt did not mean I was gay, nor could such an ensemble even be considered to look gay. But that is not the point I'm trying to make here or why I bring up this story.

The point is that girls don't "just approach guys at bars." More specifically, if something seems weird, or off, or just plain too good to be true, then you're right, there IS something wrong and you're the target of a scam or a trick. And you must understand this because on occasion you will be the subject or intended victim of such a ruse.

Now, for the most part these tricks or ruses will ultimately be harmless, much like the gay bet made against me. You will not sustain any real damage. You will not sustain any financial costs. They are nothing more than (an admittedly) sick or twisted girl deciding to toy with your emotions (or more likely, hormones). An innocuous example would be two girls "fake making out" at a dance club. If you let these minor, childish attempts affect you, then you will unnecessarily suffer, and so you should blow them off. Admittedly, for a young middle school or high school boy that's easier said than done, any attention you think is sincere and you thusly vest some measure of emotional investment in it. But, by the time you're 17 or 18, you should realize who is really being the adult and who is really being the child and such games can largely be dismissed.

However, **not all such ruses are harmless**. Additionally, it's not so easy to just "identify and dismiss" an attempt by a woman trying to trick you with her feminine wiles. And here is where the true risk lies.

Understand no matter how good you think you are, no matter how cynical, jaded or distrusting you think you are, no matter how aware and on top of your game you think you are, understand you are GENETICALLY PROGRAMMED TO RESPOND POSITIVELY TO POSITIVE FEMALE BEHAVIOR.

This forces an undeniable disadvantage on you whether you're aware of it or not. Even your old Captain has to catch himself every once in a while because on a sub-conscious level you will respond positively to warm and receptive behavior of women. Your guard is down and you're letting a girl get away with something you wouldn't normally let her get away with, or you're granting her more trust and credit simply because she's cute and is treating you kindly.

Of course, for the most part this "disadvantage" or "weakness" doesn't last long enough for you to be hoodwinked. You'll inevitably figure out something is wrong, or 95% of the time, they girl is just using this ploy to get attention or a free drink (again, the girls fake-making out at a dance club) But to a woman who is a pro AND has more SINISTER OR CRIMINAL aims, that is all the window of opportunity she needs to spring her trap as she has rehearsed it.

Now most of you think I'm going down the route of marriage, divorce, alimony, faking being on birth control, etc. etc. But that's not really what I'm talking about. I'm talking more like "getting clubbed over your head in a dark alley" because you thought the buxom blond was genuinely interested in you and your exciting career as an economist.

Oh you all laugh, and think I'm being over-cautious, but one final tidbit to my tale.

When a pro gets taken (potentially, the story hasn't ended), the rest of us ought to take heed. (language warning).

Stay frosty, boys.

Why Leftists Tend to Be Uglier

Liberal Open-Mindedness Disclaimer - If you are a liberal and are reading this, you must read the whole thing. Do not claim to be "open minded" and then not get to the meat of the post below then blather on uninformed about this post. Thank you.

Study comes out showing that republican women candidates tend to be more feminine looking than they're liberal counterparts.

No duh.

I'll say it again for the cheap seats and see if I can succinctly summarize my theory (which is right) about why this is so.

Liberals and leftist in general tend to be lazy. They eschew hard work, they're afraid of rigor, and this shows in their ideology. ANYTHING to avoid having to support themselves or work an honest day. Yes, I know some work hard, but it's more or a less a monopoly of the left to hear:

"Life's unfair."

"I'm discriminated against."

"The glass ceiling."

"The Man is holding me down"

etc. etc.

Now, even though it's disingenuous and intellectually dishonest, they can get away with this in an economic and political sense because this is a democracy. Socialists and leftists with heart-tugging sob stories can get the majority of voters to vote in policy that transfers wealth and essentially allows them to be lazy and avoid real, productive work. We all have to abide by this because we live in this democracy.

HOWEVER, while a democracy may force different economic policies on society through the government, IT CANNOT CHANGE HUMAN NATURE. Specifically, no matter what policies socialists and leftists try to implement, you will never change what a woman is attracted to and what a man is attracted to.

Women like strong, tall, big men.

Men like long legs, long hair, big boobs, tight asses and feminine features.

This means liberals and leftists (just like all humans and animals on this planet) ARE FORCED to compete when it comes to courting and mating, whether they like it or not. However, when I say "compete" I don't mean, "be lucky enough to be born handsome or pretty." I mean "work out, stay in shape and make yourself sexy to the opposite sex."

Which means, again, just like any other job, just like any other degree, just like any other pursuit, it *requires effort, discipline, rigor and hard work*. Things liberals and leftists abhor.

And it shows.

Now, keep in mind what I'm saying here because I don't want to be misquoted or taken out of context.

I do NOT believe liberals and leftists are born uglier than their average conservative counterpart. It's not like they're genetically inferior or anything. What I am talking about is that they put A LOT LESS EFFORT into their physical appearance. Ergo, this is not a criticism of their basic, physical beauty, let alone their genetics, but it *IS* a criticism of their psychology. You could take that Prius-driving, 45 year old, gray haired, super skinny yoga woman who never wore make-up, never did her hair up, give her a make over and she'd come out looking just fine. Just as you could take the cowering, tubby orbiting beta with the Seth Rogen beard, through him in the gym for 3 months and have him come out looking just fine.

But that's the not the point.

The point is to your average leftists such working out and maintenance requires effort. That AND the added risk they may still "fail" in attracting a mate. It is their pure hatred and fear of effort and competition that not only drives their political and economic ideologies, but also drives their "romantic" or "mating" ideology.

Therefore, since it takes too much work to don a pair of heels and gussy yourself up or hit the gym and lose some inches, what do liberals do?

Try to change reality.

Thus why you have "fat acceptance."

Thus why men are "shallow" for liking big boobs and tight asses.

Thus why liberal women don't "lower themselves to objectifying themselves for men."

Thus why "I don't need a man, fish bicycle, test tube babies."

All while exuding that same pompous, arrogant, hypocritical attitude they lord over the rest of us adults as they "go green" and drive their Priuses.

In the end you have a group of people living in denial. They're so lazy and afraid they will never try and thus, they will never achieve their best. They will not re-define reality (because reality is reality, it bends for no liberal), but will only manage to delude themselves what reality is. And thus you end up with wimpy, pansified men dating or marrying homely, ugly, unpleasant women pursing a "life" of pursuits and hobbies that require no real effort (going green, joining a political crusade, claiming you care about the children, majoring in "**Lesbian Chinese Sculpture Studies**," drum circles, yoga, you name it).

It is a life they really don't enjoy and it is the reason you never really see any of them smile as you pass their bumper-sticker-laden Prius on the highway.

Enjoy the decline!

The Captain's Declaration of Independence

In light of the impossibility to work

1. honestly
2. efficiently
3. void of politics
4. void of drama

in Corporate America, it has occurred to me that I (and many others) are simply just not cut out for the type of work that is being offered to us. It is not an issue of laziness, sloth or unprofessionalism, it simply boils down to the fact I (and many others) do not have the patience, lack of self-respect or tolerance for ineptitude, incompetence and idiocy that is required by today's modern employers. We psychologically cannot withstand the pettiness, the power trips, the nepotism, the cronyism and the outright psychological bullshit that previous generations have imbued into today's corporate America culture. Our lives are too short and too valuable to us that the price you pay us in terms of a wage is not worth the psychological costs we must bear in terms of lying, deceiving, ignoring, politicking and whatever other immoral "skills" you require of us to be a "team player" or deemed a "successful employee."

Instead of standing for virtue, efficiency, professionalism, profit and excellence, you instead embrace ass-kissing, brown-nosing, compliance, submission, rent-seeking, lying, affirmative action, CSR and anything else that goes against common sense and profitability. You are corrupt entities no longer worth engaging and participating in and certainly not worth any of us "dedicating" any small percentage of our finite lives.

Everybody, and I mean EVERYBODY wants nothing more than to quit their jobs and tell you to ef off. Nobody has any loyalty to you, just as you have no loyalty to them. And frankly, most would have no problem showing up the next day and plugging you full of holes if there were no legal ramifications. And while you have the upper hand when it comes to parents with mortgages and children they can't afford, and can make them your "corporate bitch for life," there is a group of us who do not have to suffer your corporate sadism. Those of us who live cheaply, without children, and without debts.

Without children, without debts, and with the simple skill of fiscal austerity, I and people like me are not owned by you. We don't need you. Matter of fact, as long term corporate profit prospects dwindle and tank, you could probably do with outside-the-box people like us. Regardless, we don't need your jobs. We don't need to suffer the HR ditz pelting us with stupid questions and 5 subsequent rounds of interviews to get that whopping $55,000 per year job. We don't need some middle aged gray hair changing our job description every 3 months, nor do we have to suffer the psychoses of your wholly psychologically unstable labor force prone to sexual harrassment complaints, filing complaints and bitching and whining about petty and irrelevant things.

We don't need a Corvette. We don't need a McMansion. We don't need luxury trips to Europe. We don't need children. And we don't need you. The life we would suffer with a 2 hour round trip commute and a mind-destroying 40 hour per week job is nowhere near worth the crappy salary you pay us, along with the 0% job stability. The minimalistic life and the psychological health that comes with it is more valuable than you could ever pay and we can do it on the cheap (especially with all those taxes your hard working employees and you are paying to subsidize low-income people like me!)

And so, in light of such obvious logic, I would like to declare my independence.

As of today, the Ole Captain is no longer working for anyone. Because of his fiscal austerity, cheap living, financial discipline and the lack of children his expenses are so low he can now officially afford to live off of blogging.

I want to say that again.

I can actually make a living off of blogging.

How pathetic and sad is it that you corporate schmucks are slaving away, working all those hours, hoping to get promoted, while suffering what can only be described as psychological torture while I get to wake up at 1030AM every morning. Go for a run or a motorcycle ride. Have my coffee, do what I want to do, oh, and subsequently, barely pay anything in taxes. And how sad is it that it's easier to make a CAREER IN BLOGGING than working a CORPORATE CAREER????

And let's be VERY clear about something. The reason I can do this is because of 100% me. Not because of any guidance or "leadership from my "elders." There's no middle aged fart complaining or asking me how Excel works. There's no moron, washed up former high school football player saying, "well, we didn't do that back in the 80's." And it certainly isn't because of any "wisdom" or "tricks" I picked up working for corporate America or some old blowhard in finance.

It's because I'm so efficient.

because there's only ONE BOSS (ME)

because of my ideas and thoughts I have translated and implemented into reality,

because I HAVE SET UP AND DESIGNED THE SYSTEM MYSELF

I can make an actual living off of **BLOGGING**!

Did you hear what I just said? You morons slaving away 60 hours a week, paying for parking, and then walking blocks to go to a job you hate with a boss equally as miserable as you and underlings as insufferable as me. And then you get to go home to a family that (probably) hates you. Certainly you bring home more than I do. Why you're a "successful corporate man!" What, $70K? $80K? Heck, even if it was $100K you take out taxes, living expenses, cars and houses you don't need, but the spouse demands. No, no, I'm sure your insufferable life and the brain damage you've suffered over the past 3 decades working in corporate America is much more enjoyable than my minimalist life financed by a blog. Yes, you just keep telling yourself late at night that I'm "disgruntled" and a "loose cannon." Just irked I couldn't make it to the "big time." Whatever helps you sleep at night and keep your mind off of whether you've pissed away your finite life on this planet and your wife is more on the 60/40 slash of divorcing you.

As for my readers, let me just say this.

It has been a long and painful road. I have saved up my pennies and dimes. I have refused to have children. Refused to buy cars I could (but shouldn't) afford, and have only allowed myself the very rare and occasional luxury. All of this has paid off.

After my return from Wyoming I now officially can afford to live off of blogging.

This is of course in part because of drastic financial decisions I've made in the past, but it also and equally has to do with all of my readers who made this possible.

Readers who help boost my stats.

Other bloggers who have linked to me.

Fans who have purchased my books or recommended me to other people.

People who have purchased items on the Amazon Affiliate program.

And the kind people who donate to my paypal account (although they could actually BUY THINGS and get something in return instead of warm Cappy Cap fuzzies).

It may not seem like a lot, but (then again) I don't need a lot. And all of you with your readership and patronage have made it possible I eek out a small enough income from this here blog to live. I wanted to say thank you and that in the future there will be more higher end quality posts as well as new book releases coming out as I am now allowed to solely focus on this venture.

My sincere heart felt thanks to all of you guys. YOu have no idea how happy you have made me and how much easier you have made my life.

It is now time to really start enjoying the decline.

The Reliability Factor

Let me tell you about my buddy Trixie.

Trixie is a girl I met in Wyoming. I met her in the last two months of my sabbatical there and I wish I had ran into her before. The reasons are many.

First, she is a spectacularly nice person. Very kind, very humble, not arrogant, and, frankly, altruistic and patient enough to put up with the ole Captain's brash and blunt personality. She had the maturity to know when I was joking, and was a spectacular sport when it came to me joshing her. AND no favor was too big for her to do. She even drove 4 hours to pick me up at the Rapid City airport late at night.

Second, she was able to keep up with me physically. In a state where the official state sport is drinking for men and having illegitimate children for the women, very few people are able to run 3 miles, let alone hike up a mountain. It is ironic that in a state where mountains and trails are not only numerous, but trailheads are no more than 10 minutes away, the people never avail themselves of those opportunities and opt instead to essentially sit on their asses. However, my buddy Trixie was always up to the physical challenges of a hike and was even in a hair better shape than me (though she was too kind to admit it as I would start to wane behind her in the later stages of some hikes).

Third, she was always game. I don't think she ever said no. "Want to go to Sturgis?" Yes. "Want to go on a 14 mile hike?" Sure. "Want to go pan for gold?" Yep. "Want to shoot guns?" Sure. Whether she had done these things or not, she would at minimum entertain the idea and try them.

But fourth, and arguably most important, she was reliable. I had ran into girls/women before in Wyoming and at first they may have looked to make for good friends, but in the end, inevitably all of them would flake out. They'd say they want to go for a hike, only not to return calls when it came time to go. They'd say they'd want to go for a motorcycle ride, only come up with an excuse at the 11th hour. They'd want to go out, but only to get drunk and go to loud bars where intelligent conversation was impossible. And keep in mind this was just to be FRIENDS, you aren't even trying to get romantic (though I surmise they viewed any requests for social outtings as romantic interest). Regardless, the reliability of the average woman in Wyoming was that of a middle school girl when it came to social activities.

But not Trixie. No. If she said she'd be there at 530PM ready for a hike, by god she was there at 530PM ready for a hike. If she said she wanted to go dancing, she meant it and would show up with her dancing shoes. And if she said she wanted to go for a motorcycle ride, she was there, with the appropriate gear, raring to go.

Unfortunately, I knew my time in Wyoming was going to be limited. And this saddened me a bit because I had found a really cool friend. And since I was leaving and because she was so kind, outgoing and reliable I had no problems "splurging" on her. Not that I was buying her attention or paying her to be my friend or vying to become a boyfriend, but because I hadn't met anybody in the entire state that was kind enough to hang out with me (not to mention I did feel some guilt leaving her to fend for herself in Wyoming's social life). Additionally, she wasn't loaded either and was the type of gal that wouldn't afford herself the occasional luxury. She was that "nice, sweet, American gal" of 1940's yore. So drinks were on me. I would pay for gas, grab her a sandwich. Got her a birthday cake for her birthday. And knowing the girl would pick me up in Rapid City, I got her a hair/salon/appointment/chick-thingy for her birthday that she'd never afford herself.

Sure enough, my two months were up. I made several trips transporting what meager worldly possessions and vehicles I own back to Minnesota. And as logistics would have it, I had to make one final trip out to Wyoming to pick up my motorcycle (which Trixie was kind enough to store for me). I flew in, did one final hike the next day, taught one final dance class the next night, and left the next morn at 615AM to avail myself of as much sunlight as possible as I dead-headed my bike back to Minnesota.

Of course, like hiking, riding your motorcycle for 12 hour stints grants you a lot of thinking time which results in a lot of SAEG (TM) epiphanies and philosophical observations. And it dawned on me that Trixie was a member of a small and elite group of girls in the ole Captain's life. Namely, a group of women that I had no problem spending a little money on.

Understand this "group" is NOT girlfriends. This group includes girls that are friends and girlfriends, but above all else nice girls who have treated me kindly. I have mentioned it before, I do not buy women drinks in an effort to impress them. I have only bought ONE woman ONE drink who I had just met at a bar and it did not work. I therefore save any kind of "drink buying" or "effort spending" on girls that treat me kindly and that I care about.

But as I drove I realized there was something much more precise about this elite group of girls than them merely just "treating me kindly." I realized that for them even to be around long enough to become friends or girlfriends they all had to have one thing in common - reliability.

My life, as is yours, is short and finite. The most valuable thing you or any other person has on this planet is time. Therefore, through a very simple Darwinian process of elimination, the people closest to you in your life are reliable on account you plain don't like wasting your time. People who flake, cancel out, etc. etc., don't make it to that elite group on account they are unreliable and waste your time and you don't want to hang out with such people (that or they also don't want to hang out with you either). The flakes never get to know you, spend time with you, and therefore never form friendships or romances. But by default then the flakes never get any of your attention - be it social, financial, romantic or favors.

And I want to say that again, so we all hear it.

"by default then the *flakes never get any of your attention - be it social, financial, romantic or favors.*"

Are all you flaky women paying attention? Are you starting to understand the ramifications for your flaky behavior?

It is here now we must make a distinction or a discernation because I know some of you know where I'm going with this and are saying, "yeah, but but."

So let me explain further.

I understand that there are women who "flake out" at the last minute because they never had any intention of going out with you in the first place. I am also fully aware of women feigning interest to score free attention be it at a bar, a night club, at work or any other place on the planet. And I am also fully aware that there are men who will pay attention (in whatever form) to flaky women because they have no game and don't know any better.

That is not what I'm talking about here.

What I am talking about is a woman who does have interest, but still insists on playing the inane "hard to get."

If there is a logic or a geometric theorem that debunks that myth I hope it is the Reliability Factor. Because IF you are playing "hard to get" and then flaking out on purpose, you will quickly eliminate yourself from any kind of long running chances of getting future attention from your target. But my observation about The Reliability Factor goes well beyond that logic with Trixie.

Ask yourself a question:

"How many girls have you met in your life that are as reliable and game-free as Trixie?"

I look back and I can't think of more than maybe, MAYBE a dozen women that were that reliable, straight forward, and forthright. Where there was no games, no BS, no drama. Just "hey, you wanna go do activity X?" "Yeah, let's go do activity X!"

Now ask yourself another question:

"How many girls have you had any kind of "positive" (romantic or friendly) relationship with?"

I look back and I'd say easily hundreds. And that's dating alone. Friends, even more. But I can only recall 10-12 women in the past who didn't play games and just straight up Joe's like Trixie.

The reason I bring up the math is that it shows the MAJORITY of women who have become friends, girlfriends, dates, etc., DID have an interest, but *still* engaged in some kind of "play hard to get" tomfoolery. However, those same girls, either because they played "*too* hard to get" or such game-playing psychologically precluded them from any kind of long term relationship, didn't make it into the "Elite Girl Pool." They went by the wayside of life. The ones that DID make it into the "Elite Girl Pool" DID have an interest and DID NOT engage in such tomfoolery - ie -they were RELIABLE.

What did this reliability get them?

Frankly, the best men have to give.

Lifelong friendships, marriages, fun, and yes, sure, "free drinks" or other forms of "attention." But the point I'm trying to make is not "look at all the attention you can get," but rather the irony of how reliability is the single most sure fire way to get "attention," but so few women engage in it.

In the end The Reliability Factor paid off for young Trixie. Because she was so reliable, her and I were able to create a great friendship. Part of that relationship (not to brag) was her going from a noob ballroom dancer under my tutelage to probably the most accomplished dancer in town (heck, the state even). The dancing also gave her a reason to wear some dresses and heels she never had an opportunity to wear. So in the two months I was there, she went from an innocuous, quiet girl with jeans and tennis shoes, to not just the best dancer on the floor, but the prettiest-dressed as well.

The women noticed she was the center of attention on the dance floor.

The men noticed she was very prettily dressed and wearing heels.

No woman ever had that much attention in the history of Wyoming.

Then again, no woman has ever been that reliable.

Made in the USA
Las Vegas, NV
21 July 2023